Disability, Liberation, *and* Development

Peter Coleridge

'In nature there's no blemish but the mind;
none can be call'd deform'd but the unkind.'

(William Shakespeare: *Twelfth Night*)

Oxfam
K and Ireland

ISBN 0 85598 194 6
ISBN 0 85598 195 4 pbk

Published by Oxfam (UK and Ireland)
274 Banbury Road, Oxford OX2 7DZ
(Oxfam is registered as a charity — No. 202918)

in association with
Action on Disability and Development
23 Lower Keyford, Frome BA11 4AP
(ADD is registered as a charity — No. 294860)

Designed and typeset by Oxfam Design Department.
Printed by Oxfam Print Unit.

112/PK/93 Palatino 9.5/12pt 80gsm Bookwove PMS 130&342

Contents

Arrangement of the book

This book is arranged to proceed from the general to the particular,
and is divided into four parts:

Part One explains the point of the book, and provides an
    introduction to the issues that will be discussed.

Part Two outlines the social, political, and developmental aspects of
    disability in general terms, mainly through interviews with
    disabled people who are engaged in development.

Part Three illustrates these issues through concrete examples from
    selected developing countries, and shows how social action on
    disability has been approached in widely different cultural and
    political contexts.

Part Four draws things together and tries to resolve some of the
    contradictions that are apparent in the arguments.

A note on language

Throughout the text the phrases 'the Third World', 'the South', and 'developing countries' are all used to refer to countries which are, in the main, not industrialised and which are the targets of 'Western' aid and development efforts. Similarly, 'the North', 'the West', 'developed countries', and 'the industrialised countries' are used to refer to the wealthier nations of the world which are, in the main, donors rather than recipients of aid.

I am only too conscious that these terms are most unsatisfactory in all respects: their use implies a view of the world which I certainly don't like and do not wish to reflect. But what to do? These phrases are understood, and when making generalisations and comparisons it is more or less impossible to avoid such widely current labels. I can only say that I deeply regret their use, but have not been able to come up with reasonable alternatives.

The use of language in discussions about disability is a matter of sensitivity and concern. It deserves more than a cursory note at the beginning, and is treated in depth in Chapter 7.

Acknowledgements

It is impossible to thank in person all those who have helped in the writing of this book: they number in the hundreds. Some of them are quoted and named in the text, and that is the best thanks. Although I take full responsibility for what is written here, it really has been a collective exercise.

To those who helped to organise my research trips I owe particular thanks: Peter Dube in Zimbabwe (tragically killed in a car accident some months later), Khalfan Khalfan and Ibrahim in Zanzibar, B. Venkatesh in India, Omar Traboulsi, Lina Abu Habib, and Nawaf Kabbara in Lebanon, Roberta Contin in Jordan, and Abdul Qadir Awad and Hussein Hussein in the Occupied Territories.

For their detailed comments on early drafts I owe warm thanks to Lina Abi Habib and Omar Traboulsi, Oxfam staff in Lebanon; Brother Andrew de Carpentier, Director of the Holy Land Institute for the Deaf, Salt, Jordan; Angela Coleridge, my wife; Roberta Contin, Oxfam Disability Trainer in Jordan; Pippa Cope, occupational therapist working with CIIR in Zimbabwe; Rita Giacaman, Director of the Community Health Unit, Birzeit University, West Bank; Rachel Hurst, board member of Disabled People's International and of ADD (Action on Disability and Development) and Director of Disability Awareness in Action; Helen Lee, physiotherapist who has worked for Oxfam in Lebanon and Jordan; Nawaf Kabbara, director of Friends of the Handicapped, Tripoli, Lebanon; Jabulani Ncube, formerly director of NCDPZ (National Council of Disabled People of Zimbabwe) and now a consultant for ADD; Catherine Robinson, who edited this book; James Tumwine, of Oxfam's Health Unit; Chris Underhill, Director of ADD; B. Venkatesh, Director of ADD India; Bridget Walker of Oxfam's Gender and Development Unit; and Pam Zinkin, Director of the CBR course at the Institute of Child Health, London.

Many authors owe a great debt to their partners for patience during a period of intense preoccupation, but in this case the debt to my wife Angela goes way beyond that: she has been a steady source of encouragement, inspiration, and stimulation throughout.

Finally, my thanks to Oxfam for giving me the opportunity and resources to undertake the work for this book, which has been one of the richest learning experiences I have ever had. ADD (Action on Disability and Development) also contributed financially to the project, thanks to the generosity of Joel Joffe, and Chris Underhill gave unstinting support in many other ways.

The book's strengths derive from all these people. Its weaknesses are mine.

Peter Coleridge
Oxford
February 1993

PART ONE

Introduction

A village school near Anantapur, Andhra Pradesh, India.

CHAPTER 1

Why this book?

de-ve'lop: *v.t. to unfold more completely; to evolve the possibilities of; to make active (something latent); to advance; to further; to promote the growth of; to make more available or usable. v.i. to grow, evolve, expand, mature, ripen, to unfold gradually (as a flower from a bud).*[1]

Charity or development?

Attitudes to development during the past forty years have, across the world, recognised that charity on its own is inadequate, and that the only meaningful development is when people plan and implement solutions to their own problems.

What creates change? Is it achieved by feeling pity towards people who are poor and oppressed — or by poor and oppressed people recognising their own strength to solve their own problems? Is it achieved by one lot of people, the 'haves', trying to meet the individual needs of another lot of people, the 'have nots' — or by people feeling their own power to meet their own needs?

We could, crudely, characterise these contrasting approaches as *charity* and *development*. Charity does nothing to challenge or change the status quo; indeed, it perpetuates it. Development is about people understanding the causes of their under-development, and with that understanding working to change their situation. In other words, development is ultimately about people having control over their own lives. Charity is about people remaining as victims, controlled by others.

Attitudes to development have indeed shifted in the past forty years, away from charity towards the empowerment of people. But this shift has not, generally speaking, been apparent in work with disabled people. Programmes and projects in disability, especially in developing countries, are still in the main designed exclusively by able-bodied people, and tend to leave disabled people out of the decision-making process. The case for regarding disabled people as an integral part of the development process, capable of running their own lives and acting as full partners rather than passive recipients of rehabilitation, has hardly been made.

This book is an attempt to make that case. It is a personal examination of some of the social, political, and developmental aspects of disability, as they are encountered in a few widely differing developing countries.

Welfare or empowerment?

The situation of disabled people provides a microcosm of the whole development debate and process. Disabled people are oppressed and marginalised in every country of the world, in both North and South. They are oppressed by social attitudes which stem from fear and prejudice. By examining these prejudices and studying examples where they have been overcome, we gain an insight into the processes of liberation and empowerment that lie at the heart of any development effort.

The literature on disability is vast and growing. There are many excellent books on the medical aspects of rehabilitation in both the industrialised countries of the North and in developing countries. In the North there is also a growing literature on the politics of disability and empowerment of disabled people, written mainly by disabled people themselves, and already creating major changes in perception.[2] Outside the specialist field, popular books and films like *My Left Foot* by Christy Brown and *Children of a Lesser God* have made an undoubted impact on public awareness and attitudes in Britain. At the same time, stereotypes and negative images are still portrayed in films like *Hook*, and all countries still have a long way to go in overcoming institutionalised prejudice towards disabled people.

In developing countries the disability literature tends to focus on the medical and technical aspects of rehabilitation, especially nowadays Community Based Rehabilitation (CBR). But very little work has been done on the social and political aspects of disability in developing countries. The voice of disabled people themselves in the South has hardly been heard.

In many developing countries disability is often perceived by governments and aid agencies as a problem, but not as a priority. Income, access to land and/or jobs, basic health care, the infant mortality rate, and the provision of sanitation and clean water are all seen as greater and absolute priorities. These are the pressing problems, and disabled people can be attended to later. Among people working in development, a common reaction to my proposal to write this book was 'What has disability to do with development?' Even people who are 'progressive', 'gender-aware', and in all other respects 'developmentally minded' perceive disabled people as belonging to a category marked 'social welfare', which is the new term for 'charity'. The implication is that disabled people can be ignored altogether in the development debate.

So charity rules OK. Paradoxically, money is available from governments, aid agencies, and private donors for institutions and programmes in disability, usually prompted by the sense that 'We must do something for disabled people'. There is an enormous industry based on disability, in which charitable institutions vie with 'community-based programmes' for major funding; vested interests are well entrenched among rehabilitation professionals; UN agencies and NGOs debate disability at their conferences.

However, all this completely misses the point: most decision makers in development organisations are able-bodied and have never been exposed to the full potential of what disabled people can do for themselves. Existing models of project design, no matter how 'community oriented', tend to treat disabled people as recipients rather than participants in the decision-making process. In the conference rooms of Geneva and New York, disability programmes are discussed, planned, and funded with hardly a disabled person present. The disability movement and organisations of disabled people tend to be regarded askance by rehabilitation professionals, with the argument that if the aim is integration, there is no point in creating a separate disability movement. Among professional carers and the general public there is a dislike of militancy exhibited by disabled people — who, it is assumed, should keep quiet and accept their situation as unfortunate but unchangeable.

A different vision of disability

Most disabled people in developing countries, if they have been exposed to any services at all, have experienced only a medical or institutional model of rehabilitation, which treats them as passive.

The idea that they are capable of organising and running their own lives, including their own rehabilitation, has hardly been tested in most places. The result is that the individual medical model of rehabilitation, which treats disabled people as patients who need to be cured or cared for, whether in institutions or 'in the community', is perpetuated without serious questioning, even by disabled people, for want of a different vision.

But there is a different vision, in which disabled people themselves play a full part in the decision-making processes that shape their own lives. It is in every sense a liberation struggle, akin to the struggles of oppressed groups everywhere, in which some human beings are struggling to be taken seriously by other human beings and to overcome the imbalance of power that consigns them to the lowest ranks in a pecking order dictated by vested interests rather than values. This book is an exploration of that vision.

The individual medical model of rehabilitation creates dependency and patronising relationships; it is also inadequate to reach the millions of disabled people throughout the world, given the limited resources of developing countries. The evidence presented in this book demonstrates that a social model, in which disabled people play a full part in development decision-making, is not only a realistic and achievable goal, but offers perhaps the *only* viable way of extending opportunities for rehabilitation and decent lives to as many disabled people as possible.

Disabled people are engaged in a liberation struggle, but there is one crucial difference from other liberation struggles by oppressed groups. If we speak of the struggle by indigenous people to survive in the Brazilian rain forest (an extreme but topical example), we are speaking of a clearly defined group of people to which the vast majority of us do not, and never will, belong. The same is not true when we speak of disabled people. Disability is an issue that touches us all. It is not only, or even mainly, associated with poverty: disability can affect anybody of any background, in any country at any time. Per head of population, there is a greater proportion of disabled people in industrialised countries, where better health care means that disabled people live longer, than in poor countries, where survival rates are much lower. Many people in industrialised countries will experience disability in some form when they get old. So disability is an issue 'in here', not 'out there', whether we live in Birmingham or Bombay. It is 'all our' problem, not 'just their' problem.

How this book was written

Oxfam (UK and Ireland) generously released me from my normal post in its Middle East programme for seven months to undertake a study of disability in Zimbabwe, Zanzibar, India, Lebanon, Jordan, and the Occupied Territories, places where there are attempts to find a new vision based on development not charity. There are many other places where a new wind is blowing, and my choice of countries may appear somewhat random; but they all illustrate widely different political and cultural contexts for development, and between them represent a large part of the spectrum of diversity in approaches to development work.

The common starting point in each of these countries is a realisation that the medical model of disability, in which the disabled person is treated mainly as a patient or client with only medical or physical needs, is wholly inadequate. The evidence from these countries illustrates a recognition that, whatever form of service is applied — whether institution-based, community-based, or whatever — disabled people are human beings with all the economic, emotional, physical, intellectual, spiritual, social, and political needs that other people have. The main implication of this is that unless they are involved in the planning and implementation of services, these services will always be inadequate in extent and in philosophy, whatever form they take. A disability programme, no matter how 'community based', is not developmental unless disabled people play a leading part in its design and implementation.

The material for the book was gathered principally from conversations with disabled people in the developing countries named. The people interviewed included disabled people in villages, leaders of the disability movement in each country, and disabled people running their own organisations. Over 300 people in all were interviewed, with most of the conversations recorded on tape. Numerically people in villages were by far the largest group. There was a preponderance of men over women, a factor perhaps determined by my own sex, but also reflecting male dominance among disabled people too: men tended to come forward and women did not.

I greatly regret that I was not able to meet and interview more women: there are obviously clear parallels between disability issues and the issues surrounding the role of women generally. I recognise that the small number of women interviewees is a serious flaw in the book. I also recognise that neither the women's movement nor the disability movement has adequately begun to address the double disadvantage that disabled women face: that of sexism and 'handicapism'. I have tried to illustrate this in the country case studies, and sincerely hope that this crucial issue will be addressed in greater depth by other writers with more direct experience than me. (Some material already published is listed in the Further Reading section at the end of this book.)

A personal statement

For me personally the discoveries recorded in this book have been a transforming experience. It has immeasurably strengthened my faith in the power of ordinary people, even in the most desperate circumstances, to effect real change in their own lives. It has led me in particular into a deeper understanding of the psychology of being disabled: the sense of loss, but the discovery of hidden strengths; the feeling of being rejected, but the ability to overcome rejection and be accepted as a full human being; above all it has shown me ways in which the demoralising patterns of negative attitudes and patronising relationships can be broken — by disabled people themselves. It has also been a discovery of the whole psychology of helping and being helped: in the final analysis we are all, whether disabled or not, both helpers and helped.

I began the project with some misgivings at not being disabled myself, aware that the most effective message will come from disabled people. But there are three things to be said about that.

First, the disability movement is not an exclusive club. Non-disabled people do have a role to play in helping to move the issues forward, as friends and allies. The disabled people interviewed for this book have given me nothing but encouragement. We are all part of a common humanity. All my contacts with disabled people have enriched my own life immeasurably: we can all contribute to each other's growth. But they are apprehensive about non-disabled people speaking on their behalf: that is indeed their main criticism of the professional carers and those with a stake in the rehabilitation industry who feel they have the final word on disability. The reader must judge whether I have fallen into this trap. I have tried to write as an able-bodied person with a deep interest in human development, for whom the situation of disabled people represents a microcosm of the whole human condition. A different kind of book would emerge from a disabled writer.

Second, the process of researching and writing the book has been an ever-deepening journey of discovery for me. My own attitudes as a non-disabled person have been transformed by what I have learnt. The change in my attitude is best summed up in the question, when I am with a disabled person: 'Am I the reason why this person feels disabled?' Everybody is affected by the attitudes of those they are relating to, and everybody knows what it feels like to be 'disabled' by another's manner, when we are treated with disrespect or in a patronising way. Conversely we also know what it feels like to be 'enabled' by another, when we feel that he or she respects us as an individual and relates to us as an equal. I hope that this book will help those who read it to be enablers rather than disablers. In this sense the book goes well beyond an examination of 'disability' and is really about how all of us, whether disabled or non-disabled, can live lives of greater value to each other.

Third, it is conventional to identify a segment of the human race as 'disabled'. But, as a visitor to a French naturist village recently observed, 'physical perfection is so rare as to be an oddity'.[3] In other words, human beings are ranged along a continuum between 'disabled' and 'able-bodied'. Disability is relative to culture and circumstances. It is important to hold this paradox in tension: disabled people need liberation, but defining who is disabled is not an easy matter. We all have differing abilities.[4]

Values and interests

My own concern about disability results from a growing disillusionment with an approach to development based chiefly on material and economic factors. The division of the world into 'rich' and 'poor', or 'developed' and 'developing', is as problematic as dividing it into 'able-bodied' and 'disabled'. To determine a people's 'state of development' by income levels or gross national product alone is a one-dimensional, materialistic attitude that leaves out the whole range of social, cultural, and spiritual factors that give meaning to people's lives. It is obvious to me that those unencumbered with material possessions often have a deeper wisdom than those who live their lives in an unending pursuit of material gain. More wealth does not imply more wisdom. I believe that aid agencies, including Oxfam, carry a large responsibility for perpetuating (albeit unwittingly) the ridiculous notion that those in 'the South' are automatically 'worse off' in every way than those in 'the North'.

Of course I agree that poverty is a blight on the face of the planet, and that in the final analysis we are talking about the need for resources to be distributed fairly; but tackling poverty only through economic programmes has solved none of the massive problems with which we live. There is an increasing awareness among those involved in development activities that there are no easy solutions; the glib optimism of the 1960s and 1970s has given way to a more sombre realism. Neither the mega-programmes nor the micro-projects have managed to 'abolish poverty'. Poverty will never be 'abolished' by a system that is run only on materialistic principles; indeed, 'development' based on the notion of acquiring more material benefits will always enrich some and impoverish others. The myth of economic growth as the key to development needs to be challenged.

There are values and there are interests. Values are what we believe in — things like democracy and respect and empowerment. Interests are the actual forces, usually economic, that drive political activity. Governments on the whole behave according to what is in their economic interests, seldom according to values. Refusing to sign an environmental treaty protecting bio-diversity because it is bad for business is a glaring example of operating by material interests rather than universal human and planetary values.

Values define how we would like the world to be; interests dictate how it actually is. It is probably inevitable that interests will be the main engine of action in the world, and the economist Adam Smith believed that a 'hidden hand' ensures that self-interest will always serve the common good in the end. I'm not so sure. It is clear from the environmental debate that unless political action is based on the fundamental values of respect for life and a responsible husbanding of natural resources, the planet is doomed. In other words, unless our actions are actually based on the eternal values of respect for life and for each other, our long-term interests will not be served. So in the final analysis, values and interests do coincide; but this has not been grasped, on the whole, by those who determine the course of things.

The problem with a purely materialistic approach to development is that it is based on short-term and short-sighted interests, rather than the deep values which actually serve our ultimate interests. Disability leads one into different pathways, different mind-sets, a different way of looking at the world and what development means, because it does indeed challenge the prevailing ethic of measuring 'success' by material achievement. There is something else, and it is more important:

> *The earth does not argue,*
> *Is not pathetic, has no arrangements,*
> *Does not scream, haste, persuade,*
> *threaten, promise,*
> *Makes no discriminations, has no*
> *conceivable failures,*
> *Closes nothing, refuses nothing,*
> *shuts none out.*

(Walt Whitman: 'A song of the rolling earth')

What is our vision for the world and for the society in which we live? Is it one in which the fittest, the toughest, the most agile, the most aggressive, those with the strongest self-interest, thrive — and the rest merely survive? Where anybody who is 'different' is shunned, and where there is a worship of uniformity? Or is it a society in which diversity is welcomed and individuals are each valued for what they are? Do we want a world which makes discriminations, or do we want a world where none is shut out?

Development based only on material interests inevitably implies the success of the strong. Disabled people can show us a different way, and lead us into an approach to development based on the profound human value of respect for each individual life. The key words are *liberation* and *empowerment*, the liberation and empowerment of all human beings to fulfil their own potential. The liberation and empowerment of disabled people provides an insight into the liberation and empowerment of all oppressed people: the process is similar, but in the case of disabled people the focus is extra-sharp.

An early draft of this text triggered a comment by one reader that there are two books here wanting to get out: one on development and one on spiritual values, and I should make up my mind which the book is actually trying to deal with. My response is that I see no difference between true development and spiritual values; they are the same thing. 'The earth ... has no conceivable failures, closes nothing, refuses nothing, shuts none out.' That is the credo of this book.

It is a process book, not a handbook or a definitive analysis of a complex subject. It is a beginning, on which others can build.

Opinions, attitudes, and ideas among disabled people about themselves, about development, and about disability issues are just as diverse as those held by non-disabled people. Those interviewed for this book range from militant leaders of the disability movement to people who want nothing to do with the movement, and all shades between these two extremes. What unites them is the common desire to be accepted as fully paid-up members of the human race.

In October 1987 a large group of people in wheelchairs staged a peace march with other disabled people, to demonstrate against the war in Lebanon. They trundled through all the main cities on the coast, from Tripoli in the north to Tyre in the south. They had many critics, and many supporters. Some said they were mad, some said they were brave. By the time they reached Tyre, the march had become a cavalcade and the city dignitaries turned out with thousands of others to meet them. They had passed through numerous militia check posts along the way, and the armed men had nothing to say.

Who creates the vision for society? Do we leave it to the men of power and violence? For evil to triumph it is enough that good people do nothing. If we want a more humane society based on the values of respect and compassion for each other, then we have to create it. The people in wheelchairs who trundled from Tripoli to Tyre were setting out to do just that.

CHAPTER 2

Setting out the issues: an interview with B. Venkatesh

'If people feel good about themselves, they can start to create change.'
(Venkatesh)

This book is intended primarily as a stimulus to thought and discussion. It is certainly not a prescription or a gospel. If you find yourself disagreeing strongly with a particular view, that is all to the good: only through critical discussion can we move away from slogans and the pernicious idea that there is one view that should prevail.

B. Venkatesh, or Venky as he is generally known, is director of Action on Disability and Development (ADD) India. He has been blind since his teens as a result of *retinitis pigmentosa*, a condition which accounts for about 2 per cent of blindness in the world today. In the interview that follows, Venky speaks about the central disability issues that will be discussed in this book.

I imagine that many able-bodied people and perhaps some disabled people reading this book will be rather similar to me when I started out on this project: aware that there is something drastically wrong with the way disabled people are regarded and treated, but not able to define precisely where the problems lie. In approaching Venky, I wanted views on the basic questions as he saw them. The answers he gave are not the only answers. They are his answers, which can be considered and agreed with or challenged. Complete answers or final solutions do not exist except as dogma; anyone who claims to have the complete answer has probably not understood the question.

An interview with any one of the many disabled people met during the research for this book could have been used as the starting point; each would have had its strengths and weaknesses. The point is, we have to start somewhere. This is a process book which sets out to explore, not to define.

I asked Venky first about language (which will be discussed in detail in Chapter 7).

Venkatesh: I prefer to be called 'blind', rather than a 'visually impaired person'. 'Visually impaired person' is such a mouthful. Whether you call me blind or visually impaired is not important, the most important thing is what I feel about myself. It's about self-esteem. I don't get hurt by being called blind. It's a mechanism I've built within myself. It's a matter of survival, of self-defence. What you are called makes no difference, because your sense of self-worth rises above that.

Q: So does that mean that blindness is part of your identity which you feel quite happy with?

If I am what I am today, you know, deep inside, the way my mind works, it is because of my disability. Disability has enriched my life as a person.

Q: How has it enriched your life?

What gives worth to this life? It's not what you have or what you don't have. It's the ability to enjoy what you have, no matter what. If you don't have that grace, you can't enjoy anything, whether you have sight or not, or even if you're a millionaire. That fundamental realisation has been crucial to me.

Because being disabled is nothing wrong; there is no value on it. If anything, the human value of being yourself can increase immensely, because of the sensitivity to yourself that can develop. I mean pain is part of growth. I think trauma is also a source of motivation. You can channel the trauma. Anger is a very powerful emotion. But properly channelled and directed, anger is very positive, socially and to oneself.

Venkatesh (Venky), Director of Action on Disability and Development (ADD) India.

Q: How have you yourself dealt with this question of other people's attitudes?

Like anyone else I have had to play many roles, as a child, a teenager, an adult, and so on. I have not been blind from birth. I could read and write until I was ten years old; I could play cricket and football; I could move about using vision until I was eighteen. My blindness came upon me gradually, so in the early years I had internalised what you may call 'normal behaviour'. In each of the roles that I have played and will play until I die, the issue for me is to be a good student, an effective manager, a good lover, and be good at having fun as well. I have continued to play the roles I played when I could see, which means simply being myself. I have not worked consciously at trying to get positive attitudes from people. I believe that a positive attitude in me will beget positive attitudes in them. I have always worked at being positive in anything I do, whether sighted or blind.

Of course I have met negative attitudes, especially from strangers when I travel, and I have to deal with them. But I have found that even in these situations, if I have a positive attitude, it gets a positive response from them.

At one time I also had a kind of determination to beat people at their own game, to refuse to admit defeat, to show that I was as good as anybody else at anything I tried.

This was the trip I was on, and it was a mistake. It came from a sense of insecurity. I wanted to prove that being blind did not stop me from being as good as the next person. From there it was also natural to go for status: good money, a good job, and all that. But I realised I was losing touch with myself in trying to be that superman. I've been fortunate enough to be sensitive to that and come out of it. I've passed a stage where I don't have to do that, because I've got there. I mean not in a smug sense, but in the sense of being accepted for my work and what I am. And so I can be just myself now. But it took a long time.

Q: What convinced you that working in disability and not in the able-bodied corporate sector was the right way to go?

It was a matter of realising that the sector of disabled people needs people of competence and vision, and for some reason I believed that I have those qualities, rightly or wrongly. So I said, 'Let's work here.' And from there on I have grown far more than I ever grew in the corporate sector, chasing status and a 'good career'.

Q: Can you point to how your ideas have developed since starting to work in the disability sector?

I joined the Association of the Physically Handicapped, Bangalore, in 1980, and realised the need to reach more people than they were doing then. Services have to be provided to disabled people, but this country cannot afford a five-star rehabilitation service. Therefore the disability issue should be built into every sector, be it banking, or industry, or government. There should not be anything separate for disabled people. We must use existing structures.

Q: Do you see disability as fundamentally a social problem or as an individual problem?

It's both a social problem and an individual problem. Primarily it is a social problem, because what stops the individual disabled person from contributing is the attitude of non-disabled people towards him or her. It is attitudes which disable. These attitudes disable to the extent that disabled people do not have self-worth, they lack confidence, they believe that they are good for nothing, and therefore they become consumers rather than contributors to society. Once they become only consumers, then they are labelled as useless. So it is a vicious circle, but the starting point is attitudes by non-disabled people, and that is where change has to begin.

Q: So you've got limited resources, limited time, limited people: where do you put your efforts?

My whole work now is about human resource development, developing people, enabling disabled people who are psychologically stunted and disempowered by social attitudes and religious prejudices. The primary aim of my work is to enable disabled people to feel good about themselves. How people feel about themselves has a direct impact on what they do and how they do it; unless they feel good about themselves, they won't be able to do very much. Furthermore, if people feel good about themselves, they can start to create change. So my effort is also in getting disabled people to understand the root cause of their own situation, and getting them to act to change the situation, if they want to. If they don't want to, no one can change it for them.

Q: What has influenced you most in that approach? It's quite revolutionary.

Work with disabled people is like a coin with two sides to it. One side is the special needs of disabled people; the other is attitudes. The services that exist today, as far as I know everywhere in the world, cater to special needs, but they do not address the whole issue of what it means to be a disabled person: what it means to be a disabled person in terms of psychology, and the social aspects of being disabled, the politics of disability. These two sides of the coin are crucial to the total development of the disabled person as a socially conscious creature. If there are not strong movements of disabled people in different parts of the world, it's because those disabled people who have had access to opportunity do not have this consciousness, and that is the tragedy of 150 years of rehabilitation work.

Q: You mean that the traditional rehabilitation approach has perpetuated a spirit of dependency?

Precisely. The rehabilitation process has reinforced the phenomenon of dependency, which we may call the disability mentality. It is evident even where disabled people have organised themselves in different parts of the world into self-advocacy groups. If they demand special concessions and privileges rather than equalisation, then they are perpetuating the disability mentality.

Q: You mean they are arguing for separate development?

Yes. It's so much in the consciousness of the elite in the disability movement, and it's the result of the whole process of rehabilitation. This mentality is evident everywhere. It all amounts to the same thing: an attitude of separateness and therefore dependency. It derives fundamentally from an attitude of religious charity: do good to a disabled person and you will find a place in heaven, as though disabled people are incapable of looking after themselves. These attitudes have always been there, and they are taking new forms today.

Nothing fundamentally has changed. If we want change, then disabled people have to become more aware. We are aiming at human dignity, not separate services.

Q: So if you were in the position of being a member of a national organisation of disabled people, what would be the things that you would be pressing for, say at the legislative level?

I would get disability work or disability policy taken out of Social Welfare. I would influence the government to have a unit for disability in every one of its ministries, be it integrated rural development, or women and children, or finance, or commerce and industries. That's what I would be aiming for. It means that at the policy level you are integrating work with disabled people. Education, health, employment, housing, whatever. Which means that at the policy level we are not marginalised. So if that takes place, I think that's the beginning of integration at the national level.

Q: There are quite a lot of disabled people who will always be dependent. Quadraplegics, for example, who have to rely on other people to do things for them. Or another category would be children born with severe cerebral palsy who are in effect physically helpless. What would you do about people with that kind of disability?

If we are talking about education, they would come under the Ministry of Education; if health care, then under the Ministry of Health. It is not to say that disabled people do not have special needs. They do. But these special needs should be met by each ministry as appropriate, not by some separate ministry which is shoved away round the corner with a very small budget to work on.

Q: So what's the main disadvantage of having a specialist ministry?

The first thing is that by the very fact of having one, you are saying that we are marginalised. Second, the amount of money provided for such ministries is very small. Out of every rupee that we spend, 21 paise[1] are spent to service international loans, 19 paise are spent on defence, 2 paise on education, and 3 paise on health. So you can imagine what disability gets: it would be 0.000001 paise or something. So that shows that they want to marginalise it right from the word go. The resource allocation is so small that it's not worth it.

The third point is that by this process you would be trying to segregate disabled people in terms of institutions or whatever. Right from top to bottom what you see is segregation: that's what I'm dead against.

Q: Following this logic on, if one is looking for complete integration and not ghettoisation, how would you argue for or against movements of disabled people? I mean organisations which are exclusively composed of disabled people?

I have been talking about an ideal world, but it doesn't exist. Therefore there is a need for a movement, to press for this change: equalisation of opportunities.

Q: So you would argue for a movement of disabled people on the grounds that you have to be noticed in order to get equal opportunities?

You must demand equalisation. Unless you demand it, you're not going to get it. You've got to see the issues clearly: you can take advantage of disability: begging, or jumping the queue because you are disabled, are manifestations of that. But that means marginalisation. If that's what you want, then you don't want a movement. But in fact you probably still want a movement, because you still want to propagate that attitude of dependence — you know: 'poor me'.

Q: Obviously there is a vicious circle to be broken here. Many disabled people do not have access to education and therefore their levels of awareness are quite low, and therefore their political awareness is low. It would perhaps be unusual for them to have reached the level of understanding that you have. How do you aim to deal with that problem?

That question brings us straight to the work we are doing. I believe that disabled people who are not educated, who have no access to literacy, are no less capable of being politically conscious about being disabled than those who have had access to literacy and education.

Q: You mean that levels of education do not necessarily correlate with awareness about disability?

Exactly. But the point is, disabled people do not have access to education, to childhood, to motherhood, property, housing, transportation, whatever. All these of course are basic rights of the human being. Given that they don't have these things, how can we get to a stage where they feel these are the things they want to work for? So in small groups of disabled people we sit with them and think through what it means to be a disabled person. 'I am a disabled person. I have brothers and sisters, and they are doing this, this and this. Why am I not doing these things? Whatever is going on in my village, I'm not party to it, I don't participate. Or it's a marginalised participation. Why? Is it because I am disabled? Or is it because someone else has decided how it shall be, because they have not seen anything different?' That's the reason: they have not seen anything different. They are seeing the same role-models for disabled people: you know, being a shepherd, or looking after children, or being a watchman.

Q: So creating different role-models is an important part of the task.

Absolutely right. Both disabled and non-disabled people need to see different role-models for disabled people in villages. They need to widen their horizons. There's a new project I've got funding for: 'Communications, Disability and Development'. It's to produce audio-visuals, street-theatre materials, and workshop material to promote this message of disability and attitude. It's about challenging disabled people who are stuck in this charity thing to decide whether they want change. Do they want to remain dependent? It's not just a question of asking for things from the government, for example, which is just a perpetuation of the dependency role. They have to believe that they can actually get from point A to point B if they want to. If that belief does not come from within themselves, if it's not internalised, I don't think anything can happen. This is a crucial first step with the disabled people with whom we are working.

We are working for fundamental change. We say to disabled people, 'It's for you to decide, whether you want fundamental change or not.' That is the issue. The questions of getting a government loan or a bus pass or a scholarship are all steps in this process of getting there, of building self-confidence, and finding strength in being disabled together.

Q: Would you support the idea of special facilities or special passes on the buses for disabled people?

I am not saying whether I support or don't support it. The point is that it is what disabled people out there want. I cannot change anything myself on my own. If they want radical change and real equalisation, they have to have belief in their own ability, and these interim measures help towards that. If you want to believe in collective action and see that it works, they have to have issues that they will succeed in. So if they want a shop, or a loan, or whatever, I think it's our job as activists to help them to attain those objectives. It's a question of how far our ambitions go. Do they stop at getting a bus pass or a loan, or does equalisation mean more than that to you? It's a process of growth, of development, of enabling people to be together and to find their strength.

We work across disabilities because we can then get disabled people to see that the problem they are dealing with is a common problem: it is a problem of attitude.

Q: What would you say is the role of the community in dealing with the question of service provision?

In an ideal world I would like service delivery to be done by organisations of disabled people. That is truly community-based. They would make the decisions about what services they want and who is going to be trained, and these people would come back and report to the disabled organisation. And the organisation would be responsible for getting the funds and administering the service.

Q: What would you see as the role of professionals in any kind of service delivery?

This professionalism is a non-issue in India. I don't want to make it an issue because some Western friends are trying to make it an issue. There are not nearly enough professionals anyway in India, so the question of their controlling disability on a large scale does not arise. But having said that, I think that professionals, in an ideal world, should be managed by organisations of disabled people. Their job is to deal with the impairment only. But to get them into an activist role is a very dangerous thing, because they have so much power, from their expertise. Already they have enough power; we should not make them more powerful than they already are.

Q: And what would you define as the role of the State in service provision?

The State should look after disabled people as it looks after any other of its citizens. In an ideal world it should look after their special needs as a matter of routine. That's my utopia. No fuss. Routine.

Q: Why do you think the disability issue is so important in the development context?

First, disabled people are a substantial minority in the world, and most governments have not reached even 5 per cent of them. Second, disability dehumanises people. It dehumanises them because it drives them into total hibernation, like vegetables. That's not on. It's the worst form of human-rights violation. Many disabled people, especially mentally retarded and communication-impaired people, are left without any stimulation from the time they are infants. They have no childhood, boyhood, girlhood; they are not aware that they are 18 or 20 years old. They are in a state of permanent senility.

Q: So they are the opposite of socially conscious people.

Yes, they just live at the level of hunger and thirst. This is what social attitudes have done to them. That is why disability is a development issue: it dehumanises people. Those are extremes I have quoted; but the same phenomenon is manifested in all disabled people to some degree. But unless disabled people themselves want to change that dehumanising situation, then there isn't much hope that the situation will change.

Q: And you think it's only disabled people who can make the change?

Absolutely right. Because being disabled is so comfortable! We can just sit on our backsides, and let it all happen. But if we do that, we gradually lose our sense of self-worth, and these expectations are not there. You just become resigned and do not demand any more. Disabled people have to get out of that shell. They have to be sensitised. People not calling you by your name, but by your disability, is just not on.

This interview reveals a mixture of idealism and realism. The key issues that Venky talks about are attitudes towards disability and the empowerment of disabled people. It is prejudice, fear, and negative attitudes which create the 'problem' of disability: if attitudes were not negative, there would not be a problem. So the task is to understand why these attitudes exist, and how they can be altered. Venky's view is that the process of change has to start with disabled people.

In the pages that follow, it is these two issues that form the constant theme of enquiry.

PART TWO

The issues

Huda, a member of the Baqaa community centre for disabled Palestinian children, Jordan.

CHAPTER 3

The experience of disability

'Social change initially comes from us, from disabled people. It has to.'
(Rachel Hurst)

Disability: who accepts?

Disability is perceived, by able-bodied people, as a tragedy, a loss, or a deficiency; these powerful negatives elicit either fear, pity, or admiration, depending on how the disabled person 'copes'. But is that the way disabled people see it? When we speak of 'acceptance' of an impairment, what do we mean? Who has to accept it — the disabled person, or everyone else?

What we have to examine is why negative attitudes are held, and how they can be changed. The negative response of most able-bodied people to disabled people is based mainly on ignorance: they assume that disablement is a catastrophe, and they fear it; fear creates awkwardness, avoidance, and prejudice. But a first step in changing perceptions and attitudes is to understand the experience of disability for those who are disabled. We will look at the question of prejudice and discrimination later in this chapter ('Attitudes: breaking out of the vicious circle'), and in Chapter 4 ('The politics of disability'). Here we will explore the way in which the impairment[1] itself is viewed by a number of disabled individuals.

Is it possible to accept an impairment? Many disabled people would say they can never 'accept' it, in the sense required by an able-bodied and non-understanding world. They resent being told that they have to 'come to terms' with their condition; rather it is the able-bodied world that has to accept or come to terms with disability. What disabled people have to 'cope with' is not their impairment, but the hostility, prejudice, and discrimination that they meet every day of their lives — for no other reason than that they are disabled.

This is true. But it is also true that there is a process of adjustment by the disabled person which is essential if life is to have any meaning for him or her. The road to adjustment for the disabled person is a lifelong process of self-discovery, the discovery of a new identity, with all the ups and downs that self-discovery for anyone entails. But adjustment requires an understanding of that identity, not only by the disabled person but by those who relate to her or him. Negative attitudes, prejudice, and discrimination make it impossible or very difficult for this adjustment to take place. At what point can the circle be broken?

It is at the beginning a question of identity. We have already seen in the interview with Venkatesh that for him blindness is not a loss, but an opportunity for deeper development as a person:

What gives worth to this life? It's not what you have or what you don't have. It's the ability to enjoy what you have, no matter what. If you don't have that grace, you can't enjoy anything, whether you have sight or not, or even if you're a millionaire. That fundamental realisation has been crucial to me. Because being disabled is nothing wrong; there is no value on it. If anything, the human value of being yourself can increase immensely, because of the sensitivity to yourself that can develop. I mean, pain is part of growth. I think trauma is also a source of motivation. You can channel the trauma.

Rachel Hurst, of Disability Awareness in Action, is a wheelchair user as a result of a form of congenital muscular dystrophy; the condition was not diagnosed until many years after the symptoms had appeared, and for her the diagnosis was a breakthrough to her real identity:

I was actually born with a disability. But it was not diagnosed for a long time, until I was 39 in fact. But once it was diagnosed, it was like recognising myself at last. It was a total liberation. It sounds crazy, and obviously there are times when I wish I could walk, but I now feel much more secure in myself, now I know what I myself 'am'.

Actually when they diagnosed it and told me that I must have had it since I was born, I did not believe them at first; but then I realised it was true and it altered the whole way I had perceived myself ... I mean I had always perceived myself as aggressively able-bodied, which meant that for years I had been trying to do things I couldn't actually

*Rachel Hurst, of Disability
Awareness in Action: 'Social
change initially comes from us, from
disabled people. It has to.'*

*do. I feel very much more comfortable with the me that I know now
than with the one I was trying to be. There was an uncanny feeling
that that wasn't the real me.*

Moses Masamene is a blind lawyer from Lesotho who, like Venky,
lost his sight gradually in his late teens through *retinitis pigmentosa*.
Now in his thirties, he sees his blindness as part of his personal
identity, in the same way that maleness is:

> *I take it to be another endowment, in the sense that if you are a male or
> a female, it is what you are. I take my blindness to be an identity; it is a
> human attribute, which should not prevent anybody from achieving
> his aspirations. So it is a question of counteracting social barriers
> which oppose unsightedness.*

Both gender and disability are 'constructed', in the sense that on top
of the biological facts of sex and an impairment such as lack of sight
there are social expectations which determine the options for those
concerned. But Moses recognises that adjusting to this new identity
is not necessarily easy. For those who were born disabled, the
question of identity is obviously easier than for those who become
disabled later in life.

> *There is early disability and late disability. With early disability there
> is no problem, because you grow up with it. But with late disability*

there is bound to be some emotional instability as you try to get over that. But with time, through contact with other blind people, and counselling from your peers, you do get over that.

Be aware that in life anything can happen, because disability is like the air that we breathe: it doesn't give you any notice. When it happens, it is important that one should cry over the loss and then accept it and accept a new identity.

Of course, becoming disabled does involve a loss, and the disabled person may go through all the agonies of denial, anger, and rejection before reaching the stage of adjustment which amounts to acceptance. Some may remain stuck at anger and rejection and never reach the stage of acceptance at all, living out an existence of bitterness and regret because they cannot accept the stigma. On the other hand, a recently disabled person may not experience any difficulty in adjustment at all, and may slip straight into the new identity. Whatever the case, the experience of millions of disabled people all over the world demonstrates that 'acceptance' in the sense of believing in the new identity is the necessary prelude to leading a fulfilled life with the new reality.

Acceptance or resignation?

But what does acceptance mean? Is it just a question of getting used to a loss, a kind of resignation in the face of unalterable odds? If acceptance means nothing more than resignation, then little of positive value can happen. Resignation is tantamount to fatalism. Acceptance is more: it involves a positive adjustment to the new identity, in which self-image and self-esteem are not impaired, but remain very much intact; they may even be enhanced, as in Venkatesh's case.

There are no simple prescriptions for how to attain acceptance, but it is a process which certainly involves all the non-disabled people, especially the family, who relate to the disabled person. Pity, neglect, or over-protection by them obviously make it very much harder. This is especially the case when a child becomes disabled; the whole family will be faced with the problem of how to react to and accept the new situation, and it may well be harder for the family than for the child.

Alexander Phiri lost both legs at the age of ten when he was hit by a car. He came from a very poor family in a village in Zimbabwe, and once his parents realised he had lost his legs, they abandoned

him in hospital as no longer of any use to the family; he had become
a major economic burden. The hospital placed him in an institution
from where he was able, against considerable odds, to get educated,
and eventually graduated from college into a good job as a designer.
Once established, he decided to trace his family, and after much
enquiry tracked them down in a different village, driving up to their
hut in his own car. His brothers and sisters had been told that he
was dead, and his mother had the greatest difficulty in dealing with
the astounding situation of his sudden reappearance after a gap of
15 years. (His father had meanwhile died.)

Alex is now the main provider for his extended family. He holds
no bitterness for the childhood rejection:

*They thought I was hopeless. But in fact I am the only educated
member of my family, thanks to my disability. So it was like a blessing
in disguise that I became disabled. Otherwise I would not have got to
where I am today.*

He has become a leading and highly articulate member of the
disability movement, not only in Zimbabwe but also in the southern
Africa region. The irony is that rejection by his parents led to his
present position as the family's main breadwinner.

Rejection of a disabled child as an economic burden certainly
happens, especially in extremely poor communities. Other dramatic
stories similar to that of Alex were told by several people
interviewed for this book. They were the lucky ones: others rejected
do not survive. But perhaps more common than rejection is over-
protection by the parents, fearing that their child will not be able to
cope and must therefore be treated as an everlasting baby.

Samir Ghosh from Jemshedpur in northern India had both arms
amputated at the shoulder after being electrocuted at the age of
eight. His parents, unable to accept this catastrophe themselves and
sure that he would not be able to deal with it, told him that his arms
had been taken away 'to be washed', and that they would soon be
brought back. As the days went by and no arms appeared, he asked
the surgeon when his arms would come back:

*'When are you going to bring my arms and hands back to me?' But he
had no answer. He just took a chair and sat with his face in his hands.
Then he realised that my parents had been telling me all these things.
But he didn't blame them. He realised they just didn't know how to
react. I was in hospital for three months. But the doctors felt I was*

fairly strong to take things. So the doctor said, 'I don't think your
arms are going to come back, but we will try to help you get some new
"hands".'

It was Samir who surprised his parents. He did indeed acquire new 'hands': within weeks he was writing with his foot, and announced he was going to return to school; his parents objected, thinking that he would be an embarrassment (presumably to them, if not to himself), but he insisted. Fortunately the headmaster was enlightened: he welcomed him back at a school assembly when he announced, without great drama, that Samir had had an accident and 'might need a little help from time to time'.

Samir, positive and outgoing, was accepted by his peers as a full member of the school. His classmates helped him with homework at first, but he was soon able to write as quickly as them with his foot. He completed his studies in India, and eventually gained a doctorate at the London School of Economics. He now holds a senior post as management consultant in one of the largest firms in India. He is more or less independent; the only aid he uses is a dressing hook which he holds in his mouth to pull up trousers and socks. He eats, writes, uses the telephone, and drives a car entirely with his feet. This acquisition of independence has been gradual, and he is still, in his late thirties, discovering an increasing range of techniques for doing things differently.

This story is not included here to portray heroism, but to make the point that positive acceptance of such an apparently appalling loss is possible. An impairment need not be an obstacle to a deeply fulfilling life. Samir was accepted by the school because he refused to see his impairment as a bar to a normal life, despite his parents' attitude, and that has been his story ever since. Without a positive attitude from him, none of this would have happened. If he had sat at home 'demanding his rights', no change would have occurred.

But inward, positive acceptance of impairment is a journey which not only the disabled person has to make. We have seen in the case of Alex Phiri and Samir Ghosh that parents may have difficulty in coping with a disabling accident to their children. Likewise for a mother to give birth to a disabled child can be a traumatic experience: with all the social and cultural prejudice against disability, coupled with the feelings of failure and guilt in herself, what should have been a joyful event turns into an apparent tragedy. The arrival of a child who may be eternally dependent seems like a blow of extra cruelty by fate. The father will almost certainly have similar feelings, deepened perhaps by the sense that somehow his manliness and family honour have been besmirched.

Some people in the disability movement say that they look forward to the day when a mother who gives birth to a disabled child will rejoice as deeply as if the child was not disabled;[2] that would be the real indication that disability is no longer feared or abhorred. We are into difficult territory here. If disability is not a negative, should it be prevented? If it should be prevented, what does that say to people living now who were born disabled? Should they have been 'prevented'? For now we will simply note this deep dilemma and return to it in Chapter 4, 'The politics of disability'.

Whatever the ethics, there is a certain reality that must be faced. The reality in many cultures is dismay when a disabled child is born. **M. Mathias** is the Secretary of the Karnataka Parents' Association for Mentally Retarded Citizens, based in Bangalore, south India. His daughter Tanya, now grown up, was diagnosed as having a mental disability at the age of four months.

> *The doctor told us: 'You have a mentally retarded child and she will be the ruination of your family.'*

At this time, in the early 1970s, there was very little awareness in India, even among educated urban people like him, about mental illness and mental disability; the two were lumped together, and there was a general fear that 'madness' was a hereditary disease which must be kept out of the family at all costs. His brother had warned him not to marry into a family 'where there was madness'. How did he and his wife react to the arrival of a little girl diagnosed as 'mentally retarded'?

> *I felt I had let my family down on three counts: to start with, my first child was a girl; second, I had brought 'mental illness' into the family; and third, the doctor had said she would be the ruination of my family.*

> *What was my reaction at that point? The normal human response: shock, guilt, denial. I think it took me about 20 years to accept my daughter's disability. My wife reacted the same way. But she is over-protective to some extent, which is another form of escape. I think I personally have finally accepted her, although I have had a few knocks when it has been clear that I have been kidding myself. I have adapted to the situation. But I have suffered the loss at each stage of what she would have been had she not been disabled.*

The family also has to face relatives and friends; they too have to find a way of dealing with the situation.

Our relatives and friends reacted with a studied indifference. They didn't know how to respond, so they pretended the problem didn't exist, like us. It was the first time in our whole family that such a thing had happened.

Eventually, when Tanya was in her teens, Mathias and his wife were instrumental in setting up the Karnataka Parents' Association for Mentally Retarded Citizens. This organisation provides support and counselling to parents, lobbies for changes in laws governing disability, and runs training courses for teachers in special education. Out of their own trauma has grown something positive and life-changing for many people.

It is important to point out here that the sex of their child was considered a matter for regret: the double rejection of girls and women who are disabled is a huge topic that has received very little attention in the literature on disability. As mentioned in Chapter 1, neither the women's movement nor the disability movement has previously addressed this issue adequately. 'To be male in our society is to be strong, assertive and independent; to be female is to be weak, passive and dependent, the latter conforming to the social stereotypes of the disabled. For both categories the disabled woman inherits ascriptions of passivity and weakness.'[3] Indeed, one feminist academic asks: 'Why study women with disabilities? They reinforce traditional stereotypes of women being dependent, passive and needy.'[4] At this point we can only note this enormous gap in understanding. It will recur in the country case studies, especially on Zanzibar and India.

Support and counselling for the parents of a disabled child are extremely important. It is no use pretending the problem does not exist, nor is it at all helpful if everybody, including the medical professionals, treats the whole matter as an unmitigated tragedy which will be 'the ruination of the family'. Doctors, midwives and other health workers need training in how to counsel parents and to give them support in the vital early stages. In particular, realism is essential. A common reaction is for parents to refuse to believe that their child has a permanent impairment and spend many fruitless years and money they can ill afford on trying to find a 'cure'. Good medical care at the beginning can certainly reduce the effects of the impairment, but the medical profession in general, especially in

Patricia Mazambani and Anita attend a mothers' support session at a township in Harare. 'When I am together with other mothers, I feel free. We feed each other with ideas.'

developing countries, is hooked on the 'cure or care' model which encourages the fruitless search; we will return to this subject in Chapter 5.

Acceptance of disability is a complex and life-long process involving many people and many factors. To regard permanent impairment, either in a newborn baby or in an adult, as a loss, is an understandable reaction; but if it is allowed to persist, such a reaction is not likely to lead to any constructive life process, either for the disabled person or for the non-disabled people around him or her. It is a new circumstance, which everybody has to adjust to — and come to terms with.

But let us be very clear and very careful about what is being said here: permanent impairment may or may not be a personal tragedy for the person concerned, but whatever it is, there is no reason for society to turn it into a handicap. Acceptance of an impairment does not mean accepting the role placed on disabled people by an able-bodied society. The social expectation of disabled people is that they will shut up, sit at home, and not complain. Acceptance of the impairment is one thing; but acceptance of such a passive, unconstructive, and disempowered role imposed by society is of course quite out of the question. What we have examined in this section is how some disabled people relate to their impairment. Of far greater importance is how the rest of the world relates to them.

Attitudes: breaking out of the vicious circle

It is attitudes that disable. If able-bodied people did not react with horror, fear, anxiety, distaste, hostility, or patronising behaviour towards disabled people, then there would not be a problem. Discrimination and prejudice create the sense of being disabled that leads to further discrimination and prejudice. How can this vicious circle be broken?

The testimonies from the disabled people interviewed for this book emphasise again and again that the process of attitude change starts with disabled people: their attitude towards themselves and their own disability. This perhaps sounds the wrong way round: surely it is able-bodied people who have to alter their attitudes first? But as with people suffering oppression of any kind, the truth is that the oppressor is not likely to change behaviour unless the oppressed person makes the first move. The harsh reality is that if disabled people see themselves as victims, they will be treated as victims; if they are sunk in self-pity, they will be perceived as pathetic; if they are hostile towards non-disabled people, they will be shunned; but if they refuse to see themselves as victims, if they claim their own dignity, see themselves as positive and able to contribute, they will be seen as positive and able to contribute. This is not at all the same as saying that disabled people should be quiet, stop complaining, and settle for some kind of half-life. Absolutely not. The issue for disabled people is ultimately one of self-esteem, of refusing to accept the role of victim. There are many different ways of expressing that dignity, but it lies at the heart of whatever choice disabled activists make, whether strongly militant or quietly persistent. In the words of Rachel Hurst of Disabled People's International: 'Social change initially comes from us, from disabled people. It has to.'

Samir Ghosh from Jemshedpur subscribes very strongly to the idea that disabled people will be treated according to their own attitudes towards themselves. In his opinion, much of the awkwardness displayed by able-bodied people is more the result of ignorance, fear, and lack of familiarity than outright prejudice. Because disabled people in India tend either to be in institutions or confined at home or are beggars, able-bodied people have few opportunities to meet them or form strong relations with them.

Samir therefore makes a point of putting people at their ease and has no hesitation in talking about his impairment if that helps the process. He feels that every person he meets is probably curious about how he manages with no arms, and is basically anxious to be able to relate to him normally.

Furthermore, says Samir, disabled people should not be deterred by one or two negative experiences:

> *I take the attitude that people are nice, people are good. But I think human beings tend to bank on their bad experiences, rather than their good experiences. We tend to judge the whole human race on just one or two bad experiences. For example, I once went into an office to ask for an address, and they told me to get out because they thought I was a beggar. That used to disturb me, but it doesn't mean that I am not going to go to any other office to ask the way.*

But it is very hard. Every time a disabled person goes out into the street, he or she has in a sense to start from scratch: the looks, the avoidance, the awkwardness, the prejudice are all there, every time. Dealing with these things positively time after time gets very wearing. Disabled people are, after all, only human; they may be forgiven for getting impatient with other people for not recognising that simple fact.

The dynamics of prejudice ✳

For many disabled people, rejection is catastrophic: it provokes despair and retreat, which in turn widen the gap and produce further rejection and stereotyping. They become literally disabled by the social attitudes they meet every day of their lives. They end up with a profoundly damaged psyche that is also a feature of other oppressed people: children molested or beaten by their parents, women living in fear of violence, or whole peoples subjected to institutionalised discrimination down the generations.

How can human behaviour be changed? How can this most vicious of vicious circles be broken? There are basically two views on this. One view insists that human nature is fundamentally flawed, and human beings must be prevented from transgressing through coercion and legislation: make it illegal to discriminate against disabled people, and prosecute when it happens. The other view contends that human beings can be influenced, enlightened, and persuaded, and that prejudices and fears can be altered only by the people who are the targets; change has to start by disabled people taking the initiative, by refusing to see themselves as victims, and by being outgoing in their relations with able-bodied people. Both views were expressed by people interviewed for this book, with the second by far the more dominant.

The truth, I think, lies on both sides. People can be influenced, but legislation is vital. Laws need not be viewed as an instrument of oppression; they are an essential expression of the values of a civilised society. A society without laws is indeed lawless. That is why getting disability legislation on to the statute book is a major objective of most disabled people's advocacy groups in the world today.

The validity of both views needs to be recognised by the other. Certainly we need laws, but they will not have any effect if attitudes do not change; we cannot ignore the need for influencing people through example and modifying our own attitudes. On the other hand, if our view of human nature is that it can be changed only through legislation, then that rules out the whole enterprise of development, not to mention education.

Let us stay with the view that people can be influenced. It is not an easy matter at all. On the one hand, changes in attitude must begin with the disabled person's own self-esteem: unless that is positive, nothing can happen. It is very difficult to form a constructive relationship with someone who is bitter and hostile to the world, or lost in self-pity, or angry that they are still alive. On the other hand, self-esteem cannot be raised in isolation from the social environment: we are all, whether disabled or able-bodied, a mixture of many influences, hereditary, environmental, and social, and our own attitude towards ourselves is not usually, except in rare cases, something which we as individuals have complete control over. If the social environment is oppressive and casts us in the role of victim, then inevitably that is the way we tend to see ourselves; it is very difficult to break out of this strangle-hold.

The question then becomes: if the answer lies inside the disabled person, what are the mechanisms by which an inner source of strength can be discovered? How do you start building self-esteem in an environment which continually undermines it?

Both disabled and able-bodied people need to be sensitive to the dynamics of prejudice, and they must work together to deal with them. There has to be acceptance of the disability by the disabled person, and a realisation that the process starts with a positive self-image. Able-bodied people need to make an extra effort to understand the difficulty of this process and avoid pandering to self-pity or indulging in over-protection. Robust friendships are needed, not kid gloves.

I am convinced by the testimonies of many people that attitudes can be changed, even in the most unpromising circumstances and under the weight of apparently insuperable cultural discrimination. The many examples quoted in this book illustrate how the circle may be broken. It is significant that all the disabled activists I interviewed insist that their work is primarily with disabled people, in enabling them to understand the causes of their oppression, to feel good about themselves, to walk tall. From that position change can start.

Heroes, heroines, and haloes

There is another aspect of negative attitudes that is possibly more insidious than outright rejection, because it appears to be benign. It is the phenomenon of hero-worship. Some people surround disability with a kind of halo which designates the disabled person as a hero or a saint. But both rejection and hero-worship are equally disabling.

Nawaf Kabbara from Lebanon was paralysed in a car accident in his twenties. Before his accident, he had what he describes as the 'normal' attitudes towards disabled people: pity for their condition and admiration for them if they coped well. For him disabled people were in two classes: beggars or heroes. But after his accident his ideas changed. He did not see himself as a hero:

> Why is it wrong to regard disabled people as heroes? Because we are not heroes. It just happens that things have changed in the way we do things; we are doing them in a different way. Of course there are challenges. You have to 'cope'. Some do that better than others. But it is not heroism. It is just a life you have to carry out.

Regarding disabled people as heroes or heroines is another form of labelling. Labels disable because they do not present the person for what he or she really is. Being regarded as a hero is ultimately very discouraging if you know perfectly well that you are not; it implies a shallowness, artificiality, and lack of seriousness in the relationship which is profoundly unsatisfying for the disabled person. It also inevitably entails failure when he or she does not live up to the expectations that hero-worship imposes.

While non-disabled people must be aware of the dangers of hero-worship in relating to disabled people, disabled people themselves also have to be sensitive to the risk of playing the hero, especially if the trauma of disability fires them to succeed and 'beat the able-bodied at their own game'. Building self-esteem can go over the top. Venkatesh recognised this danger in himself:

> There's a kind of determination to beat people at their own game. But one should not get lost in it. I got lost in it, and came out of it. Because you can overdo it, and therefore lose touch with yourself in trying to be that superman. The trip becomes getting a better job, earning more money, having status. These are the social parameters of someone who is doing well in life. So I was caught in that, and I had to get out of it. I've passed a stage where I don't have to do that because I can be just myself now. But it took a long time.

Such an awareness is not reached quickly. We all, whether disabled or not, spend our lives on a journey of discovery about ourselves in relation to our own character and the way it reacts to events. Disabled people have an added dimension to their journey, which is the identity created by their impairment, and they are, like everyone else, continually going through shifts in perception about themselves. The process of attitude change is life-long. And for everybody, whether disabled or not, the way people relate to us is determined by many factors, but most of all by the way we feel about ourselves.

The point about attitudes, finally, is that disabled people just want to be themselves and accepted for what they are. They are people with different abilities, like anyone else, with their own desires, ambitions, weaknesses, prejudices, perceptions, emotions, and hopes, like anyone else. In the final analysis we all have impairments: those who are referred to as disabled just happen to have more obvious impairments than others.

Role-models: breaking with stereotypes and stigmas

Some of those already quoted in this book are examples of 'successful' disabled people. Samir Ghosh has a PhD from the London School of Economics and is a much sought-after management consultant in India. Venkatesh was 'making it' in the corporate sector in Bombay before he decided to work full-time in the disability field. It is not my intention to extol the virtues of such success, which (as Venkatesh says) can be a trap and lead one into missing the point about life altogether. And it is no help to a disabled woman in a remote Indian village to be told that she too could get to be President if she tried hard enough. Such lack of realism is certainly not the point. But it is important to examine role-models, because negative attitudes by non-disabled people and low self-esteem by disabled people have much to do with what disabled people are perceived as being able to do and not do. The process of breaking out of the role of victim involves looking hard at role-models.

It comes back to self-perception and self-esteem. Do disabled people perceive themselves as able to argue for their rights, join unions, and hold down serious jobs? Where disabled people do these things, they provide positive, confident role-models for others. Where these things do not happen, alternative role-models are not on offer and the negative syndrome of the 'helpless victim' is perpetuated. The problem, once again, is how to create the alternative role-models and break the cycle.

Rungta is the president of the National Federation of the Blind in India, and a practising barrister. He recounts an incident in a hotel restaurant in Delhi where the staff cast him in the role of a helpless blind person and treated him accordingly:

> *A few months ago I decided to go to the Hotel Meridian for a meal, with my car and driver. We got out of the car and went into the restaurant. I placed the order with the waiter. That waiter and the lobby manager called my driver and told him that such and such a dish costs 70 rupees, another dish 80 rupees, and so on: would this man be able to pay? When my driver came and told me, I went to the lobby manager and asked, 'What were you saying to my driver?' And for two minutes I spoke in English and he kept mum. He did not even expect me to speak English. Then he said, 'Sorry, sir.' I said, 'What do you mean, sorry sir? You can't say this kind of thing to the customer. If the customer doesn't pay, then you have a case. But you have no business to say such things before the bill is paid or not paid.'*
>
> *That represents the attitude and the feeling. That lobby manager did not expect me to patronise that hotel. He did not imagine that I could own a car or speak English. These attitudes are not due to economic factors; they are due to prejudice about blindness.*

No doubt the incident was an educational one for the lobby manager. Rungta makes a point of being assertive in such situations: he refuses to let the matter pass without comment, and declares his disgust with vigour. It is a way of breaking out of the vicious circle, although to do it day after day must indeed be wearing.

We are talking about the need for major shifts in perception in both able-bodied and disabled people. What are the forces that can produce these shifts? **Muhammed Osman** is a founder member of the Nyala Association of the Disabled in the Sudan. He has a condition called spinal muscular atrophy, which means that his muscles are growing progressively weaker, and he now uses a wheelchair. The event which triggered a change of attitude in him was when he finally heard the truth about his condition:

At the beginning it was so hard to live with such a reality, to realise that you would never be like the others. But in 1980 I went to Egypt and there I met a doctor who told me certain facts: it was a genetic disease, and it was incurable.

This was a turning point for me, because I realised that if I couldn't can't get a cure, I should do something that will help other disabled people. It was a real turning point, because I realised that I should no longer waste any time in pursuing medical treatment. I should instead take a social approach to it. Realising this, I began to think about doing something. Well, it turned out to be bringing disabled people together to discuss these problems.

Once it was clear to him that he was disabled rather than 'sick', Muhammed was able to relinquish the role of 'patient' and become

Muhammed Osman, founder of the Nyala Association of the Disabled: 'I realised that if I couldn't get a cure, I should do something that would help other disabled people. ... It turned out to be bringing them together.'

active: he brought disabled people together in his home town of Nyala, which led to the founding of an association of disabled people. (We will see more of this example in Chapter 1.)

The question of role-models is also linked to that of stigma. For many people who become disabled as adults, it may be very difficult to accept that they are now part of a population referred to as 'disabled'. This is particularly true of ex-combatants and war veterans, who by the nature of things have lived aggressively able-bodied lives, may have always identified with 'macho' behaviour, and cannot accept that they are now, as they see it, incapacitated and classed with people they may have formerly despised. This may be one reason why, in a country like Zimbabwe, it is rare to find ex-combatants in the disability movement.

At the age of 18, **Mike du Toit**, a white South African, became hemiplegic (one side of his body was paralysed) after a car accident. But even though he trained as a social worker and clearly has a well-developed consciousness for social justice, he was determined not to identify himself with 'the disabled' after his accident, perhaps subconsciously influenced by the tough, rugby-playing ethos of his society, and therefore not willing to join a group he instinctively saw as carrying a stigma. But as a social worker, he attended a Rehabilitation International (RI) congress on disability in Winnipeg in 1981. RI is an organisation consisting primarily of able-bodied professionals dealing with disability; out of 3,000 delegates at the congress, only about 200 were disabled. These few disabled people demanded 50 per cent representation on the board of RI, but this request was refused. The refusal was a watershed in the whole politics of disability: in a dramatic moment of self-discovery and self-assertion, the disabled people responded by leaving the hall, meeting in another room, and setting up their own alternative organisation, Disabled People's International (DPI), run entirely by disabled people.

For Mike, this moment was a turning point in his self-perception: he suddenly understood that it was not only credible but important to be identified with this group; having gone to the congress as a 'social worker', he returned as a 'disabled person', and he has been active in the disability movement ever since:

> *I think until then disability for me was very definitely a personal thing, and it was a tragedy; it was something you felt sad about; it wasn't in any kind of way something that was exciting. Winnipeg for me changed all that. There were all these professional carers giving*

their papers about what they were doing to help disabled people. And there were disabled people confronting them head-on, asking pertinent questions and exposing the complete inadequacy of services for disabled people. On a daily basis they produced a newsletter during the conference that satirised the speakers from the previous day. It was exciting and positive.

The point is that both non-disabled and disabled people are part of the business of stigma-attachment and stereotyping. For disabled people, breaking the stereotype means being proud of their identity and creating role-models that do not perpetuate the syndrome of the 'helpless victim'. For Mike du Toit, excitement at the power revealed by disabled people when they were speaking for themselves in their own interests was enough to trigger a major shift of perception in him. The role models available in Winnipeg showed him another way: he had finally overcome the stigma and accepted his impairment as a positive identity.

CHAPTER 4

The politics of disability:
what is at stake?

'Disabled people have not benefited from charity,
because charity is not part of the development process.'
(Joshua Malinga)

An individual or a social issue?

Politics is about power and control. Ultimately, whether we engage in active politics or not, the central political issue is how much control we have over our own lives and the decisions that are important to us in shaping our lives.

Throughout the world, regardless of culture, disabled people have generally been seen as incapable of taking control of their own lives. There are three broad attitudes towards them among able-bodied people: they may be regarded as lesser beings to be rejected; or they are seen as objects of charity; or they may be viewed with 'benevolent neutrality', which is another way of saying: 'I don't wish to become involved.'[1]

Rejection in an extreme form is advocated by the exclusive ideology of fascism. The glorification of the 'perfect' human being resulted, under Hitler, in an effort to exterminate disabled people altogether as 'imperfections which contaminate the genetic stream'. The Nazi Euthanasia Programme saw disabled people as 'useless eaters'; that is, they were perceived as making no contribution to society, and as a drain on resources. But Hitler was not the first to advocate getting rid of disabled people: in medieval Germany Martin Luther strongly endorsed the killing of disabled babies as 'incarnations of the devil', and many centuries before him the Spartans insisted upon it by law for the same reasons as Hitler. And the Nazis were themselves following the Eugenicists, English Victorian scientists of the nineteenth century who, influenced by Darwin, held that 'survival of the fittest' required the elimination of 'defectives'.[2]

It is perhaps tempting to assume that the world has moved on from such crude and overt rejection. But have we really moved? The Nazi doctors declared at the Nuremburg Trials that they were doing no more than doctors everywhere did, but without official sanction. Nowadays, when market forces are the dominant factor shaping social policies, it is not uncommon for doctors and health planners to argue that 'the country cannot afford too many disabled people'. The medical profession and planners of health services are ambivalent about the wonders of modern medicine: it can prolong the life of, for example, a person with spina bifida, but at what cost to the exchequer? And what if they have children? Who will pay for the consequences?

Muhammed, a blind person in the village of Unguja Shangani in Zanzibar. Disabled people experience rejection in all societies.

Social Darwinism and charity

There is no doubt that the allocation of financial resources in health is a complex matter, beset by profound ethical dilemmas. But an approach to health care guided by nothing but economics is not a great improvement on the nineteenth-century Eugenicists. And what about education? Transport? Housing? Are all these going to be planned in a way that says it is too expensive to cater for disabled people? The Nazis and the Eugenicists may belong to history, but today we have 'social Darwinism': the (usually unspoken) assumption that only the fit and the fully functional have a right to real life. It is this attitude that lies at the heart of the discussion on the politics of disability.

The Nazi and fascist vision of society is one based on the glorification of health, fitness, perfect specimens, and uniformity. In this vision, being different calls for rejection. At the other end of the spectrum is a vision of society based on a celebration of the whole diversity of creation, in which individuals are valued for what they are, not rejected for what they are not. Which of these opposing visions do we prefer?

It is unlikely that paid-up fascists will read this book. Can the rest of us then be excused from reading further on the politics of disability? I'm afraid not. There is the matter of charity. The 'charitable' approach to disabled people is also a form of rejection that is actually more insidious than fascism: it turns disabled people into objects who only receive and who do not participate in the processes which shape their lives. It sees them as individuals, with individual problems: according to the 'charity' approach, if you solve the problems of individual disabled people, then the 'problem' of disability is solved.

Except that it isn't. The 'charity' approach is more damaging than rejection as a cause of oppression of disabled people today, because it is more prevalent; with charity the assumption is that 'the problem is taken care of'. Out of sight, out of mind. It is assumed that if disabled people are looked after in separate institutions or by separate services, then that is OK; it may not be ideal, but it is better than nothing. But apart from whether institutions are humane or not (and some certainly are), or the effect they have on disabled people, there is the question of human and financial resources: in India there are an estimated 15 million disabled children requiring education, but existing institutions cater for about 100,000, or 0.6 per cent. Charity cannot cope.

The 'charity' approach grows out of social Darwinism: as long as the underlying assumptions about society are shaped by notions of 'perfect' and 'imperfect', there will always be a need for someone to pick up the pieces, the 'imperfect' pieces. But there are more such 'pieces' than can ever be picked up in this way. If disability is seen as an individual problem, services will always be inadequate, because individual needs can never be fully met.

The crucial distinction that has to be made is between universal rights and individual needs. Charity is about attending to individual needs; what disabled people want is for their rights as ordinary citizens to be recognised. Both able-bodied and disabled people are caught up in an unquestioned attachment to the charity model, often in very subtle and unrecognised ways, and both need to break out of it because, in the final analysis, it cannot deliver.

The dilemmas are the same in both developed and developing countries. Sheer survival in very poor countries like Sudan also poses major ethical dilemmas for decision makers. **Muhammed Osman** describes vividly how attitudes and decisions shaped by social Darwinism operated in Sudan during the famine of 1983-84. His home town of Nyala became a major food-distribution point:

It was famine, and I live in Nyala, over 1,000 km from Khartoum. People were dying at that time of starvation, and people were moving from neighbouring Chad or northern Darfur to southern Darfur, so Nyala became a meeting point for many different people. And you could see that in this situation disabled people were becoming victimised. Always disabled people, women, children, the elderly, are left behind when it comes to survival. Only the fortunate ones were able to come to Nyala.

Not only were disabled people not able to reach Nyala, but many of those who already lived in the town could not stand in the queues at the food-distribution centres. In the last chapter we saw how Muhammed discovered his identity as a disabled person through learning that his condition was incurable, and that with this discovery he determined to work with other disabled people. There was no movement or organisation of disabled people in Sudan, let alone Nyala, at that time. He was uncertain what he should do. The famine provided an opportunity. He approached the representative of an aid agency which was donating relief food, and explained the problem faced by disabled people:

The aid agency rep. said, 'Well, first of all, who are you? Whom do you represent? We have an agreement with the government of Sudan to distribute food according to certain rules; you know, we give it to councils, or district committees, and this is the way we have agreed to do it. If you have any complaints, you go to the government.'

So Muhammed went to a government official:

Now it happened that the one who was in charge of food distribution in what they called the technical committee there in Nyala was an old school mate of mine. I remembered him well. So I went to him and asked, 'Well, what are you going to do for disabled people?'? He said, 'What's the problem?' I replied, 'We can't come out and queue.' He said, 'Well, you're complicating things; if we make an exception for you, the women will also say: "We want a special allocation".' I said, 'Yes, if there is a need, you have to think about it.' But he said, 'No, no, no, it is not in my power to do so, so please do not complicate these things.'

For Muhammed this was the second major trigger in the formation of his consciousness in the politics of disability. The first was when he assumed positively the role of a disabled person. Now these replies from officialdom made him aware that unless disabled people take action together, nothing will change; he recognised at this point that it was not an individual problem: if he approached it as an individual, nothing would happen. It turned out, despite its apparent negativity, to be the beginning of a process of empowerment for him and other disabled people in Nyala.

Private troubles or public responsibility?

Is disability an individual or a social issue? Is it a question of 'private troubles' or 'public responsibility'? Should decisions on disability be made on the basis of 'individual need' or 'universal right'? On the answer to these crucial questions rests all policy planning for disability, the training of professionals, the provision of services, the quality of life for millions of disabled people and of able-bodied people who will become disabled. Is disability an individual or social issue? It is *the* crucial question.

At the individual level there is the question of how the disabled person relates to his or her impairment, and that is conditioned, as we saw in the last chapter, by the attitudes of society towards disability generally. It is true that the way in which disabled people feel about themselves will influence the way they are treated, as individuals, and it is true that social change has to start from disabled people. But the grave danger of pursuing that argument too far is that it places the onus back on the disabled person, when it really belongs in the public domain.

The bottom line is that disability is in the eye of the beholder, not in the eye of the person with an impairment. It is social attitudes which create the 'problem' of disability. It is not disabled people who create the problem. If that sounds too theoretical, consider the practicalities. The 'public responsibility' is created by currents well beyond the reach of the individual disabled person. Social, cultural, religious, economic, and political practices all play a part in creating disability and the negative attitudes that go with it. For example, impairment in the workplace may be created by shoddy safety standards resulting from a quest for maximum profits at the expense of humane employment. Once impaired, a worker may then lose not only income but also a role in life, self-respect through not being able to provide for a family, and respect within his or her community. The driving force which creates the impairment here is greed; the impairment is then turned into a handicap by an assumption that unless someone is productive, he or she is useless.

But society is composed of people. Society cannot change unless individuals change. A change in consciousness happens at the individual level, in both disabled people and non-disabled people. This change in consciousness consists in understanding that it is a social and political issue. Individuals on their own can achieve little.

What is empowerment?

Empowerment is a word much used in development circles. What does it actually mean? This is a somewhat murky and misunderstood area, and it is important to explore what we mean when we speak about the empowerment of disabled people (or any people who are oppressed and disempowered).

Politics is about the struggle to change power relationships. Those who hold power feel threatened by the idea of others being empowered, if it means that these others slip out of their control or, worse, challenge their own comfortable position. This holds true in the politics of disability just as in politics generally: those perceived as holding power are the professional carers and administrators, and the powerless are disabled people themselves. This was graphically illustrated in Winnipeg in 1981 (as described by Mike du Toit in the previous chapter), at the 14th World Congress of Rehabilitation International (RI). RI is an organisation which principally represents professionals, but also service providers, government officials, and others involved in rehabilitation; disabled people may also be members. When the request by disabled participants for 50 per cent representation on the Board was turned down, it was a classic case of the professionals in power feeling threatened at the prospect of their position being challenged. The power of professionals in the rehabilitation business depends on disabled people remaining as passive recipients, not active participants.

But imbalances in power between disabled people and the able-bodied world are manifested in other forms too. Instead of vested interests being threatened, as in Winnipeg, there may be plain inertia, as in the example from Nyala quoted above: harassed officials, whether in famine-relief systems or in local councils, plead that they just do not have the time to grapple with what they perceive as yet another complicating problem. Or it may be argued that there simply isn't room in the organisational budget to make the extra provision for people with 'unusual' needs.

But does the process of empowerment need to be seen only in terms of winners and losers, a zero sum game in which if X wins, Y loses? There has to be a different way of viewing empowerment, one in which everyone wins. When the word 'empowerment' is used in development discussions, I submit that it is not the zero sum game that is being suggested. We are talking about a vision of society in which everybody ultimately benefits, not one in which some are dominant and others are oppressed. There is not much point in 'empowerment' if it means that the oppressed become the new oppressors.

In the case of disability, we are definitely not talking about that kind of pendulum swing, but about a change in power relationships from which everybody ultimately benefits. The present system, because it has grown out of the 'charity' model that is based on individual needs, cannot deliver. No matter how much power they may have, the professionals will never be able to see to the individual needs of all disabled people, at least not in developing countries. The only realistic option is for disabled people to take action on their own behalf. There is nothing inherently threatening about that; it simply makes sense from a practical and pragmatic point of view, apart from all other considerations. We are not speaking of an irrelevant or marginal rebellion, but of absolute necessity.

The process of empowerment

So how does empowerment happen? It comes back largely to attitudes. We can show the contrasting attitudes of people who are empowered and people who are not empowered like this:

Empowered	Not empowered
open to change	closed to change
assertive	aggressive
proactive	reactive
self-accountable	blames others
self-directed	directed by others
uses feelings	overwhelmed by feelings
learns from mistakes	defeated by mistakes
confronts	avoids
lives in the present	lives in the past or the future
realistic	unrealistic
thinks relatively	thinks in absolutes
has high self-esteem	has low self-esteem

The characteristics of an empowered person are immediately evident. Empowerment comes from these positive attitudes finding expression. But nobody loses by meeting an empowered person — quite the contrary. Disabled people need to see themselves and their roles positively, and they can be given the power to do so if other people relate to them positively. Does this mean that able-bodied people are somehow losing some of their own power? Not at all. In fact they are becoming more powerful, in the sense of more enlightened and more human, through the act of enabling a disabled person to feel empowered. This is where it is difficult to understand why medical professionals feel so threatened by disabled people becoming empowered. When the professionals grasp the point and work in a way that truly liberates the disabled person, they themselves are liberated. It's a pretty good feeling.

Venkatesh, in his explanation in Chapter 2 of how he works with disabled people ('my work is the development of human resources'), is following the ideas of Paulo Freire (developed in *Pedagogy of the Oppressed*).[3] Freire introduced the concept of empowerment through what he termed 'conscientisation', that is, the process by which oppressed people come to understand the root cause of their own

The politics of disability 53

oppression. Once such an understanding has been reached, they can begin to do something about it.

Outsiders can act as catalysts in a complex process where the right environment for a change in consciousness is created. That catalyst role is sometimes unpredictable. The aid agency official in Nyala was presumably not even thinking of empowerment when he asked Muhammed, 'Whom do you represent?' But his question acted, unwittingly, as the trigger for a shift in consciousness in Muhammed that was itself empowering.

How consciousness is changed is indeed unpredictable, but there are certain common themes in the experience of disabled people which provide pointers for a strategy. 'Whom do you represent?' is the key question. As an individual, Muhammed represented no one. The need, he suddenly realised, was for disabled people to form themselves into a group which could be recognised as significant, with its own voice.

So you see what happened ... at that time we were just beginning. Certain challenges were presented to us. In fact this man helped us a lot, because it was only then that we realised the importance of coming together. We realised that unless we could bring disabled people together and present a petition to a minister or something, nothing would happen. These people would do nothing to help us as individuals.

For millions of disabled people all over the world, isolation (both physical and social) is the main obstacle to this realisation. But once this isolation is broken, dramatic shifts in consciousness result. The case studies in this book supply many examples, mainly from rural settings, of the extraordinary empowerment that results from breaking the isolation of disabled people. The effect is not just in terms of changes in their consciousness, but in showing a far more effective way of dealing with the practical problems of disabled people than the existing 'charity' model provides.

Joshua Malinga is the Secretary General of the Southern Africa Federation of the Disabled (SAFOD) and the Chairperson of DPI (Disabled People's International). He is outspoken in his criticism of the 'charity' model:

Charity has not really solved the problems of disabled people. What it has done is that it has entrenched the negative attitudes; it has made the position of disabled people worse. Disabled people have not

> *benefited from charity, because charity is not part of the development*
> *process. It is not part of national socio-economic development.*
> *Disabled people want to be treated as normal citizens, with rights.*
> *They want to be treated equally and participate as equal citizens in*
> *their own communities. To achieve this, you need political and social*
> *action to change society.*

It is to challenge the 'charity' model that Joshua believes that social and political action is necessary, and that is why there is a disability movement.

The need for a disability movement

The growth of the disability movement, which is a fairly recent development of the last two decades, flows naturally out of the kind of individual changes of consciousness illustrated in the preceding pages. **Rachel Hurst** of DPI found that her own personal experience led inevitably towards collective social action:

> *I've actually been disabled for most of my life, but when I became*
> *disabled in society's eyes, when I started using a wheelchair, I realised*
> *overnight that I wasn't, in society's eyes, the person I was supposed to*
> *be, or knew myself to be. So I immediately wanted to change the world to*
> *get them to think appropriately, and tried to do it myself, which was a*
> *complete waste of my time. It was a very salutary lesson that you can't*
> *do it alone. You can only do it by coming together with like-minded*
> *people and being very clear. When you come together with other disabled*
> *people, you have the time and the opportunity to discuss what the*
> *situation really is — what oppression is, who is oppressing you, where*
> *oppression comes from; what discrimination is and where it comes from.*

> *Those are the issues which need to be discussed; and you as an*
> *individual cannot possibly see the light over all these issues on your*
> *own, and particularly if you are battling, as an individual, with*
> *starvation, segregation, and deprivation. You are actually much more*
> *worried about where your next meal is coming from than about the*
> *whole political thing.*

The same story is told in different ways in virtually every one of the hundreds of interviews conducted for this book. We are not speaking of some kind of way-out political radicalism that can be dismissed as 'left-wing' or whatever. 'Left' and 'right' actually have nothing to do with it. It is a matter of the logical progression of ideas in a section of the population that has normally been denied any

A disability group in a village in Andhra Pradesh, headed by Ramu (centre) who has leprosy.

kind of self-awareness and self-expression, let alone social and political action.

A question immediately arises, however, over the logic of forming a separate group called 'disabled people'. If integration is the eventual aim, so that disabled people are regarded as nothing unusual and are accommodated as a matter of routine into the affairs of everyday life, then surely forming a separate group runs counter to that aim?

Segregation is when people are kept apart — not through choice, but against their will. The crucial issue for disabled people is whether they have the choice to form their own groups. 'Being in the same boat, knowing what it is like, sharing experiences, and helping yourself by helping others all add up to a fellowship that is the key feature of self-help groups.'[4] It is that choice, the possibility of forming common-problem groups with the rich sense of fellowship which they bring, that marks the beginning of empowerment for disabled people, as we shall see in detail in the country case-studies.

Creating a movement
Fellowship in disability groups is one thing. But there is a need to go beyond fellowship and take on the question of advocacy, to create a

movement. As Venkatesh said in his interview, an ideal world would regard disabled people as nothing out of the ordinary, and there would be no need for a separate movement. But in the very unbalanced world in which we live, run by the comfortably-in-power as well as by well-meaning but harassed officials and administrators, there has to be a separate movement struggling to make its voice heard. **Nawaf Kabbara**, a founding member of the Friends of the Handicapped in Lebanon, explains the dilemma, which was particularly acute over the organisation of the peace march by disabled people in Lebanon in October 1987:

This is a discussion that is going on all the time. There is much misunderstanding. There is a process to be taken. When you are managing a life outside society, you have to make society aware that you are there. Only then can you be integrated into society. We have hardly started the beginning of this process. I mean, you can't be integrated if you are not even recognised as being there! This is what people do not understand. I have been challenged on this many times in Lebanon. Over the peace march, they accused me of trying to use disabled people for political purposes. But this is the way for people to see that we are there. That we exist.

Joshua Malinga, who attracts the same kind of criticism, echoes this:

If you see yourselves as a minority and as a group that is not taking part in society, you have to find a solution, and one of the solutions is that you organise as a group to create a voice, and then you get listened to by the powers-that-be.

But once this awareness has been reached, itself a major milestone, the path that lies ahead is very tortuous. Because of their isolation, disabled people tend not to have had practice in even the rudiments of a democratic process. It would be unrealistic to expect people who have had little or no education, who are unable even to meet with people in the next village, and who have never been involved in a decision-making process, suddenly to acquire all the skills needed to form and run an organisation aiming at major social change. It is one thing to realise the need for a movement, quite another to form one which is dynamic, democratic, and effective. The next stage in the events in Nyala, described by Muhammed Osman, is instructive here:

At the beginning we were a group of nine who set up the Nyala society. Now there are differences. At the beginning there was nothing that people could argue about. But once there is an office, a vehicle and some sort of funding, once you come to tables and desks, then there is something to argue about.

The early excitement of beginning to feel a sense of empowerment through acting together was dampened by the reality of trying to run a democratic organisation. Muhammed recalls that once they had established themselves as a group and scored a first success in persuading the officials to make provision for disabled people in the food distribution, they then had to sort out their own distribution principles and priorities.

I chaired the committee which was to decide on the distribution, and I realised how undemocratic we were: just a group of nine were asked to set the terms for distributing the food to our own members. Now from the group of nine there came voices that we on the committee should get two bags each and give the others one bag. I asked why, and the excuse was that the others would not have got any food, had it not been for us.

So much for equality and justice! Muhammed goes on:

So I said, 'Look, what are we going to say to the members? Are we going to say that we take two bags and you take one simply because you are not on the executive committee? This means that seats on the executive committee are privileged.' But they were adamant. In the end I refused, because it was quite clear that we were inviting problems.

Muhammed was in a lonely position. But he had one other person who was committed to fairness.

So I said to myself and to the person who was with me and supported me, 'We need to find a way round this.' So at the next meeting I suggested, 'Why shouldn't we set up sub-committees? So that the social secretary sets up a social committee, and instead of just being on the Executive, he has to represent that committee. So that at least the decisions in the social sphere are not taken by only one person.' The point is, we needed to democratise the whole thing. By having nine people elected every two years, we were giving power to a group of disabled people at the expense of the others, because once they are in power, they cannot be challenged.

A common criticism of disabled groups is that they tend to squabble among themselves; it is implied that because they are disabled, they should somehow be above normal human behaviour. But normal human behaviour, when big issues like social change are at stake, is frequently unedifying; one only has to listen to a debate from the House of Commons in the British Parliament to be reminded of that. And development agencies themselves are notoriously fractious. Being democratic is an immensely arduous process that takes years of experience and a sophisticated ability to grasp complex and entangled issues. It does not come naturally and is not learnt in a day.

It is important to stress at this point that part of the process of empowerment for disability groups is to be allowed the freedom to fail. If failure is not a possibility, that is, if others come to the rescue too often, then it is unlikely that much of substance will be learned. A sustainable organisation is one that has learnt from its failures. Muhammed Osman is very open about the difficulties that face the movement in Sudan, which are the same issues that face disability groups — or any social action groups — everywhere. A common difficulty is leadership: it is frequently the case that disability groups are led by disabled people whose own consciousness, sense of the issues, and ability to articulate them owe a good deal to educational opportunities not enjoyed by others. In other words, leadership tends to come from an elite. In Muhammed's case he was the only one in the group with a university degree and good English, which gave him access, for example, to the powerful world of aid-agency representatives. He therefore came to be perceived by the group, despite the role he played in setting it up, as 'one of them' rather than 'one of us', especially when he had to challenge their plans for an unequal distribution of food. The principal need, in his view, is to be very clear about why the organisation is being set up and what its objectives are:

> *The first thing we have to do from within our ranks is to agree what we want to do through this organisation. I mean, we disabled people have to ask ourselves frankly why we are setting up organisations of disabled people. Is it just to sit in committees, or is it a means to an end, which is social change, by which I mean changing attitudes? Because we are individuals in our own communities; disabled people themselves need to understand why the community is behaving like that, and the community needs to understand why disabled people are behaving like that. Now we as disabled people have not yet reached that level of understanding.*

Then there is the question of their own prejudices to deal with, just as in the world of the non-disabled:

> *In our meetings we often just beat around the bush; we raise the issues, but we never settle them. We say, for example, that the community discriminates against disabled people, but we disabled people also discriminate against our own disabled people. For example, the representation of the blind is not as it should be, nor of the deaf, let alone the mentally retarded. The challenge to the disability movement is how to overcome this.*

Yet another problem to be faced is how far disability groups interact with mainstream political parties. In the Nyala case, starting with such enthusiasm and, it must be said, innocence, it suddenly dawned on the committee that they were entering the political arena. What would that mean? It came up in the context of having to register the organisation with the Ministry of Social Welfare. Muhammed explains:

> *So I discussed it with the group, and they said, 'Well, we've never heard about this Ministry of Social Welfare; we should go to them.' But one of the members raised the point that doing disability is doing politics. At that time it was Nemeiri's regime, you know, a one-party state, and there was the problem of how to operate outside the party system. Because there was a rumour that the Sudan Socialist Union was trying to bring us into their party.*

This is an increasing difficulty in Sudan. It is possible that the formation of self-help advocacy groups like the one in Nyala is possible only in a country where there is at least a degree of official tolerance for this approach to development. This rules out some countries in Central America, for example, where even to be a rural health worker is to risk your life, and animation of communities is quite out of the question.

In countries where there is some form of democracy, a further consideration for disabled people working on the political level is whether to involve themselves in mainstream politics. Both Joshua Malinga and Nawaf Kabbara, of those so far quoted, are city councillors in their home towns. In the country studies we will deal in greater depth with the practicalities and difficulties in the mobilisation of disabled people, in particular the difficulties of democracy and representation.

Integration, segregation, normalisation, and participation

We have already considered the question of whether a separate disability movement runs counter to the ideal of integration. From the viewpoint of the disability movement, this was answered in the previous section: you cannot ask for integration if people are not even aware of your presence. If integration is the aim, the problem is how to get there. There is also the question of integration within the disability movement: Muhammed Osman mentioned the problem of how to integrate those with communication impairments like deafness into the disability movement, which tends to be dominated by the conventionally articulate.

Communication-impaired people pose a double problem for integration: they find themselves excluded both from non-disabled society and from the disability movement. It is rare to find deaf people, for example, as leaders of cross-disability groups. Deaf people are frequently excluded from educational opportunities, and go unnoticed because their impairment is not visible. They are heavily dependent for their education and information on hearing

Like many deaf children, Fadwa — who lives in a refugee camp in Gaza — has been denied educational opportunities. But now, aged 13, she is making good progress at a neighbourhood disability centre. Here she is working with Shafiq al Bis, a volunteer helper.

people, who are in the role of 'benevolent oppressors'. With access to communication through sign often denied, and poor oral/verbal skills, how can they assert themselves? I attended an all-Africa DPI conference in Zimbabwe in September 1991; the organisers had made no provision for interpretation in sign language; a speech-impaired lawyer in Zimbabwe who has offered his professional services to the disability movement has consistently been refused. Deaf and speech-impaired people, because of their lack of oral/verbal language skills, and in spite of physical 'able-ness', go to the bottom of the power ladder. It is oral ability which carries power.

The words 'segregation' and 'normalisation' raise all sorts of questions. Should disabled people be treated as though they are not disabled, or should their disability be recognised? On the one hand, disabled people seem to be saying: 'Don't treat us as anything unusual.' On the other, they seem to be saying: 'It's not us who have to change: it's society that must recognise us and accommodate us.' It is exactly the same issue that confronts any social action group advocating its rights as a minority. How far do you 'normalise' and how far do you remain segregated? Because they tend to be excluded from both non-disabled society and from the disability movement, deaf people in particular have created their own culture and communication system which gives them a distinct identity. Deaf people are proud of their deaf culture with its own language, and many deaf people would say they do not want to be viewed as 'normal'. And yet obviously oral communication is very important for their own development, and written language even more so. So the answer lies in 'bi-lingualism', with ability to relate to both worlds.

Lessons from the Peto Institute

The issue of normalisation comes into sharp focus through the experience of Vic Finkelstein, a wheelchair user who teaches a course on disability through the Open University in Britain and who was one of the first people to become active in the politics of disability in Britain. In an article in the journal *Therapy Weekly*,[5] he described a visit he made to two cities with very different approaches to disability: Budapest and New York.

New York is a city which has a policy of accessibility for all public buildings and buses; in consequence wheelchair users are a familiar sight in the city, and are thus half-way to being socially integrated. In dramatic contrast, in the Hungarian city of Budapest there are no ramps on pavement kerbs, and neither public buildings nor public transport are accessible to wheelchairs. The policy in schools is that if a child wants to attend, he or she must be able to walk. The result is that disabled people in wheelchairs are not seen at all on the streets of Budapest. Those who cannot walk are stuck at home, presumably living out a kind of twilight existence, because they cannot go anywhere without an enormous effort and a great deal of help. They certainly cannot go anywhere on their own.

In response to the situation of Hungarian children with cerebral palsy, the dedicated staff of the famous Peto Institute in Budapest work 8 or 12 hours a day in efforts to teach them to walk, through a process known as 'conductive education'. 'Normalisation', in the sense used in the Peto Institute, sets out to make disabled people as much like non-disabled people as possible, so that they can fit into 'normal' society. And that is indeed what many disabled people and their families would like, especially the parents of children with cerebral palsy who are willing to make enormous sacrifices for their children to be taught to walk by conductive education; there is now a vigorous parents' campaign in Britain, for example, to set up such centres across the country.

It may well be right for individual children with cerebral palsy to learn to walk, rather than use a wheelchair. It undoubtedly does a great deal for children's self-esteem and self-confidence to be on their feet, especially if the only option is being stuck at home staring at the ceiling. There is nothing wrong with conductive education in itself. But where Budapest has got it wrong is that it insists on normalisation — and the Peto Institute endorses this insistence.

Such a policy is highly detrimental to the interests of disabled people in Hungary generally. It stands as the ultimate example of the 'cure or care' approach: parents come to the Peto Institute in the hope that their child will be 'cured'. But in terms of physical rehabilitation, techniques like conductive education can only do so much: they cannot produce a complete 'cure', and there will always be those who are in wheelchairs whatever therapists can do. The point is that disabled people themselves must decide what normalisation means for them as individuals, and how far they want to go along that road. What is unacceptable is for an entire rehabilitation policy to be founded on the insistence that 'disability must be overcome' if disabled people are to benefit from what is on offer to 'normal' people. To throw all of a country's resources into professional efforts of this type, with no awareness of the need for creating a barrier-free environment in the country at large, is tragically misguided. It is obvious that for developing countries the Peto model, even if it were possible, would be an irresponsible and unrealistic use of scarce resources.

The point at issue is whether disability, represented here by wheelchairs, is accepted as an ordinary part of human existence, or whether it is so unacceptable, threatening, and inconvenient to able-bodied people that disabled people are allowed to join in life only if they play by the rules of able-bodied people with all their functions. Integration means opening up social structures and attitudes to include disabled people, not changing disabled people to fit in an able-bodied society. There is richness in diversity. A society in which 'deviants from the norm' are rejected is not only repressive; it is also exceedingly dull.

A further key concept is *participation*. Much disability literature speaks of integration as the ideal, when in fact participation might reflect more accurately what disabled people aspire to. To take the example of deaf people again, they would like to retain their identity as deaf people, but they also want to participate in the non-disabled world. They certainly want to participate in the decisions that affect their own lives.

Society cannot change unless individuals change. The women's movement has had an effect on men: more men are prepared to listen to and understand the women's point of view, to exchange roles with women, to recognise the central importance of the feminine in the whole of life. It is possible to speak of the 'transformed man', the one who has gone through a quantum shift in perception on gender and come out the other side a very different person from his previous personality. So with disability. For 'men', read 'able-bodied people'. The disability movement is slowly creating changes in consciousness among able-bodied people who recognise the importance of what disabled people have to offer. Disabled people do not want to be seen as heroes, or as saints. They just want to be treated as human beings, and this realisation is gradually gaining ground among able-bodied people.

CHAPTER 5

Disability and development: the basics

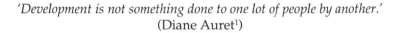

'Development is not something done to one lot of people by another.'
(Diane Auret[1])

Why is disability a development issue?

There is a close relationship between poverty and disability: malnutrition, mothers weakened by frequent childbirth, inadequate immunisation programmes, accidents in over-crowded homes, all contribute to an incidence of disability among poor people that is higher than among people living in easier circumstances. Furthermore, disability creates and exacerbates poverty by increasing isolation and economic strain, not just for the individual but for the family: there is little doubt that disabled people are among the poorest in poor countries.

However, it is important to stress two vital points that contradict much received wisdom on the prevalence of disability. The first is that impairment is not only a function of poverty, and is not restricted to poor people. An important factor is cultural behaviour, such as early marriage in India, female circumcision in Africa, or marriage between blood relatives in the Middle East. Wars, which since 1945 have taken place chiefly in the South, have maimed hundreds of thousands, mainly civilians, irrespective of class. Disability affects all strata of society.

The second point is that more technical development does not mean less impairment. Statistics on disability are extremely unreliable but, while the *incidence* of impairment may be high in developing countries, there is strong evidence to suggest that improved health care in industrialised countries leads to increased *prevalence* of impairment, simply because those with severe impairments survive longer, and people live long enough to acquire the impairments of old age.[2] ('Incidence' refers to the numbers of cases which actually occur; 'prevalence' refers to the numbers of people who survive.) Thus disability is also an important development issue in industrialised countries. (We will examine the question of numbers and statistics more closely in Chapter 7.)

The profile of impairment types changes with medical advances and demographic factors: polio may have been virtually eliminated from most countries, but, as people live longer, the impairments of old age such as cataracts and arthritis come into play. The proportion of disabled people in industrialised countries now is therefore probably higher than it was in the nineteenth century. Disability cannot be eliminated by medical advances; medical advances simply change the proportions of various impairments in the population.

I am not trying to diminish the importance of the discussion about disability in developing countries. On the contrary, what I am saying is that this is very much a development issue shared by the rich North and the poor South. The age-range of disabled people in

Leprosy is a disabling illness associated with poverty. Ramu's husband has left her because of her leprosy, but she is a forceful member of the disability association in her village of Dampetla in Andhra Pradesh, India.

industrialised countries is weighted towards the later years of life, while in the South disability tends to occur in the earlier, productive years. Society, whether in the North or South, therefore has no choice but to come to terms with disability as a part of life.

An analysis of disability based on poverty alone is not only inaccurate; it is also misleading, because it somehow puts disability 'out there', whereas it is very much 'in here', close to each of us. Disability is a major feature of life in both developed and developing countries, and can affect anybody of whatever background at any time. Nobody is immune, and nearly everybody is likely to experience disability personally or through a family member or close relative to some degree at some point in their lives. Disability is therefore not a separate issue from which we can choose to remain detached: it is woven into the fabric of all our lives, whether we like it or not.

This works both negatively and positively. On the one hand, the realisation that disability can affect anyone may make people more afraid of it; on the other hand, greater familiarity in industrialised countries has led to a greater awareness. In some countries there has been progress in making significant changes to give disabled people an equal chance through, among other things, legislation, adapting the environment, and mainstream integration of disabled children. There is still a long way to go, especially in the way in which the whole medical world relates to disability, and books like Colin Barnes' *Disabled People in Britain and Discrimination*[3] make it very clear that institutionalised discrimination is still the norm in countries like Britain. But the process has started. Disability is on the map.

Official assumptions about disability
In developing countries the scene is less encouraging. Development policy in the South is formulated by governments and international agencies, and both tend to give disability a low priority in overall development planning. But that is not to say that nothing is done about disabled people: there is a huge industry based on disability, especially among private voluntary agencies — and that in itself poses another set of problems. According to Rachel Hurst, 'There is a vast network of medical, charity and social work experts who have, as it were, cornered the market in disability.'[4] Disability is big business, but it is in the hands of the wrong people.

The disability 'industry' is driven largely by attitudes that are more 'charitable' than 'developmental'. It is rare to find disability being considered systematically with developmental attitudes by development planners at the level of governments or international agencies. It is worth looking at some of the arguments used by planners in development when they are challenged on disability:

• Rehabilitation is complicated and expensive, requiring trained professionals; it is beyond the abilities of ordinary villagers.

• Aids and equipment for disabled people are too expensive to be budgeted for in normal primary health care programmes.

• If they survive, disabled children will become disabled adults who will be an economic burden all their lives.

• Disabled people are taken care of in institutions; there is a whole industry to cater for them, with millions of pounds poured into it, mainly from private sources; 'real' development is about empowering people to help themselves.

• Disability is not a priority when so many children die before their first birthday anyway of such causes as diarrhoea; let us bring down the infant mortality rate first, and then we can think about things like disability.

Underlying all these arguments is the undeniable influence of social Darwinism, with the implication that unless a person is 'normal', he or she does not qualify for the same chances as everybody else. But these arguments are based not so much on prejudice as on ignorance and a lack of awareness of what is possible. The country studies in this book illustrate that rehabilitation can be effectively practised by uneducated people; aids and equipment are not always complicated or expensive; and disabled adults do not need to be an economic burden.

As for institutions, we have already seen that they can cater for only a tiny fraction of disabled people in developing countries: it is precisely the inadequacy of this approach that demands a different way and the integration of disability into the heart of the development process.

As for the last argument, we must ask when can the infant mortality rate be considered low enough to move on to dealing with disability? When it reaches 100 per 1,000? 90? 50? Who is to say? The idea of 'solving' one problem in this way before moving on to another is in any case misleading and unrealistic in development terms: not only are problems of this magnitude seldom solved in such a discrete manner, but this argument implies a materialistic and mechanical approach based on dealing with faceless masses of human beings with no individual identity and no say in their own lives. It is implied that it is the development agencies' or governments' job to reduce these figures. 'Development' becomes a kind of numbers game in which the appalling indicators of under-development must be reduced — by people making plans in offices.

Fertility control and self-determination

There is no question that the infant mortality rate must come down, and there should be fewer babies born in the first place. But how can these figures be reduced? If people feel they have some control over their lives, they are more likely to make responsible decisions. The evidence points to an improvement in the quality of life, coupled with a greater sense of being able to take decisions over the factors which influence one's life, as the most effective way to bring the birth rate down, not mass sterilisation campaigns. The best way to improve the quality of life is by focusing at the community level and giving people a real voice in the decisions that affect their lives. Once people feel they have some control over their immediate concerns and are not just ciphers in someone else's plans or hostages to an unknown and fickle fate, then their whole attitude to themselves, their children, and their future becomes more hopeful and more structured.

This is an important point. It is often said that having many children is an intelligent response to the conditions in which people live in developing countries, because children provide some kind of security in old age. The interviews conducted for this book give the lie to this view: many people in villages in Zimbabwe, Zanzibar, and India said that having many children made poverty worse; they argued that the problem of inheritance is greatly exacerbated by large families: they expressed the view that the increasing division of land leads to increasingly uneconomic plots; two educated children are more likely to be better off than six who have had little or no education; therefore two children are more likely to take care of their parents than six or seven. A number of elderly disabled people interviewed said that their children were not looking after them, and that it was a mistake to rely on them.

I stress this point partly to question an assumption that seems to have become enshrined as a dogma in development doctrine (that having large families makes economic sense to the parents), and partly to stress that community development has much to do with hope, and with people feeling that they have some control over their lives. Having many children seems, according to the testimonies of the scores of people I have interviewed, to be a response more to uncertainty than to hope, a reaction to an unknown fate and a future which they do not in any way control. But once people begin to feel they do have some say in their future, then they take more rational decisions — and this is reflected in having fewer children.[5]

Action on disability can enrich the whole community

Positive action on disability is an important part of the process by which a community gains more control over its life and more hope about its capacity to solve immediate problems. So to see work on disability as drawing resources away from other aspects of development, or as deserving a lower priority, is to miss the point of what development is actually about. Work on disability raises levels of community responsibility and civic consciousness; ignoring disabled people simply perpetuates despair and hopelessness in the whole community, not just for disabled people and their families. It is very rare to find a parent who does not want to do the best for a disabled child; neglect is not usually wilful, but often the only option when no services are on offer: as soon as some kind of service is available at community level, there is always a flood of applicants to use it. In Jordan, the West Bank, and Gaza Strip the experience of starting neighbourhood centres for disabled children in refugee camps shows that the presence of such centres provides a source of pride and raises morale in the whole community, not just for those who directly benefit. The truth is that people operate more effectively when they feel valued and are able to value each other.

Development is not simply about finding a solution to the problem of poverty on the grand scale. Poverty is a symptom of a greater malaise, an intrinsically flawed materialism which fails to value the earth and its resources and all the people who live on it. Poverty cannot be 'solved' using materialistic attitudes and mechanisms. Disability provides a key to unlock the secret of where the deeper values lie; it challenges all of us over our fundamental attitudes to what determines the value of life. A society which ignores its disabled people or shuts them away in institutions

> ... is deprived of its necessary corrective. It mistakenly believes that only the disabled are dependent persons. It fails to see that

society itself is invisibly dependent on the disabled for a critique of its humane norms and values. In view of both our domestic social problems and the problems of the world community (for example starvation, apartheid and the gap between rich and poor), it is becoming ever clearer that the solution to these problems depends less and less on power and money and increasingly on the challenge of a radical thinking, that is learning.[6]

Disability is a development issue because it dehumanises. It dehumanises because, on the practical level, disabled people are left out of development planning and their voice is not heard in decision-making circles. On the philosophical level we know instinctively that if we deny the humanity of another, we ourselves are dehumanised.

We who have disabled friends, family, or workmates owe to them our affirmation of the value of their lives. It is for us to show the

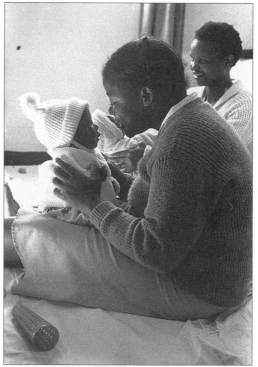

'... the contribution that any infant can make simply by being alive ...'. A rehabilitation session for mothers and their children born with cerebral palsy, Harare Hospital, Zimbabwe

Photo: Chris Johnson/Oxfam

achievement of the disabled life, but more importantly the enriching contribution that life can make to the community.

It is a great mistake to believe that one can only contribute to society in the active physical sense. After all, what we do in the office, the home, the factory, is ephemeral, whether we do it as an able-bodied or a disabled person. What counts is what the great philosophies and religions of the world are all agreed upon, and that is the spirit of man. It is this that gives worth to what is basically the daily grind.

It is not enough to say that in extinguishing the life of the blind infant we may be destroying a Milton, or an Einstein in a deaf one. In extinguishing the life of any infant we are denying the world the contribution that infant can make simply by being alive, by laughing and loving, hurting and needing, simply being a human being.[7]

The contribution that disabled people can make to a more holistic understanding of the world is enormous:

We have noted that many disabled persons — especially those who have managed to learn skills and lead fulfilling lives — have developed an exceptional 'view of the world'. They feel a sort of brother-and-sisterhood with other disadvantaged, exploited and oppressed peoples — the Earth's 'socially handicapped'. They are committed to working in their own different ways toward a fairer world, one in which the silent speak out and the weak grow strong by joining hands. They feel that all who are disabled should be given an equal chance. They would like to help in the rehabilitation of a socio-politically disabled Human Race on ecologically disabled Earth.[8]

Three models of disability

A model is a framework by which we make sense of information. For the sake of clarity we shall consider three models or approaches to disability: the traditional model, the medical model, and the social model.

The traditional model

The traditional model is the construct created by religion and culture in any society. In most religions and cultures, disability is seen as a punishment, or the result of ancestral anger or retribution by divine forces. Such beliefs are not confined to religions regarded in the

West as 'primitive'. Christianity is no exception: where it is mentioned in the Bible, impairment is linked with being unclean, an outcast, and/or possessed by demons. We have noted that Martin Luther, imbued with these ideas, recommended the killing of impaired babies. Such beliefs are still widespread in many parts of the world, both Christian and non-Christian. A blind person I interviewed in Madras, India, was refused entry to a theological seminary because, he was told, 'a priest must be without blemish'. The traditional model regards disabled people as unfortunate, different, 'blemished'.

The medical (or 'individual') model

In the West the traditional model based on religious and cultural attitudes has been largely replaced by the medical model, which is an extension of the same idea. The medical model views an impairment as an 'abnormality' — which assumes that there is 'normality'. An abnormality needs to be 'corrected', 'cured', 'overcome'. The medical model has value in certain contexts, but when it is used as the *only* model for approaching disability, it is seriously defective: based on the concepts of 'normality' and 'abnormality', it sees the human body as flexible and alterable and the social environment as fixed and unalterable: if a person does not fit the social environment, then that person — not the environment — must be made to change.[9]

In Chapter 3 we considered the question of whether disability is an individual or a social issue, and concluded that any approach to it has to start with the understanding that it is primarily a social issue. The approach to individual disabled people has to be within a framework of understanding the whole social context of disability. The problem with rehabilitation based on the medical model is that it focuses on the individual, without relating to the overall social and environmental context. For this reason it is sometimes referred to as the 'individual model'.

The example of Budapest quoted in Chapter 4 is relevant here. The obstacles to disabled people's development in Budapest, at least those with mobility impairments, are the physical barriers imposed by a society that either has not understood or is dismissive of their needs for mobility. The rehabilitation model in Budapest evident in the Peto Institute represents a struggle to fit disabled people into a society which makes no allowances for them: if children want to go to school, they must learn to walk. The Peto Institute is endorsing the barriers set up by this model through its efforts to get children with cerebral palsy to walk at all costs. This is the logical conclusion of the medical, individual model.

A rehabilitation model is needed which does not accept and endorse the barriers placed in the way of disabled people by society, but breaks them down.

The social model
The social model of disability starts from the point that integration is ultimately about removing barriers, not 'normalisation', cure, or care. Rehabilitation conducted within a comprehensive social framework is about the removal of barriers at the individual level; it is also about the removal of physical and attitudinal barriers in society at large. This book is, in general, an exploration of the social model.

Both able-bodied professionals and disabled people are caught up in the medical model of rehabilitation, largely because this model is only now beginning to be questioned, and the vast majority of disabled people and professional therapists have never known anything else.

The role of the professionals
This is a difficult section to write. I am aware that many of the people who will read this book are professionals working in the field of rehabilitation who are interested in development as an issue. They are therefore likely to have progressive and open attitudes towards their work, and to have moved away from a narrow devotion to the individual medical model. Many rehabilitation professionals in developing countries work in this way with an increasing willingness to welcome a partnership with disabled people in planning and delivering services. Growing numbers of disabled people themselves are becoming professional therapists and carers.

Nevertheless, a book like this would not be complete without taking a critical look at the role of the professionals, for two reasons: first, the medical model is still dominant in the West, despite a minority of professionals who have moved on from it; and second, training in developing countries tends to follow Western models, with all their inappropriate attitudes. It is also the case that a great deal of Western funding for disability projects in developing countries is directed at the medical model run by professionals wedded to it. The rehabilitation industry is dominated by such professionals.

There are two fundamental points. First, nobody is arguing for fewer professionals: let us be very clear about that. They are vital. What is at issue is the underlying attitude they bring to the job. What disabled people want is to join with professionals in formulating policy on rehabilitation, and then to work with them to implement it. This is an exciting, positive process which in no way detracts from or undermines the importance of the professional task; on the contrary, it enhances it.

Second, professionals, from orthopaedic surgeons to occupational therapists, are needed in order to give disabled people choices about how far they wish to go along the road of 'normalisation'. If, for example, a disabled person has difficulty holding a cup, there may be two solutions: change the design of cup, or operate on the hand. If there is no orthopaedic surgeon, there is no such choice.

Agents of social control?

However, despite these points it remains true that many people in the disability movement see the control of their lives by rehabilitation professionals as one of the main causes of their oppression. Why? The oppression, in their experience, derives from two things. First, an attitude of 'cure or care' which sees them as everlasting patients: if they cannot be cured, they must be cared for. In the words of **Joshua Malinga** from Zimbabwe:

> *The point is that they believe that they have solutions to our problems. They do not see us as belonging to society, they think we belong to them, they have to keep files on us throughout our lives, and decide when we should see the doctor and so on. But I want to decide when I see the doctor! They have enjoyed power and control over us for a long period. We have to understand that we are talking about an attitude here. Changing attitudes is a very difficult thing.*

Second, the 'success' of professionals working with the medical 'cure or care' model depends on disabled people co-operating in the process of treatment or cure, 'to get better at all costs', to return to productive function. But this approach is devastating for disabled people because, if it fails (that is, if it does not return them to productive function and leaves them 'disabled'), the implication is that, because they are unproductive, they are classed by society as non-people, people who have nothing to offer, rejects. It is hardly surprising that disabled people find such an implication dehumanising.

Professional rehabilitation therapists are generally well-meaning and committed people: they are not blatant agents of social control, and do not sign up for their jobs with the intent to oppress disabled people. So what has gone wrong? They are obviously part of a bigger problem which is above and, in a sense, beyond them as individuals, an oppressive system in which they are unwitting cogs. This system can be analysed in several ways; for example, an historical overview of the development of capitalism would reveal the way in which 'being productive' has become crucial to defining a person's value; people are defined by what they do and what they can produce, not by what they are.[10] Or an analysis from a religious perspective would show the development of the medical model from the traditional one. But whatever the historical reasons, what we have now, across the world, is a highly professionalised system in which trained experts relate to disabled people from a position of power and dominance, not equality.

In the industrialised countries this situation has provoked a crisis of confidence which sparked, most notably, the formation of Disabled People's International at the 14th World Congress of Rehabilitation International in 1981, already referred to twice in previous chapters. This momentous event drew the lines for the battle that has been raging ever since. Over the last decade there has been a major growth of organisations of disabled people across the world, which have certainly succeeded in some countries (Zimbabwe is a good example) in opening up the debate about disability, and in gaining recognition among people in power for the rights of disabled people. But the medical model is institutionalised, and institutionalised ideas are very hard to shift. There are also vested interests involved. Attitudes among professionals, the very group where a change in attitude is most crucial, have been slow to change, and there remains on the whole a deep division between organisations of disabled people and the professionals.

As specialists, professionals 'tend to diagnose a problem in relation to what they themselves can offer'.[11] Everyone is busy and formed by their daily experiences; it requires a huge imaginative leap to form a wider view. So policies, programmes, and projects are designed not only on the principle of 'cure or care' and 'returning to productive function', but also in a way which divides up work with disabled people into different professional tasks classed mainly under 'health'. There is a good deal of squabbling over professional boundaries; trying to cross these boundaries, for example into education, then becomes very difficult, and amalgamating them almost impossible.

Professionals without a wider view tend to express a certain weariness about the hostility of the more militant disabled people towards their efforts, and may dismiss the disability movement and organisations run by disabled people as non-essential, a kind of extra for those who feel that way, with the implication that they should be jollied along, but not taken too seriously. They question the effectiveness of disabled groups, and point out that they tend to be fragmented. Similarly people who run institutions for disabled people, especially in the South, often see themselves as having a mission and living sacrificially in order to achieve it; the idea that they are oppressing disabled people would strike them as ludicrous, insulting, and profoundly ungrateful. (We will see a good example of this in the Zimbabwe country study.)

Thus the two sides are divided by mutual misunderstanding. Disabled people feel oppressed by the professionals, and the professionals do not understand why. But disabled people are very ready to acknowledge the value of professionals, and are quick to point out that developing countries have a severe shortage of therapists anyway, so control of disabled people by them does not arise in the same way as it does in the North. But unless therapists throughout the world begin to think differently about their role and see it within a wider social context, there is little hope of radical change.

The whole psychology of helping and being helped is a big and important subject: it is outside the scope of this book, but there are many excellent books which tackle it.[12] However, it may be useful at this point to hear the experience of one person (in the North) who was grateful for the therapy he received and had nothing but admiration for the therapists, but still remained profoundly dissatisfied:

> I've been chronically ill for years. Stroke. Paralysis. That's what I'm dealing with now. I've gone to rehab programme after rehab programme. I may be one of the most rehabilitated people on the face of the earth.
>
> I've worked with a lot of people, and I've seen many types and attitudes. People try very hard to help me do my best on my own. They understand the importance of that self-sufficiency, and so do

I. They're positive and optimistic. I admire them for their perseverance. My body is broken, but they still work very hard with it. They're very dedicated. I have nothing but respect for them.

But I must say this: I have never, ever, met someone who sees me as whole ... Can you understand this? Can you? No one sees me and helps me see myself as being complete, as is. No one really sees how that's true, at the deepest level. Everything else is Band-Aids, you know.

Now, I understand that this is what I've got to see for myself, my own wholeness. But when you're talking about what really hurts, and about what I'm really not getting from those who're trying to help me ... that's it: that feeling of not being seen as whole.[13]

Wholeness is the key. To be cast in the role of perpetual patient means to be seen only in part.

So what advice would an active member of the disability movement give to a young person contemplating a career as a physiotherapist? **Mike du Toit** from South Africa offers these thoughts:

I would certainly encourage them. I mean, particularly in my country we have such a severe shortage of people like physiotherapists. Of the few that there are, something like 80 per cent are in private practice, which means that they serve only the rich. A remarkable percentage work on horses! So obviously I would encourage them, but at the same time qualify that by urging them to have exposure to the movement of disabled people, and have their attitudes formed there, rather than in the professional circles.

And what does 'the movement' think the role of professionals should be? Mike du Toit again:

The movement does not reject the role of the professionals. What we reject is the inappropriateness of so much of the work that is being done, and the inappropriateness of their attitudes, and the complete inappropriateness of their seeking to represent us. We do need professionals, we need services, we need rehabilitation. But I would hasten to add that rehabilitation is something that happens to us for a very short period of our lives. It's by no means the most important thing in the life of a disabled person. But we need professionals, there is no doubt about that.

New skills and new relationships

The role of the professionals does need an overhaul. Fortunately there are very clear indicators of what is needed and how it can be done. The key word is *resource*: rehabilitation professionals need to 'change from management of the patient to that of being a resource for the disabled person to use in reaching their own goals'.[14] This does not mean that professionals should become passive and de-skilled. Quite the contrary: acting as a resource actually requires a higher degree of skill than treating someone who is merely an object in the process. But it does require a different attitude and different training:

> Professionals acting as a resource to be used by others need special education and training so that they are able to promote control by disabled people. ... To do this, professional workers will need new communication skills, new professional codes of practice, new ethics, new rules of confidentiality and new concepts of clinical responsibility. In all this the professional rehabilitation worker needs to learn how to listen to clients, while at the same time helping the client to identify the central rehabilitation issue. ... The need is for new relationships to develop between helpers and those they help.[15]

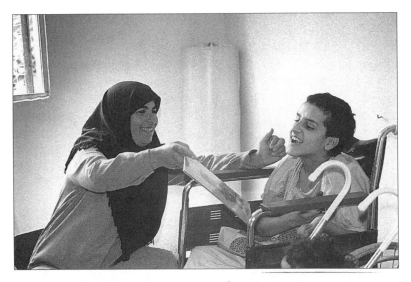

A new relationship begins in Jarash community disability centre, Jordan.

Such an approach will also ease the problem of professional boundaries and what disabled people see as the 'farce of professional teamwork', where they are shunted around from one professional to another, none of whom sees them as a complete person. If rehabilitation is a process controlled by the disabled person, and professionals are skilled resource people, then the whole context in which rehabilitation happens will change: the power balance will shift in favour of the disabled person, but without reducing the effectiveness or job satisfaction of the professional; rather, these essential elements will be enhanced. Working towards 'resource-based rehabilitation' is the major challenge facing both professionals and disability organisations.[16]

Ultimately the way in which professionals relate to disabled people depends on the image that professionals have of themselves. Ram Dass and Paul Gorman express it this way:

> Implicit in any model of who we think we are is a message to everyone about who they are. It's not as if there are any real secrets. If we are seeing only one part of the picture about ourselves, positive or negative, that's all we will be able to make real to anybody else. Caught in the models of the separate self, then, we end up diminishing one another. The more you think of yourself as a 'therapist', the more pressure there is on someone else to be a 'patient'. The more you identify as a 'philanthropist', the more compelled someone feels to be a 'supplicant'. The more you see yourself as a 'helper', the more need for people to play the passive 'helped'. You are buying into, even juicing up, precisely what people who are suffering want to be rid of: limitation, dependency, helplessness, separateness. And that's happening largely as a result of self-image.[17]

Who needs rehabilitation?

For the sake of clarity it is useful to distinguish three main categories of disabled person: children; adults who have been disabled from childhood; and recently disabled adults. Each of these groups relates to disability in different ways and has different needs; in particular, their needs for professional input are different.

The needs of disabled children

Disabled children need focused rehabilitation and educational opportunities in order to maximise their potential and minimise the effect of impairment. For example, a child with severe cerebral palsy, if left unstimulated and over-protected at home, will suffer even greater impairment, unable to sit up, feed herself, or play any kind of independent role. But if the parents are shown how to stimulate the child, to encourage her to use her limbs, and enable her, with supportive seating, to sit up so that her view of the world is not confined to a few square feet of the ceiling, then the effects of the impairment by cerebral palsy can be mitigated. Such an intervention needs a person trained in this kind of physical rehabilitation who can pass the necessary skills to the parents and other family members.

Similarly a deaf child, if left to cope without specialist care and discouraged from using sign language, may acquire hardly any language at all, with no tools for forming concepts, and may suffer serious intellectual impairment as a result. It is important for this child to have professional help at an early age, so that he acquires a means of forming concepts (either by signing or conventional language) as early as possible; otherwise his mental development will be impeded.

The needs of adults disabled from infancy

An adult disabled since early childhood or birth, if he or she has undergone some kind of rehabilitation process in childhood, will probably be outside the need for professional rehabilitation services, but may still have regular but probably fairly straightforward needs, such as checks on internal infections. Such a person's world view and awareness of disability issues are very likely to have been heavily influenced by the type and quality of the rehabilitation received earlier, if indeed there was any.

Both disabled children and adults disabled from their earliest years have always been part of the population marked 'disabled', and will probably have learnt to cope with the implications of that in various ways. Disability is part of their identity.

The needs of recently disabled adults

A recently disabled adult may have had feelings of fear and pity towards disabled people before being impaired, and may therefore find the whole experience of becoming disabled extremely distressing, with all the emotions of anger, rejection, and despair that are common when facing grievous loss. In particular, such a person may not want to be identified as disabled at all, as we saw in

Chapter 3 when considering ex-combatants. In analysing the biographies of 80 adults disabled since childhood, Erika Schuchardt at the University of Hanover found that 'two thirds of them remained at the stage of aggression, negotiation and depression and never reached acceptance; this results in a condition that is 0equivalent to social isolation'.[18]

Recently disabled adults definitely require professional rehabilitation, again to minimise the effects of the impairment and to maximise their chances of adaptation to the new circumstances. The presence or absence of good rehabilitation is a matter of life and death: the life expectancy for a spinally-injured black person in South Africa is about one year, in stark contrast to a spinally injured white person, who can expect to live many years. The difference is that the white gets proper rehabilitation, while the black does not, and will probably die from bedsores, urinary infections, and other complications.[19]

The point is well illustrated by a study of spinally-injured people in Zimbabwe carried out by Veronica Brand in 1984.[20] An earlier study had revealed that there was 'a very high mortality rate for paraplegics discharged into rural areas'. She set out to discover the reasons why, and found two main factors: first, there was almost no attempt at social work or preparation for life beyond the hospital; second, there was very little contact between the hospital and the family of the injured person during treatment, because the family could not afford to keep travelling to the city from rural areas. Thus even if there had been some attempt at preparation for returning to the village, the family could not have been involved in it. 'Lack of contact between relatives and hospital personnel, either in the form of family counselling sessions or through home assessment visits, contributed to a situation where discharge was likely to be a traumatic experience, both for the paraplegic and for the family.' Thus the family had little idea of the recently disabled person's needs or how to meet them.

Both disabled children and recently disabled adults have a profound impact on their families. Consequently rehabilitation needs to pay attention to the non-disabled members of the family members too.

Survival in such cases is not only a matter of avoiding bedsores and dealing with urinary infections: a paralysed person needs a reason to live, otherwise he or she may simply turn to the wall and die, seeing no point in continuing as a burden to their family and themselves. The challenge is to help such people to identify skills that can be transferred from their previous lives, and also train them in new skills. For example, a quadriplegic man in Ain el Hilweh refugee camp in Lebanon has started reading books on to audio tape for blind students; he can't use his limbs, but he still has a voice.

Rehabilitation means removing barriers

So it is clear that the role of professional therapists is primarily with disabled children and recently disabled adults and their families. But the point to be made is that their role is to minimise impairment and to maximise adaptation to a new lifestyle, and not to treat disabled people as though they must be cared for for the rest of their lives. Their task is to remove barriers at the individual level.

Many programmes in disability in the South are aimed at children, and it is obvious that resources of time, money, and expertise should be focused on them. But children grow up, and unless these programmes are set within a full understanding of the social context of disability, the negative cycle of patronising attitudes and a feeling of disempowerment among disabled people will be perpetuated, however good the rehabilitation is technically.

Finally, there are increasing numbers of cases where disabled people and professionals work closely together, several illustrated in the case studies in Part Three of this book (for example Zanzibar and Zimbabwe). Even though it is not a developing country, it is worth mentioning the example of New Zealand. In 1983 three organisations, Rehabilitation International (NZ) (a body mainly of professionals), the New Zealand Coordinating Council of the Disabled, and Disabled People's International (NZ) united to form the Disabled Persons' Assembly. At that time the Disabled Persons' Assembly 'was the only organisation in the world which had as members individual people with disabilities and their service-providing organisations working together as a partnership, but with constitutional power in the hands of the disabled individuals. The service providers are corporate members.'[21]

***

This chapter has argued that professionals and their organisations cannot dismiss organisations of disabled people as irrelevant. At the same time, the disability movement cannot dismiss the professionals as irrelevant. Changing attitudes comes through co-operation, and takes time.

CHAPTER 6

Towards social action

*'An organisation of disabled people cannot simply talk about the problems.
It has to do something about them as well.'*
(Jabulani Ncube)

Three approaches to rehabilitation[1]

In a recent survey, disabled people in Uganda were asked to list their needs in order of priority. At the top of their list came income, then housing, then transport, then sex. Rehabilitation came a bad fifth.[2] Yet the literature on disability in developing countries is predominantly about rehabilitation.[3] The normal reflex when speaking or writing about disability is to discuss rehabilitation. This accounts in large measure for the irritation that disabled people feel towards the whole rehabilitation business, and for their perceived hostility towards the professionals: the plain fact of the matter is that the constant emphasis on rehabilitation perpetuates the idea that disabled people must be normalised, taken care of, treated as perpetual patients.

It should by now be obvious that this book is not primarily about rehabilitation, but about attitudes and approaches. However, it is important to take a hard look at rehabilitation, because it is precisely here that many of the negative attitudes originate and are perpetuated. In looking at rehabilitation, we have the following basic questions in mind:

• What attitudes and approaches are needed to make rehabilitation a developmental experience? In other words, how can rehabilitation enhance rather than diminish the personal growth and dignity of the disabled person?

- How far does rehabilitation advance integration and participation?

- Is rehabilitation seen as an end in itself, or as a resource for disabled people to use for their own development?

For the sake of simplicity and clarity we can fit present-day rehabilitation services roughly into three types: institutions, Community-Based Rehabilitation (CBR), and an approach using neighbourhood centres. These three do not stand in conflict with each other, but each may be more or less developmental, depending on how close it comes to answering the basic questions listed above. CBR is not necessarily more developmental than confining disabled people in an institution: it depends on the attitudes and approaches of the people involved.

The institutional mentality

Let's begin with institutions. This section will not be a tirade against institutions and all who run them, but an examination of where they fail to be developmental, and the valuable role they can play if they are run on developmental lines. We are not talking about buildings, but about attitudes.

The charitable, medical, and individual response to disability has tended to be the establishment of institutions. But it has been clear for a long time that classic, isolated institutions are both extremely expensive and an ineffective way of supplying the needs of disabled people. Not only do they cater for a minute number, but those who are in them often find it difficult or impossible to live outside them, cut off for many years from their own contexts. **Amer Mukaram**, head of the Youth Association of the Blind in Lebanon, was blinded in a shooting accident at the age of seven and spent nearly all of his school years in a residential institution for blind children:

I come from a mountain village, and from the time I became blind I was cut off completely from my home environment. My relatives considered that I was ill. The school for the blind that I attended was a welfare school. There was no contact with family or friends at home. All the contacts with people on the outside were very unbalanced. Sighted people would come to the school, but out of pity. It was impossible to form normal relationships with them: they were just doing us a service. They regarded us as poor people who needed our help. It took me years after I left to learn how to relate to people normally.

A long-term resident of Abu Samra Institution, Tripoli, Lebanon. It is not buildings, but attitudes, which create institutions.

However, despite the obvious drawbacks of institutions, there is a feeling among some government planners, non-governmental agencies, and especially private philanthropists in many developing countries that anything less than expensive institutions 'on the Western model' is something of an insult.[4] The argument that 'disabled people deserve the best we can give them', when used in this context, is beguiling, drawing as it does on feelings of guilt. Institutions are also very visible and are an obvious way of expressing personal generosity and charity in cultures where such acts enhance esteem within the community, not to mention religious merit. They can also be an effective way to build a personal empire.

Institutions may not be a solution if you are starting from scratch, but they are a feature of the landscape and are likely to remain so. An institution-less revolution is not very likely. That being so, rather than damn them it is more constructive to see how they can be incorporated into rehabilitation planning. Large institutions on the traditional model isolate, segregate, and address only a fraction of the need. But they need not necessarily remain so: they can become a reference point for community action, or resource centres with a much wider impact. For example, the Divine Light Trust for the Blind at Whitefield near Bangalore in south India was set up in the 1950s as a school for blind children. Its director, Father Cutinha, explains what happened:

Take our institution here. It started as a school. But after about 35 years of running it as a school, it came as a severe trauma to me to discover that only about 5 per cent of blind children are in blind schools. I just could not believe it. After 40 years of national independence, all the efforts of the government and the NGOs were not able to reach more than 5 per cent. At this school we could take only about 8-10 new pupils each year. We were not even beginning to touch the problem.

So we don't run it as a school any more. We run it as a resource centre for training teachers in ordinary schools in how to integrate blind pupils into their classes. Now, with the same budget and the same number of staff, we reach out to practically the whole of India. We motivate them to start services, and they come here for training. So we have made our point and proved ourselves by de-institutionalising. We are far more productive now.

But the sad thing is that I have made this point in umpteen workshops, but no other institutions have followed suit. The reason is that when such workshops are run, hardly anybody from the management side comes. It is staff who come, but the management does not come, and so the message never gets through to the decision makers of these institutions.

Existing institutions can become valuable resources to large numbers of people, both disabled and non-disabled, if they can make the imaginative leap that was made by the school near Bangalore. Scrapping institutions is not likely to happen, because of the personal investment that they often represent; but they have buildings, facilities, equipment, and skills that could be resources of immense value to their own wider communities. The main difficulty, as Father Cutinha explains, is getting that message to the decision makers behind most institutions, who tend not to read books on disability and development. However, it is important to believe that change can happen: in Chapter 12 we shall see an interesting and encouraging example of social action to change an institution in Lebanon.

Community-Based Rehabilitation (CBR)
It was a serious attempt to de-institutionalise, de-mystify, and de-professionalise rehabilitation that led to the formulation of the CBR concept in 1979 by the World Health Organisation (WHO).[5] But unfortunately this term has been probably more misunderstood and

misapplied than any other concept in disability. It has been widely discussed in books, articles, and conferences since its introduction (there are several good summaries and critical analyses listed in the resources section at the end of this book), but confusion prevails.

'CBR promotes awareness and responsibility for rehabilitation in the community. The disabled person, the family and community members are called upon to take an active part in the process of rehabilitation.'[6] A WHO manual, *Training Disabled People in the Community*,[7] sets out how this can be done. A local supervisor is recruited from the community and trained; the supervisor then trains the family of the disabled person in basic rehabilitation supported by 'the community'.

CBR is thus based on two fundamental assumptions: that the greatest resource for helping a disabled person is his or her own family, and that the community around that family can be mobilised in support. These are obviously good ideas in themselves, but like all assumptions they need to be examined. Let us take the role of the family first. There can be no question that the family is the main building block of any developmental process; it must be the centre of a child's experience and the structure through which most learning takes place. This is self-evident. But there are a number of problems attached to making the family the prime focus of rehabilitation; they do not negate its role, but they must certainly be borne in mind.

In the first place the family has always been, in the absence of any other services, the main source of learning, support, and help for the disabled child: there is nothing new in that. But there may well be factors (either practical or attitudinal) which prevent the family from helping the child. On the practical level the family, if it is very poor, may be so hard-pressed to survive that its members simply do not have time to devote to the rehabilitation of a child. This does not imply a lack of caring, but is simply an illustration of the fact that absolute poverty concentrates the mind on the absolute essentials. As soon as services become available, parents will use them for their children, but they may not have the energy or time to do systematic rehabilitation themselves.

On the attitudinal level, regardless of whether the family is poor or not, the role of a parent is different from that of therapist or teacher. Every parent knows this. The relationship between parent and child carries a set of emotions that do not exist between the child and a therapist external to the family. In particular a disabled child may produce an undercurrent of guilt in the mother which results in coddling rather than a robust encouragement to reach for independence, or a failure to appreciate what the child is capable of. Over-protection is more common than neglect as a reason for under-development in a disabled child; but whether it is over-protection or neglect, the fundamental problem for the child is the lack of challenge and stimulation.

It also has to be recognised that looking after a disabled child or adult can be very wearing. Parents and family need regular breaks. Planning any rehabilitation programme needs to consider this factor very seriously. Parents can certainly support each other, and one of the strongest arguments for neighbourhood centres (as opposed to institutions) is that they give the parents a break and also a chance to meet each other and share their mutual problems. But even without the facility of a centre, families can be encouraged to pair up so that a disabled member spends time on a regular basis with a support family, who may or may not have a disabled member of their own.[8]

So the point about families and community-based (or rather home-based) rehabilitation is that without adequate support, disabled people may be little better off than if they are parked in institutions.

The second major assumption behind CBR relates to community action. It is very difficult to impose a community approach from the top, by government decree or a decision made by development planners. Community action means different things in different contexts. The difficulty with the classic CBR approach is that it assumes a rather bland view of community action in which the entire community — family, neighbours, health service, social workers, local authorities, employers, carpenters, etc. — all play their part in recognising the needs of disabled people and fulfilling the three major objectives set out by the World Programme of Action on Disability: *prevention, rehabilitation, and integration.*

The reality is seldom so simple. The country case studies in Part Three of this book illustrate how differing contexts require very different approaches. However, one of the main points behind those case studies is to show that, whatever the circumstances, community action of some kind is possible when people at the community level see the point of it. The key point for development workers is to discover how to tap into existing community patterns and interest, rather than simply 'set up a project'.

Closely connected with the question of community action is the

A training course in rehabilitation work for village community workers, Kunaka Hospital, Seke Communal Lands, Zimbabwe

Photo: Chris Johnson/Oxfam

role of the CBR worker; this needs much thought. One of the main misconceptions about CBR as practised in many countries is that it is seen as another way of passing the buck of 'dealing with disability' to 'experts' who are designated for that task; the CBR worker goes round the houses 'doing rehabilitation'. It becomes a modified version of 'out of sight, out of mind', which defeats the whole object, especially if all the rehabilitation is done in people's homes, which effectively removes disability from the public domain.

There is a need for specialist CBR workers, but to do the job properly requires a high level of social and diplomatic skills: the prime task of a CBR worker is to 'skill' other people, which means the disabled person, the family, and other members of the community. The CBR worker cannot be the main source of learning and therapy for the disabled child or adult: the whole point is to enable the family to be that. So he or she needs to be a rehabilitation specialist, have a good understanding of individual and social psychology, and be a good development worker. He or she must be able to see beyond the physical needs of the disabled person and see when and how to involve and inspire other members of the community, perceive where useful connections can be made, gain the confidence of decision makers, and so on. It requires a sensitivity and perspective based not on 'coming in as the rescuer', but on enabling and facilitating other people and fostering a climate of mutual trust and cooperation. This is no small task, and it is rare to find a sufficient number of people with these qualities who are not snapped up by better-paid jobs.

It has often been found that disabled people themselves do an outstanding job as CBR workers, because they have a perspective not shared by non-disabled people. This has been well-documented, for example by David Werner in the Projimo Project in Mexico.[9]

When the difficulties of implementing CBR in its 'pure' form as proposed by WHO are considered, it is hardly surprising that there are very few successful examples around, and that there is much literature which is critical of the concept as unrealistic.[10] On the other hand, the term 'CBR' has become part of the jargon of development, three magic letters that are known to trigger the right response in the minds of funding agencies. 'CBR' has tended to become synonymous with 'development work in disability'. Even institutions themselves will say they are 'doing CBR' if they start an outreach programme. All this muddies the waters of understanding.

It is certainly not my intention here to be unduly negative about CBR as a concept. What is being challenged is an uncritical or muddled application of it as a panacea or as a total solution. The aim of any disability programme must be to fulfil the three objectives defined by the World Programme of Action, namely prevention, rehabilitation, and integration. CBR is often touted as the only way of 'dealing with' disability, but one of its dangers is that it can easily become focused only on physical rehabilitation of children at home, and nothing else happens. There has to be a co-ordinated way of dealing with the other important aspects of disability: prevention, equal opportunities, the supply of aids and appliances, access, integration in schools, and general awareness-raising.

Neighbourhood centres and local disability committees

Both institutions and CBR can play an important role in approaches to disability if they are developmentally managed, and in particular if they involve disabled people fully in decision-making and implementation. A third model that has the potential for a more comprehensive approach within small and clearly defined communities such as villages and long-term refugee camps is the local disability committee. Examples of these will be considered in detail in the case study of the Occupied Territories and Jordan in

Chapter 11, so I will merely sketch the outline here.

The basic concept starts with the formation of a committee whose members accept responsibility for disability within their own community. This committee can consist of disabled people, parents of disabled children, teachers, social workers, health workers, rehabilitation professionals, and anybody else in the community interested in the issue. They then decide what to do about disability in their own community. The first step might be to do a survey to see how many disabled people there are, what different disabilities they have, what age spread there is, what the likely causes are, and what services are needed. Some workers are sceptical of surveys, with good reason, but in my experience they can be a vital process which will raise both awareness and expectations; they can also be an important way of bringing the community in general into the planning process. Those conducting the survey should emphasise that any services must be managed by, and be within the capability of, the community, and they should also stress that some enormous institutional project is not about to materialise.

The committee can then develop a strategy which includes prevention, awareness raising, equal opportunities, integration, rehabilitation, and service provision. The strategy they adopt will depend on the findings of the survey, existing services, availability of funding, and opportunities for training. They may decide to set up a neighbourhood centre for children who cannot be integrated into normal schools. Neighbourhood centres, sometimes also called community rehabilitation centres, are small, low-cost centres where children (and parents) can attend to socialise and take part in a programme geared to their needs. The committee will also need to establish links with sources of appliances and referral centres, find ways of training staff for their own centre, raise money, and build links with other committees in neighbouring communities. If a CBR programme already exists, it can be integrated into their strategy. Developing links with institutions can only be a good thing, since at worst it may lead to nothing, but at best it may open the institution up to new ways of viewing the world and the wider use of valuable facilities.

The examples in Chapter 11 show how such committees can work in practice. Where they work well, the results are impressive. But there is no such thing as a complete solution: 'There is no single pattern of service delivery that can fit all contexts. Communities differ in many respects, administrative structure, legislative provisions, population and population distribution, economic and cultural conditions, manpower resources. These variations will lead to different models of service delivery.'[11] The crucial point about service delivery is that, whatever form it takes, unless disabled people themselves play a key role in its design and delivery, working together with able-bodied people, then it will not empower disabled people and will not achieve the three goals of prevention, integration, and rehabilitation.

Before considering how disabled people can be empowered in this way, we will need to consider the role of the State in all this.

The role of the State

'Private voluntary action is the distinguishing mark of a free society.' (William Beveridge[12])

There is a tension in all countries between the role and obligation of the State and private voluntary action. Should the State act as the big daddy (or mummy) which takes care of all its citizens, or should it leave this task to private voluntary agencies? Are the causes of destitution to be found in the structure of society or in individual family lives? Who is responsible for shaping the society in which we live? These are very big questions, but they have particular relevance to the situation of disabled people, or indeed of any group who feels itself to be oppressed. Although this book is about disability and development in developing countries, the baseline principles underlying the discussion hold good everywhere. There are some useful lessons to be learned from the United Kingdom.

In the UK the foundations of the Welfare State were laid during Victorian times. The Victorians identified 'the poor' as a group, but saw them largely as a collection of destitute individuals; and so they plunged with great energy into philanthropy, setting up institutions and dishing out soup and shoes to pinched-faced people in the dark, satanic streets of industrial towns. But 'when the focus shifted from *the poor* and what could be done to relieve their distress, to *poverty* and what could be done to abolish it, then it became inevitable that the state should intervene more decisively and that the scope of private charity should be correspondingly altered'.[13]

'The poor' are the objects of charity; 'poverty' is the domain of politics. By this analysis private voluntary organisations in Britain deal in 'charity' and the State deals in 'politics'. In Britain this division is not only recognised; it is protected by law: it is illegal for private charities to involve themselves directly in 'politics' — that is, they can deal with people in need, but may not seek to change government policy as it affects such people. To people outside the UK this distinction may seem illogical and bizarre, but it is broadly accepted by the British population, for philanthropy did not end with the establishment of the Welfare State in 1948: there are today over 180,000 charities registered in Britain, increasing by several thousand each year.[14] We give our pounds and pennies to charities like Dr Barnado's for the individual child, and give our vote to whichever political party we think will deal with the problem at large, thereby affirming our belief that both politics and charity have a role to play.

But for disabled people there is a crucial issue at stake. We are back to the question of an individual or social problem, to private concerns and public issues, to individual need versus universal right. Are disabled people perceived by the government as the responsibility of the charities or of the State? Are they simply individuals with special needs, or is disability seen as an issue of fundamental rights? For **Joshua Malinga**, Secretary General of the Southern Africa Federation of Disabled Persons, there can be no question:

> *If the government passes disability completely to charity, it is avoiding its responsibilities. It is not enough to do a little CBR and provide drugs. I am a city councillor here in Bulawayo. Every year we sit down and say, What can we contribute to SAFOD, to NCDPZ, to Jairos Jiri? $400 to SAFOD, $400 to NCDPZ ... So what the council is doing is not accepting its responsibility to provide for disabled people in the mainstream. If you give $400 to NCDPZ and divide that by the number of people NCDPZ is working with, then you are contributing about one cent or half a cent per capita to the disabled population.*

Amer Mukaram, a founder member of the Youth Association of the Blind in Lebanon, believes that the crucial role of the government is to create the legal framework within which disabled people can claim their rights as citizens, like everyone else:

> *The practical way we want to achieve integration is to put pressure on the government to bring out a law which makes it possible to integrate. We must go beyond having relations with sighted people in which the sighted person is just a volunteer. Why not a friend? Just like ordinary people. The State has the responsibility to create the circumstances through which that can happen.*

And **Venkatesh** in India:

The State should look after disabled people as it looks after any other of its citizens. In an ideal world it should look after their special needs as a matter of routine. That's my utopia. No fuss. Routine.

In order to create this routine, he advocates removing responsibility for disability from the Ministry of Social Welfare altogether:

I would influence the government to have a unit for disability in every one of its ministries, be it Integrated Rural Development, or Finance, or Commerce and Industries. That's what I would be aiming for. So that means that at the policy level you are integrating work with disabled people. Education, health, employment, housing, whatever. Which means that at the policy level we are not marginalised. So if that takes place, I think that's the beginning of integration at the national level.

Livion Nyathi, formerly of the National Council of Disabled People of Zimbabwe (NCDPZ), clarifies what he believes the government's role to be:

The role of the government is of paramount importance in co-ordinating, funding, researching and stimulating agencies and its own departments in the establishment of rehabilitation services.[15]

But in stressing that disability is an issue which demands basic rights recognised by the State, we should in no way be dismissive of private voluntary action. There is much wisdom in the quotation from William Beveridge that heads this section: private voluntary action *is* the hallmark of a free society. Where the State provides all, the human spirit itself seems to wither and die. Not only that, but without a flourishing private sector there is no mechanism for making the State accountable. Despite what has been said in criticism of 'charity' as a non-developmental concept, the private voluntary sector does represent the conscience of a society. The role of the government is to create the environment where private voluntary action can flourish, strongly supported by the State. Support does not imply control: private voluntary action requires State backing in both cash and legislation, but not control.

The way of social action

'Equality for oppressed minorities is never voluntarily given by entrenched authority.' (Justin Dart)[16]

There is probably no government in the world that has given rights to disabled people voluntarily; where it has happened, it has happened through pressure from disabled people working as a movement. The task is clear, but immense. Social action on disability is fraught with the same problems and pitfalls as social action on any other issue. The problems can be summed up in a few basic questions: to what extent does confrontation encourage change, and to what extent does it hinder it? Have the very militant sections of the women's movement, for example, pushed their cause forward or driven people (more moderate women and men) away? Does militancy, in other words, work, or does it alienate those it is trying to convert? Does social action have to be militant? How do you work for radical social and political change without being dismissed as extreme and therefore losing your audience before you have started? On the other hand, anger can be an enormous stimulus to action: when the pioneering nineteenth-century English nurse Florence Nightingale was asked what drove her, she replied, 'Rage'.

Does militancy work?

Among those interviewed for this book some were very militant, while others believed that militancy does not work. There are obviously times when anger and dramatic action are fully appropriate and justified, and other times when it is inappropriate. The case-study material supplies illustrations of effective militancy, for example in Lebanon (see Chapter 12).

Samir Ghosh, whom we met in Chapter 1, explains the dilemma in these terms:

> *I have always believed that the major effort should go into building a relationship with society, so that people understand that it's of mutual benefit to society as well as to the individual. It is very important for society to understand the benefit.*
>
> *I am not of the attitude that we have got to snatch something. Because I think that's where there is a kind of indifference now. Rather than that, I would much rather bring the cause closer to society. I know it's a long process, but we've got to work in this area, where the real understanding is of mutual benefit; otherwise no matter how much we keep harping on about it, society will continue to use benevolence when dealing with disabled people and considering it a charitable act to rehabilitate a handicapped person.*
>
> *I'll give you an example. When I walk on the streets, people look at me*

. It's something I can't avoid. I'm different. But whenever I'm asked a question about my disability, I always reply nicely and positively. The same person never asks me a second time. So I have at least educated one person. And it multiplies. For example, the manager of the Taj Mahal Hotel where I am staying came and asked me about my requirements, and I told him everything about me. Then I found that it was conveyed to the room boys and everybody. So it's automatically a multiple educating process. But if I was arrogant or embarrassed and replied accordingly, that would be counter-productive.

For Samir, strident militancy is counter-productive. The key lies in the spirit with which we approach the matter of changing attitudes. What Samir is saying is that people do not like being 'should upon'. Arrogance or self-righteousness are not good starting points for social action. If we want peace, then the way is peace, not hostility.

The second point Samir is making concerns mutual benefit. Just as global consciousness is changing on environmental issues because people recognise the interdependence of themselves and the planet, so real change in attitudes towards disability will come only when non-disabled people recognise what disabled people have to offer.

We are led back to self-esteem again. 'The basic social institution is the individual human heart. It is the source of the energy from which all social action derives its power and its purpose.'[17] The spirit with which social action is undertaken will determine its outcome, so before we start, we need to know who we are. If we are at war with ourselves and with the world, it is unlikely that we will succeed in building bridges of confidence with people we wish to change. 'Our power will come from who we all are and know ourselves to be. It will be communicated in the quality of our presence, not just the substance of our message.'[18]

Jabulani Ncube was director of the National Council of Disabled People of Zimbabwe for some years in the mid-1980s. It is an organisation that has established a reputation for being militant. In his opinion:

There is a valid role for militancy. But a militancy that is not supported by concrete actions, by which disabled people have an opportunity to demonstrate a more serious commitment, runs the risk of being an empty type of militancy. What is important is that disabled people have not had an opportunity ever to plainly express their views, their own position. The vehicle of the organisation is the platform that now presents itself for them to stand up and present their position quite unequivocally. In southern Africa and elsewhere, I think disabled people have begun to do that.

The noise that disabled people are making should be a constructive kind of noise. Not a noise of simply beating drums, attracting attention but being unable to move the issues forward. Disabled people do have to take the responsibility that they can do something. More respect will accrue to disabled people and their organisations if they can be seen to dedicate themselves seriously to action and hard work.

So while it is the easiest of things to stand up and blame all the problems that disabled people are facing on the government, on the lack of coherent policy, on able-bodied people not understanding at all, on the oppressors — we can call them by many names — I think the most striking manner in which one can impress an oppressor, if that is possible, is for the oppressor to be able to see what you can do. And I think they are likely to stop and say, 'Ah! Is that what they are saying?'

These are obviously not easy things, but I think it is an important part of the militancy for disabled people to retire back to their chambers and seek to define ways in which they want to move forwards and provide concrete examples of the improvements they wish to see in society in general. And then the government and other agencies working in development could be held responsible for implementation on a wide scale.

An organisation of disabled people cannot simply talk about the problems. It has to do something about them as well.

It is the combination of practical action and advocacy that forms the heart of any social action programme: there must be both to move the issue forward. The words must be matched by the action. Justin Dart, Chair of the President's Committee on Employment of People with Disabilities in the USA, has some very direct and powerful things to say on social action:

Human society is not a magical source of truth and solutions. Society and its governments are simply the sum total of what individual humans think and do every day. The illusion, the big lie, that paternalistic government can give quality of life, has resulted in a cancerous dependency, which has debilitated the people it promised to empower. We, as individuals, are the government. We are society. We, as individuals, as a movement, must empower ourselves, our government and our society, or empowerment will not occur. This is not a philosophy. It is a fact.[19]

A meeting of a village disability group in Tamil Nadu, India. Such groups have achieved much in practical action for basic rights.

So we return to our starting point: if there is to be change, it has to start with us, with those who want change, disabled people and their allies. How disabled people see themselves is the starting point. Self-esteem means feeling good about yourself and being sure of your own value as a human being. Feeling good about yourself does not mean accepting the institutionalised injustice meted out by society: it gives you the power to begin changing it. In Part Three of this book we look at a few countries where disabled people and their allies are attempting to do just that.

CHAPTER 7

Language and numbers

This chapter forms a kind of appendix to Part Two. The book would not be complete without considering the important matters of statistics and language in relation to disability, but I have placed them in a separate chapter rather than incorporate them into the arguments of other chapters.

Language: examine the label

Our thoughts and attitudes are influenced by the language we use; we tend to slot into language patterns dictated by current usage and prevalent attitudes. For example, 'Poor Leila, who has a secretarial job, is suffering from multiple sclerosis and has been confined to a wheelchair for years.' Or 'John is a stroke victim who has been afflicted with hemiplegia and is restricted to special equipment to feed himself.'

Labels disable because they focus on the person not as a person but as a case or an object. Words like 'poor', 'victim', 'suffering', 'afflicted', 'confined', and 'restricted' all reinforce the notion of disabled people as sick and helpless. A wheelchair does not confine: it liberates the user to go out into the world to work, play, and be creative; it is a mobility aid, just as a car is for anyone who uses one. In most cases it may be inappropriate to mention that the person is disabled at all: is he or she identifiable only by the fact of being disabled? But if it is appropriate to mention it, each of these statements could be expressed positively, or at least neutrally, without any negative implication: 'Leila has a job as a secretary; she moves around in a wheelchair as a result of multiple sclerosis'; 'John had a stroke some years ago and is able to feed himself using special equipment'.

The use of language to refer to disability in English has changed over the past 40 years. Words like 'idiot', 'moron', 'imbecile', and 'lunatic' have mostly passed out of use, but are occasionally found in the press and popular writing. There are other old-fashioned words like 'invalid', 'deformed', 'cripple' which are still regrettably common.

Impairment, disability, and handicap

There is a great deal of confusion over the terms 'disabled', 'handicapped', and 'impaired'. But we need to be precise about these words in particular. Within the disabled community and among professionals dealing with disability the debate about their use continues. The World Health Organisation suggests three basic definitions:

> **Impairment:** 'Any loss or abnormality of psychological, physiological, or anatomical structure or function', e.g. paraplegia.

> **Disability:** 'Any restriction or lack (resulting from an impairment) of ability to perform an activity in the manner or within the range considered normal for a human being', e.g. inability to walk.

> **Handicap:** 'A disadvantage for an individual, resulting from an impairment or a disability, that limits or prevents the fulfilment of a role that is normal (depending on age, sex, and social and cultural factors) for that individual', e.g. lack of wheelchair access to public buildings and transport because no ramps are provided.

However, there are major problems with these three definitions. First, they are based on the medical model, to which the notion of 'normality' is central. Second, what is, in practice, the real difference here between an impairment and a disability? 'Loss of function' and 'lack of ability to perform' are pretty much the same thing.

The disability movement has generally rejected these definitions in favour of two basic concepts related to the social model of disability:

> **Impairment:** 'The loss or abnormality plus the effect on function', e.g. paraplegia plus the inability to walk.

> **Disability/handicap:** 'The disadvantage or restriction of activity caused by social factors which take little or no account of people who have impairments and thus exclude them from the mainstream of social activities.'

Most languages have only one word for the two English words 'disability' and 'handicap', so in the context of developing countries it does not make much sense to retain a distinction between them; 'impairment' and 'disability' cover the two essential concepts of *loss of function* and *being disabled by social attitudes*. That is the position taken in this book.

Language and identity

Debate also rages over the terms 'disabled people' or 'people with a disability'. The phrase 'people with a disability' has gained some currency, especially among professionals working in rehabilitation; but, apart from being rather clumsy, it is not strictly accurate according to the social model formula above, since it should be 'people with an impairment'. Most people in the disability movement would now favour 'disabled people', because that states clearly who they are. They argue that other minorities or oppressed groups do not use such circumlocutions; for example, we do not refer to black people as 'people who are black'. Black people are proud of being black, and disabled people have no reason whatever to be ashamed of being disabled: they want to claim their identity as disabled people.

What is not acceptable is to refer to 'the handicapped' or 'the disabled', because these expressions simply supply a label, without acknowledging that they refer to people. It is likewise not acceptable to refer to 'the blind' or 'the deaf'; to refer to an individual as 'a spastic', as though he or she is identifiable only by an impairment, is completely unacceptable, though regrettably still common.

Cultural differences in the use of language

In developing countries and in languages other than English there is probably not so much debate about language as there is in the industrialised North, and it is certainly not possible to be dogmatic about English language usage across the world. In India, for example, which uses English as a main form of communication, people with learning difficulties are called 'mentally retarded', even though that phrase has fallen out of use in Britain. In India the argument in its favour is that the phrase 'people with mental disabilities' could include people with mental illness, and it is important to distinguish the 'mentally ill' from the 'mentally retarded'. ('People with learning difficulties' does not seem to have caught on in India, probably because very few of these people are

*Not 'the deaf one', but
Hassan, a deaf child, playing in Jericho, West Bank.*

lucky enough to be in 'learning situations', i.e. schools.)

But language is a cultural issue in relation to attitudes and self-perception. **Naidu**, a worker at the Association of the Physically Handicapped in Bangalore, southern India, who had polio as a child, remembers: 'In my village I was referred to as "the lame one", not by my own name.' The same is true in millions of small communities across the world: people are referred to by their physical characteristics, whether disabled or not: 'the dark one', 'the short one', 'the one with red hair', and so on. In Arabic, for example, there is a whole class of adjectival nouns used to describe physical characteristics. In the West we would contend that social integration requires calling people by their real names, not by their physical characteristics. But in many small communities in the South such labelling does not necessarily imply disrespect or discrimination (although it may do). Indeed, disabled people may well be much better integrated socially in such communities than they are in industrialised environments, despite such linguistic labelling.

Does language matter?

For some disabled people, their own personal development and sense of self-worth takes them beyond the hurt caused by labelling; for example, **Venkatesh** can say:

> *I prefer to be called 'blind' rather than 'a visually impaired person'.*
> *Whether you call me blind or visually impaired is not important. The*
> *most important thing is what I feel about myself. It's about self-esteem.*

Venkatesh is perhaps unusual in having developed a sense of self-worth to this degree. Language remains an important issue for most disabled people, because it is so intimately linked with consciousness and attitudes. Drawing attention to language is an important way of exposing the unquestioned prejudices and assumptions upon which most people operate. Unexamined clichés govern the thoughts of the unthinking. Examining the clichés starts the process of constructive reflection on the issue. As Venkatesh himself says in the interview at the start of this book: 'People calling you not by your name but by your disability is just not on.'

Thomas Harris in *I'm OK, You're OK* sums up the importance of language in relationships:

> I am a person. You are a person. Without you I am not a person, for only through you is language made possible, and only through language is thought made possible, and only through thought is humanness made possible. You have made me important. Therefore I am important and you are important. If I devalue you, I devalue myself.[1]

Numbers: how many disabled people?

Nobody knows how many disabled people there are in the world. It is often claimed that disabled people constitute ten per cent of the world population, but this is a rough estimate which is not based on statistical evidence, and is not very helpful in practical terms.

Do the figures affect the fundamental argument for civil rights? No, they do not. No matter what the actual number of disabled people in the world, the case for civil rights is the same. Do the figures matter? Yes, they do, because looking at the statistics on disability reinforces the basic point that disability is defined more than anything else by two crucial factors: people's attitudes and the barriers erected by society.

The difficulty with the blanket figure of ten per cent is the implication that ten per cent of any specific population is disabled; but this is rarely borne out in practice, and it leads to some ludicrous arguments. For example, some writers have assumed that in a world population of ten million refugees, one million are disabled; but a head count gives an actual figure of a few thousand. Although in extreme circumstances some will have died, this does not account for the enormous discrepancy. The problem lies in the assumption of ten per cent in the first place.

There is a very wide variation in the prevalence of disability within a country and between countries; it may be more or considerably less than ten per cent, depending on a variety of factors. As a general rule it seems that urban areas tend to have more than rural areas and, according to UN statistics, industrialised countries tend to have higher proportions than developing countries. Both these trends may come as a surprise, since they contradict received wisdom but, as we shall see, logic is on their side.

Global variations
Differences in definition used in surveys mean that all statistics on disability are inherently problematic. The United Nations Disability Statistics Compendium[2] shows Peru, Ethiopia, Egypt, Pakistan, and Sri Lanka as having a disability rate of less than one per cent, while Austria claims 21 per cent, and Australia, Canada, Britain and Spain apparently have 11 per cent and above. In the middle are countries like China, whose national survey in 1987 showed 4.9 per cent and Zimbabwe, where the National Disability Survey in 1981 indicated 3.4 per cent. (See the chart opposite.)

Where detailed surveys of specific communities have been done *within* developing countries, the results usually give figures much lower than expected. In rural areas especially, numbers are generally low: in a village of 2,000 people in India you would expect to find about 200 disabled people according to the ten per cent estimate, but in practice the number rarely exceeds a couple of dozen at the very most. In surveys conducted house-to-house in villages near Madras by PREPARE, a local NGO working in social action and community health, the figure was less than one per cent.[3] In each of the surveys conducted in refugee camps in Jordan and the Occupied Territories before the establishment of neighbourhood disability centres, the figures were around two per cent.[4]

What do all these figures tell us? That Austria actually has over twenty times as many disabled people as Peru? Or that the Austrian

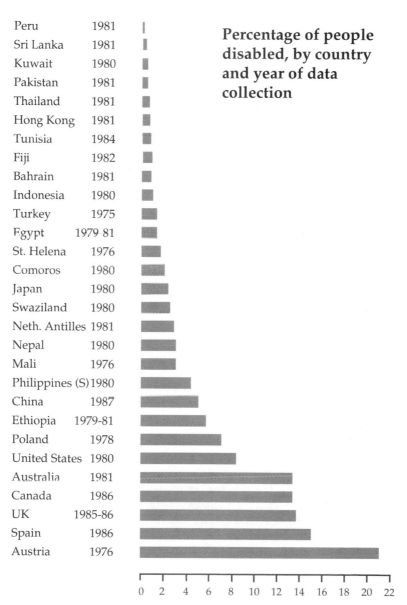

Percentage of people disabled, by country and year of data collection

Peru	1981
Sri Lanka	1981
Kuwait	1980
Pakistan	1981
Thailand	1981
Hong Kong	1981
Tunisia	1984
Fiji	1982
Bahrain	1981
Indonesia	1980
Turkey	1975
Egypt	1979-81
St. Helena	1976
Comoros	1980
Japan	1980
Swaziland	1980
Neth. Antilles	1981
Nepal	1980
Mali	1976
Philippines (S)	1980
China	1987
Ethiopia	1979-81
Poland	1978
United States	1980
Australia	1981
Canada	1986
UK	1985-86
Spain	1986
Austria	1976

Percentage disabled

(Based on 'Statistics on Special Population Groups', Series Y, No. 4, *Disability Statistics Compendium*, United Nations, New York, 1990) survey had a much wider definition and was more detailed? Or that disability is perceived quite differently in Austria and Peru? Even allowing for wide variations in definition, the figures flatly contradict the received wisdom that there is a higher proportion of disabled people in developing countries, and that impairment is a function of poverty. In the West the greater survival rate of disabled people and the demographic bias towards old age could mean that indeed industrialised countries have more. In very poor circumstances, such as Indian villages, the survival rate of children born with disabilities is extremely low. And the life expectancy of traumatically disabled adults in all parts of the developing world is dramatically lower than that of their Northern counterparts. For example, in South Africa vast differences in the standards of medical care for whites and blacks mean that a spinally injured white has a ten times greater chance of surviving until late middle age than his or her black compatriot.[5]

Urban and rural differences

Some figures show there to be an urban bias, and some show the reverse. My own observations while collecting material for this book, reinforced by a large number of specific studies,[6] strongly support an urban bias. Reasons include the greater risk of injury in road and industrial accidents, the attraction of possible services and institutions, better medical care, the higher likelihood of finding sedentary jobs, and the possibility of begging. (In Indian cities children are sometimes maimed deliberately in order to make them more profitable beggars.) It would almost certainly be incorrect to assume that because 80 per cent of the population of a country live in the rural areas, 80 per cent of the disabled population are to be found there as well. However, even in rural areas there are wide variations: in some villages in Zaire more than 30 per cent of the population may be affected by river blindness, and in some African countries there is a high local incidence of disabling diseases like filiriasis, which produces elephantiasis.

The effects of war

In a number of developing countries war accounts for significant numbers of disabled people. Cambodia has many amputees who have trodden on land mines, and in Angola a 'low-intensity conflict' (LIC) policy by South African-backed forces in the late 1980s deliberately set out to maim as many people as possible. David

Werner, who made a visit there in 1989, reports:

> The large number of disabled people visible throughout Angola is part of the strategy of LIC. Leaving people seriously disabled puts a greater economic burden on families and on the nation than does killing people. It also takes a bigger toll psychologically: disabled people remain far more visible than the dead.[7]

However, we must beware of figures which are politically manipulated. In conflict situations casualty figures are often inflated, including disability figures.

Cultural differences in the perception of disability

It is the problem of definition which renders such highly generalised figures as ten per cent unhelpful. The definition of disability used by the Zimbabwe National Disability Survey of 1981 was:

> A physical or mental condition which makes it difficult or impossible for the person concerned to adequately fulfil his or her normal role in society.[8]

This definition works well for the arguments in this book, but for a survey it is important to define which impairments are truly incapacitating and which are not. Are dyslexia and flat feet (both included in the definition used by the World Health Organisation) real disabilities in a Zimbabwean village? Almost certainly not, but total blindness or the loss of a lower limb would be. Are we talking about functional impairments or perceived disabilities? Why is it that in most societies spectacles do not carry a stigma, but a hearing aid does? How *do* you define disability for statistical purposes?

The statistics already quoted which show an urban bias and a heavy weighting towards developed countries cannot be dismissed as meaningless: they underline the fundamental point that disability is relative and depends for its definition on local attitudes and physical barriers, which change from one society to another. A mobility or visual impairment may be more of a disability in a Western urban environment than in a village in the South where there are no buildings with stairs, no pavements with kerbs, and no newspapers to read.

The problem of over-estimation

Realism is essential. There is as much danger in over-estimating the numbers as in under-estimating them. If the figure of ten per cent is used blindly and all calculations are based on it without doing specific and detailed surveys, the size of the problem is likely to appear so daunting for hard-pressed governments and those planning services with slim resources that they may be reluctant even to embark on concerted action. Inflated estimates can lead to poor project planning and wasted resources, and also encourage the myth that disability is somehow competing with other fields of development for funding. In terms of political lobbying by the disability movement, there is more credibility to be gained by professionalism and accuracy than by assertions based on inaccurate estimates. I say this with the interests of the movement at heart; I believe its credibility can only be damaged by continuing to use the figure of ten per cent.

The ten per cent figure has in any case now been discounted by WHO itself. The author of the WHO Manual on Community-Based Rehabilitation, Dr Hillender, who was responsible for declaring ten per cent to be the world average, now favours a figure of about four per cent for developing countries and seven per cent for developed countries.

The main purpose of any survey should be to lay the foundations for service delivery. A therapist and child at a clinic in Glenview, Harare, Zimbabwe.

Photo: Chris Johnson/Oxfam

In terms of planning it is the need for services that ultimately matters, and the main purpose of any survey should be to lay the foundations for service delivery. However, there are considerable dangers attached to surveys. It scarcely needs pointing out that doing a survey with no follow-up or service delivery is a very cruel blow to those identified: a survey raises expectations of a measurable improvement in their lives, and should be done only as part of a general plan for service delivery.

What surveys and statistics do not show is the economic and human impact of, for example, a disabled child on a family. It inevitably falls to the mother to care for the child, which may have knock-on effects on income, the mother's health, and the health of other children. It is therefore specially important to ask women in any survey, and not rely only or mainly on answers from men.

Case studies

Juma Juma, a self–employed shoemaker in Zanzibar Town, disabled by polio.

Introduction to Part Three

Part Three contains five case studies illustrating efforts by disabled people to work for constructive change in attitudes, policies, and practices in the field of disability and development. In each country the cultural, social, economic, political, and development background is very different. **Zanzibar,** a group of small islands off the coast of Tanzania, has a population of about 700,000 and an economy based largely on cloves; it is probably the poorest part of one of the poorest countries in the world. **India,** in vivid contrast, is a country of enormous complexity, with 850 million people and well over 1,000 languages. **Zimbabwe** reveals all the problems of a country struggling to emerge from a colonial past in a part of Africa racked by drought and enormous political change. **Lebanon** is on the road to putting itself back together after a protracted and bitter civil war, but the path is rocky. In the **West Bank and Gaza Strip,** major political conflict provides a backdrop of almost continuous emergency.

Despite the wide differences, there are strong similarities. In all examples the debate about development, whether in disability or any other field, is ultimately about empowerment: the struggle for personal dignity by people who have been disempowered through social inequality, injustice, violence, and the wearing down that comes from a life lived on the edge of survival. Disabled people are part of such a struggle, which in their case is sharpened and amplified by the fact of being disabled. But, as the case-study material will reveal, it is by no means a hopeless struggle. Even in the direst circumstances, creativity, personal growth, social cohesion, and constructive change are not just pipe dreams: they can be realities.

Attitudes towards disabled people in each country are similar, but reflect the different cultural and social backgrounds. Disability as a development issue in each of the countries is treated differently, both at government level and by non-governmental agencies. Taken together, the countries considered here illuminate, from different angles, the issues surrounding disability, empowerment, disempowerment, and development that have been set out in the first part of this book.

One should be careful of case studies: they are intended to illuminate the argument and the difficulties, not necessarily to provide models. I do not want to present these examples as models to be followed, but as slices of experience from which others can learn. Some of these efforts are clearly 'successful', in the sense that they achieve what they set out to do, which is for disabled people to influence attitudes and policy, and to take more control over their own lives. But they are fraught with the same pitfalls and difficulties as any other efforts in social mobilisation working for major change against deeply entrenched attitudes and interests. Perhaps one of the most important ways in which real empowerment and self-development can happen is when groups are given the space and the freedom to fail, and to learn from these failures on their own.

CHAPTER 8

Zanzibar: Starting from scratch on CBR and social action

'The group has enlightened me: we give each other strength.'
(Fatima Hassan)

Fact file

Population: The last census in 1988 showed a population of 640,000 (with an annual growth rate of 3 per cent) distributed between two main islands, Unguja and Pemba, and a number of other very small islands. Pemba is less developed than Unguja. The figures listed below are averaged for the two islands.

Religion: Islam

Culture: East African with Arab influence

Language: Swahili

Economy: 90 per cent of Zanzibar's income is derived from cloves, the price of which on the world market fluctuates wildly. Most of the cloves are grown on Pemba. Coconuts, coconut fibre, other spices, and tourism make up the rest. A recent addition on the east coast of both islands is seaweed farming for the Far Eastern market (used as both food and medicine). Small-plot cultivation, fishing, and boat building are the main elements of the subsistence economy.

Government: An Arab Sultanate under British protection which had ruled since 1830 was overthrown by the Afro-Shiraz Party in an armed revolution in 1964. Later in the same year, Zanzibar joined with the mainland to form the United Republic of Tanzania. In 1977 Afro-Shiraz and TANU formed the single Tanzanian Party, Chama cha Mapindizi (CCM). The Zanzibar government is headed by a President who is also chairman of the Revolutionary Council. With the exception of foreign affairs, defence, communications, currency, and higher education, which is controlled from mainland Tanzania, Zanzibar has sovereign authority and its own ministries to implement domestic policies.

Infant mortality rate: Out of every 1,000 live births, 125 babies die before their first birthday and a further 210 die before their fifth birthday. The main causes of these high mortality rates are malaria and malnutrition.

Average age of marriage: 18.6 years. About half the women of Zanzibar give birth at an age when they are not physically mature enough for childbirth. The average age of marriage is lower in rural areas.

Maternal mortality rate: 300 per 100,000 births.

Malnutrition of children under five: Increased from 37 per cent in 1985 to 51 per cent in 1990. A main reason for this rise is the reduction in income of people in the rural areas, for whom food security is now a major issue.

Immunisation rates are high, and the incidence of diseases that are preventable by immunisation has fallen dramatically over the last few years. Malaria is the single biggest health problem.

Khalfan: an interview

Khalfan Khalfan is a wheelchair user whose legs were paralysed when he was a boy. In 1984 he founded UWZ — Umoja Walamavu Zanzibar (Association of Disabled People of Zanzibar) — which he still heads. It runs a programme of Community-Based Rehabilitation (CBR) in six villages on Unguja Island, and has fostered the establishment of groups of disabled people in villages throughout the two islands. It sees its main role as influencing the government to implement services for disabled people, educating disabled people about their rights, and raising awareness in the community on disability. It also runs skill-training programmes for adult disabled people. The staff and board of UWZ consist of both disabled and able-bodied people.

Q: So you went through school and eventually became a headmaster. How did you follow that course?

When I finished my schooling, I had to take an in-service teachers' training, because the normal teachers' training was not accessible. In my first school I began to take on more and more responsibilities and learned a lot about school management and administration; I was almost like an assistant headmaster, but I was just an ordinary teacher. Then ten years later, after I had proved my capability in school and management and administration, the ministry promoted me and made me an assistant headmaster. Two years later they made me a full headmaster.

Q: Why did you stop teaching and move into disability work?

Basically I wanted to teach in another way — because, you know, I am still teaching, but I am not teaching students in the classroom! So now I am teaching the population on disability issues. I thought if I remained as a teacher and did the disability work, I wouldn't manage either properly.

Q: What was it that convinced you that there was a need to work in disability?

Up to 1981 I had no idea about the disability movement. I was just Khalfan, disabled, and I did not have contact with any other

Khalfan Khalfan, founder of UWZ, with Zwena, a CBR worker, visiting the home of a disabled child in the village of Kilimani Dole, Unguja.

disabled people or with disabled organisations on the Tanzanian mainland. In fact I did not know that disabled people had organisations. So it was by sheer chance when I corresponded with one organisation in London requesting a wheelchair and they told me they don't provide wheelchairs for foreigners, only for people in Britain, but they gave me the address of DPI (Disabled People's International), which was just formed at that time. They suggested I contact them, and they told me DPI were having a meeting in Singapore.

So I wrote to DPI — in fact not requesting a wheelchair, but asking to participate in this meeting. I told them I didn't have any organisation in Zanzibar, I was disabled and did not have the money to travel to Singapore, but I would be interested to come as an observer. DPI sent me a ticket and I went.

There in Singapore I came to learn about disability. For the first time I met other disabled people — so many disabled people coming together from different parts of the world, with very strong organisations and some weak ones too. I was focusing all the time, asking a lot of questions of disabled people. So I went home and thought, 'Now there is a need to organise the disabled people in Zanzibar so that they will be able to achieve some of their rights.'

Q: But if you had not met other disabled people, would you have been aware of a general problem in Zanzibar as far as disabled people were concerned?

No, I was not aware. I was just aware of my own problem.

Q: And how would you identify your own problem?

I had a lot of problems. I suffered negative attitudes, even with some of my employers. For example, when I was just about to travel to pursue a diploma course in educational administration and management in London, at the last minute my employer said, 'No, we don't allow sick people to travel.' He used that term in fact! And I was very angry about that. I wrote a strong letter to the Ministry, saying that if I was sick then I was not fit to teach; so I would have to resign if I was not fit, and leave the job. And they wrote back and apologised and all that. But I didn't go to London.

Then there was the problem of accessibility; it used to frustrate me a lot, not being able to go places I wanted, like the cinema. And then sometimes you meet people who insist on treating you as incapable because you are in a wheelchair. That was true even among my employers.

Q: So on coming back from Singapore, you were very strongly motivated to do something about the situation. How did you start working on it?

I wrote a report to the government about the Singapore conference, and then I made some suggestions. One suggestion was that I needed to be supported by the government to move around and talk to disabled people, to give them information about what I had learnt in Singapore.

The second suggestion was that we be allowed to form an association. But then it was not that easy. The government did not accept it immediately. It was being delayed and delayed, from 1981.

Q: What was their objection?

At that time ... maybe they were either ignorant or a little bit suspicious: I might be dealing with a political movement or something. The other thing is that some of the government officials came to the point of saying, 'Why do you want a separate organisation? What do you want, Khalfan? If the disabled people have a problem, they can go to the Social Welfare Department.'

Q: So their attitude was basically: 'The government will provide; you don't need to organise your own provision.'

That's right. That was their attitude. That went on up to 1984, when there was a change of leadership, and we got it through with the new leadership.

Q: Was that their attitude to any kind of non-governmental organisation being formed in Zanzibar?

Well, in fact we were the first one, so after ours there came others, but before then there were no NGOs in Zanzibar.

Q: What provision was there for disabled people before you formed the association?

There was very little. A very few people were provided with wheelchairs, but that was about all. There was a little bit of physiotherapy, and some provision of callipers and crutches, but it was very limited.

Q: So you finally managed to form your association in 1984. What were your immediate goals?

Our first main objective was to mobilise all disabled people under the umbrella of this organisation, and then to sensitise the disabled people about their rights and the obligations of their society.

Q: So it was educating disabled people, rather than the able-bodied community.

.Yes, at first, because the first step is to have members who accept your organisation. So we thought the first thing is, we have to educate the disabled people to know their rights.

Q: How did you reach them?

We used the structure of the party (CCM), because after forming the organisation we were registered and recognised officially. After that recognition we used the social welfare department of the party, and they were the ones who were travelling together to different villages in the two islands asking disabled people and the parents of disabled children to come together at local party branches. I talked with my members to discuss the issues of the rights of disabled people, education, the importance of having an organisation, and all these sorts of things.

Q: And did you find that people in the rural areas understood what you were talking about?

Not very much, because of the situation they were in. Whenever anyone appears in rural areas, the people normally think of charity; their first reaction is that with this organisation we might get some money or clothes or food, so at first many people did not really understand the objective of the organisation.

Q: But don't you think that people in a rural area are perhaps as well integrated into village life as they are ever likely to be, and therefore there isn't much that a central organisation can do to improve things?

Well, they are integrated, but they are not involved. I mean they may live in the community and be accepted by it, but they are not involved in its decision-making and in participating in general activities. So it is not full integration; they are, or were, still isolated in significant ways.

Q: So they were kept out of the decision-making by their disabilities.

Yes, and because of society's negative attitude. And they thought that the community could make decisions on their behalf, including about their rights.

Q: What kinds of right would a village person demand which they don't already have?

First, the village set-up in Zanzibar is very different to the set-up on the Tanzanian mainland and Kenya. There is very little difference between the village and the town in Zanzibar; village people always have a very strong relationship with people in the town. That's the pattern of our life. So they've got their rights, for example their right to education, because eleven years of education are compulsory in Zanzibar. But most disabled people do not enjoy this right. That's one very important area.

Then there is rehabilitation. It is also a right, but most disabled people in rural areas don't have the facilities for rehabilitation. They cannot afford to attend a physiotherapy unit in the town. They do not have access to callipers and so on. The only people who have access to these things are those who live very close to the town, and even then it's very few of those.

But even employment is an issue in rural areas. Two blind people told me the other day that they wanted to work in a coconut collective, but the landlord said, 'No, you can take ten shillings and go!' So employment is a major issue and a right.

Q: So it was the need for rehabilitation which led to your CBR programme eventually.

Exactly.

Q: How can it be applied more widely? At the moment you are concentrating on six villages which are quite close to the town.

In fact we want the government to implement the rest, because we as an NGO are a small organisation in Zanzibar; we have just shown the way.

Q: So you are putting the ball back in the government's court.

Yes. It is the responsibility of the government to do Community-

Based Rehabilitation. We as an organisation can work with them, show them the experience we have. They can use our workers for training other workers, and so on. But we as an organisation do not see it is our role to take on CBR over the entire country, because we cannot manage to do that; and besides, it is the government's responsibility. That is why we don't want to move into other areas. The government has asked us several times to do that, but we feel it is their responsibility.

Our organisation is a pressure group, and it has been able to influence the Minister of Education to adopt a policy of special education, and the minister has already started sending teachers to be trained to teach the blind and the deaf. They now have a few classes in Zanzibar which did not exist before. So now at least we have a few classes for the blind and for the mentally retarded, and we hope that each year the ministry will establish more and more units. So this is the impact of our organisation on the situation of disabled people. The Minister of Health has collaborated with the Prime Minister's office to set up a special task force to work on a policy for rehabilitation.

Q: So pressure to provide services is a very important part of your work.
Yes, definitely. We are also working closely with government offices in different ways: whenever disability issues arise in any of the ministries, they use us as consultants, and we are happy to do that. For example in special education we are not experts, but we know people who are, and we provide these contacts to the government. Recently I was in Oslo and visited an institute for special education, where they said they would take two people from Zanzibar on their next course.

A model of co-operation

How does action for change start? The development of UWZ is a classic story of a personal learning experience leading to effective action and social change. Khalfan had proven ability and an excellent reputation as a headmaster, and his accidental discovery of the disability movement fired his enthusiasm to start work in disability in a situation where almost nothing was being done. The story from then on illustrates insight, diplomacy, ability to inspire and mobilise others, organisational skills, and political judgement. Zanzibar has been lucky to have someone with these qualities available and exceptionally well-placed to take such an initiative. Zanzibar is also lucky, despite its severe poverty, to be a small, homogeneous, and close-knit community where many people now holding government office have passed through Khalfan's hands as pupils when he was a headmaster. There could hardly be a more auspicious basis for starting constructive work in disability.

These are very considerable advantages. There are many valuable lessons to be read in the Zanzibar example which could be remembered elsewhere:

• the vital importance of networking (in this case by DPI) on a global scale, especially for an isolated population like that of Zanzibar;

• persistence in the face of bureaucratic obstacles;

• using all available means to reach people, including the government structure itself, and not trying to set up a separate monolithic structure;

• winning the government over and working constructively with it instead of alienating it;

• keeping in focus the need to sensitise disabled people themselves as the first objective of the new organisation;

• recognising the limitations of an NGO like UWZ, and insisting that the ultimate responsibility for full service delivery lies with the government: the role of UWZ is to show the way and then provide advice, expertise, and pressure to start new services.

The result is a model of co-operation that would be the envy of most NGOs in the South. That is not to say that all the battles have been won; but given that there was almost nothing before UWZ came along, the achievements are very significant. UWZ has succeeded in a few years in both being an advocate for the needs and rights of disabled people and setting up a model for a basic rehabilitation service.

Making a start on community based rehabilitation

The UWZ CBR programme raises the dilemmas familiar in any rural rehabilitation effort dealing with a scattered population. Although Zanzibar is small by African and Indian standards, the roads are very poor and public transport almost non-existent in many places;

private cars are an extreme rarity, and so are taxis; bicycles are the most common form of personal transport, but are used almost exclusively by men; it is not uncommon to find women who have never been to Zanzibar town in their lives, and whose world is entirely bounded by their house and their village. Unlike the Tanzanian mainland, where women do most of the cultivation work on the family plot, in Zanzibar it is the men who do the bulk of the agricultural work, aided by women at peak times like harvest. But the work of, for example, drying cloves, which is done at home, tends to fall to women.

Zanzibar is a Muslim society, and while that does not place Zanzibari women in purdah or lesser kinds of seclusion found in some parts of the Middle East, it does restrict their social mobility more than their sisters on the mainland. For urban women the problem of mobility is less severe, but still significant.

Saada is 15 and was born with severe cerebral palsy. She is one of eight children: seven girls and one boy. Her father is a shopkeeper in Zanzibar town. Her mother describes her life:

I knew that she was not normal, but I did not discover what was wrong until five years after her birth. Saada was given a little physiotherapy at the hospital, but it didn't make much difference; she remained completely dependent, unable to dress, toilet herself, or even sit up from a lying position.

Then when she was 12, the UWZ CBR programme started and Zwena, one of the staff, began visiting us at home once a week. We have been working together to free up Saada's stiff muscles so that she can sit; we have also worked on toilet training. Now she can sit up from a lying position; it has made a lot of difference: she is much happier and takes more interest in what is going on around her.

In relation to my other children, I feel that Saada is intelligent and special: she is a happy and deeply affectionate child, and she has a strong sense of humour. Her brothers and sisters try to include her as much as possible. One sister in particular takes good care of her: she dresses her and toilets her before going off to school.

Now I am pregnant again. If I knew that my next child was going to be like Saada, what would I feel about that? I would prefer a normal child, but whatever happens is God's will. I love Saada, we all love her, but I feel tied.

After three years of weekly physiotherapy sessions with her mother and CBR worker Zwena (r.), Saada, a severely disabled child, is much happier and takes more interest in the world around her.

Most Zanzibari mothers of disabled children find themselves similarly isolated. The implications are obvious: if the mothers are stuck at home, so are their children. The greatest need is not so much to provide rehabilitation at home, even though that is clearly necessary, but to create the opportunities and possibilities for mothers and their children to meet, socialise, and learn from each other. For this reason, it is unsatisfactory to regard a CBR programme as merely a system of home visits: it needs to be used as a means of breaking the isolation of families with severely disabled children like Saada. That is why UWZ set up a system of playgroups as an essential part of its CBR programme. Contact with other mothers through the CBR playgroup organised by UWZ gives Saada's mother essential support: she does not feel alone.

The task of the CBR rehabilitation staff, as they see it, is to remove barriers: freeing up children, despite their disability, to realise their full potential. **Ramadhani**, now 13, is the sixth of seven children; he and his family live in the village of Kilimani Dole on the main island, Unguja. He was a year and two months old, just starting to walk, when he was struck by a high fever. His mother describes what happened:

*When he came out of the fever, I found he could not use his limbs. I did
not know what disease it was; all I knew was that Ramadhani was
paralysed. I managed to get him to hospital, where I learned that it was
polio. They said there wasn't much that could be done for him. So I
took him to traditional healers and they used local oil and massaged
him to straighten out his limbs, because he was very stiff. They
managed to loosen him up a little and he recovered the use of his arms,
though they are still weak.*

His father farms a family plot of about two and half acres growing
cassava, maize, and bananas. They consume nearly all they produce,
selling occasional surpluses to find the money for essentials like
clothes, tea, sugar, rice, and (on rare occasions) meat or fish.
Ramadhani does not go to school, although he would very much
like to:

*I am interested in machines and things that work; I want to be an
electrician. Three of my brothers go to the school — it's about a
quarter of a mile away; there are two shifts, one in the morning and
another in the afternoon. But I can only crawl and cannot get there. I*

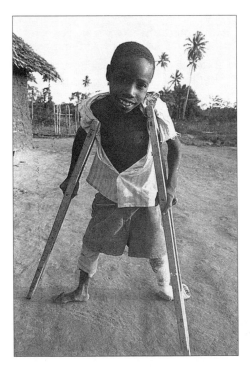

Ramadhani: 'As soon as I can
walk, I can go to school.'

don't think a wheelchair would be much use: there is no road, and the ground is very rough. My mother says that as soon as I can walk, I can go.

For the past year he has been visited by Hasan Khamis, one of the UWZ CBR staff, who has been working with him and his parents to prepare his legs for callipers. He has been wearing corrective plaster-casts and learning to use crutches. He already feels more independent, though he finds the crutches quite a struggle, because his arms are weak.

For Ramadhani, school stands as the major incentive, a goal driving him to struggle with crutches and callipers. Clearly bright and determined, he will probably make it. Are there shades of the Peto Institute here, of 'normalisation' against the best interests of the individual disabled person? Perhaps. But the poverty and harshness of his immediate environment are the reality. The choices open to Ramadhani are to struggle or wither.

In my interview with Ramadhani's family, it was suggested that perhaps his brothers and sisters could take him to school in a small handcart, which they already use to involve him in play away from the village. His parents rejected this, because they wanted him to be as independent as possible; if the crutches and callipers proved too much, the cart might be a backstop, but they felt that he should have the incentive of unaided mobility first.

Removing barriers at the individual level is the main purpose of CBR. For Ramadhani it is happening. For Saada's mother the barrier of her isolation and feeling of aloneness has been removed (at least in part) by the contacts she makes through the playgroup scheme.

Village disability groups: discovering solidarity

The UWZ CBR programme, which deals only with the rehabilitation of children, runs in six villages within easy reach of Zanzibar town, as a pilot project, in order to demonstrate the principle to the government. But what of the adult disabled people throughout the islands? As with the rehabilitation of children, breaking the isolation of disabled people is the primary objective of UWZ: in both Unguja and Pemba islands, UWZ has a network of members, who are recruited by district secretaries.

Mwantatu Mabarak contracted polio as an adult, and her right leg is affected. She is District Secretary for UWZ, based on the village of Bungi (population about 2,000), but covering adjacent villages too. Her job is to make people aware of the organisation in the villages and to mediate between the UWZ office in Zanzibar and the members.

I am also a member of the group in Bungi itself, which I started two years ago. We have 18 members, both men and women, who have a range of disabilities including hearing, mobility, and learning impairments. I feel that UWZ has achieved a real change of attitude in the villages where I work. There is a difference in the way disabled people are treated in the villages. What has made the difference? The main influence, I think, is that the chairperson, Khalfan, who is himself in a wheelchair and widely respected, passes through here and meets disabled people. Also government representatives come and talk to them. So they feel they are recognised, and other people change their behaviour towards them too as a result of this recognition. Our group in Bungi has recently opened a tea shop which sells basic necessities.

What does integration mean within a small, close-knit village community in Zanzibar? Khalfan made the point above that while disabled village people may be accepted by their communities, they are not involved in decision-making in the same way that other people are. They need recognition as well as integration.

Through interviews with many people in these disability groups in Zanzibari villages, two points repeatedly surfaced: the strength which they gained from meeting each other, and their need for better economic opportunities. Some are finding it through co-operation with each other, and some have joined forces with able-bodied people. Prospects for such cooperation in the town are considerably better than in villages. **Haji Maulidi Haji** is 27 and lives in Zanzibar town.

I had polio as a child and I can walk only with difficulty. I use a hand-powered tricycle to go any distance. When I was 20 I set up a bicycle repair shop with a friend who is not disabled. We can repair about ten bicycles a day and earn 7,000 shillings a week between us [about £35.00, a very decent wage by Zanzibar standards]. I am not married; I live with my brother; my partner is married with several children. I feel that an enterprise where a disabled person works with a non-disabled person is the best arrangement. I would like to expand this workshop and employ both disabled and able-bodied people.

Much of the effort of UWZ with village disability groups goes into finding and creating opportunities for improving earning power. In

February 1991, in Makunduchi, a village on the east coast of Unguja island, some disabled women formed their own group. The ten members have a range of disabilities including polio, visual impairment, and deafness. The group mobilised initially around an income-generating project based on coconut-fibre products: rope making, matting, and brooms. **Fatima Hassan** is a member; she had polio as a child, which left her with a weakened arm and a deformed leg. She has three children who are now more or less grown up; her husband divorced her a few years ago.

Why did we form a group? The UWZ worker talked to us and explained what was happening in other villages, and it seemed a good idea. Disabled women especially are in a very difficult situation. Take me: I'm both disabled and divorced, and my children, who are almost grown up, do not give me much help, even though they depend on me financially. I was pretty desperate.

Since forming the group, my life has changed. It has helped me in so many ways, but mainly in providing a support in my difficult situation. The group has enlightened me. It's not only about production: we give each other strength and also practical help in many little ways. We meet once a week on Thursdays. It's women only. Why? It would not be possible to have a mixed group of men and women. If we had men, they would dominate. We would rather stay as just women.

Fatima Hassan, member of Makunduchi disability group: 'Joining the group is a kind of liberation.'

We started this rope making project. It's hard work and doesn't bring much: so far 2,500 shillings for the whole group [about £12.00], but we hope we can earn more than that. We start with the raw coconut husks and bury them under the sand by the sea and leave them there for six months; that makes them easier to work. Then we beat them with heavy sticks until they become pliable, and then we start making the rope. The problem comes in the selling; we sell the rope to merchants in the village who take it to the town. Who controls the prices? The merchants, of course. The whole process of selling and buying works against us.

So if they could sell directly, they would earn more. Why don't they take the rope to town themselves, and cut out the merchants?

It would be impossible. We do not have that kind of mobility, not in this village. We need to find someone we can trust, but we don't trust the merchants. Look, I'm not complaining that much: this group is the best thing that ever happened to me. If I am at home inside all alone, that itself is a disability. Joining the group is a kind of liberation. We have so many ideas we can share with each other. I hope we can solve the marketing problem.

The situation for disabled women is difficult everywhere: they live under the double disadvantage of sexism and 'handicapism'. The testimony of women like Fatima Hassan provides a small insight into the limitations imposed not just by their disability but by a society which regards it as inappropriate for women even to travel to the town on their own. But the groups formed around UWZ, still young, are gradually opening up new horizons for Fatima and others like her, and a vision of a life where they can begin to experience something of what it means to be empowered.

CHAPTER 9

Zimbabwe: forming a disability movement

'We do not speak about politics; we speak about survival.'
(Simon Tevera)

Fact file

Population: 9.7 million (1991 estimate)
Main ethnic groups: Shona 77%, Ndebele 18%, others 5%
Religion: Traditional animist 60%, Christian 40%
Population growth rate: 3.5% p.a. (estimate)
Urban population: 27% (1989)
Adult literacy: 81% of men, 67% of women (1985)
Life expectancy: 64 (1989)
Infant mortality: 49 per 1,000 live births (1988)
Gross domestic product: £2,605 million (1990)
Average income: £200 per capita (1991)

Background

The disability movement in Zimbabwe is one of the most vigorous in Africa. Why?

Tourist brochures describe Zimbabwe is a land of contrasts; a recent Oxfam publication[1] describes it as a land divided. But the country strikes the first-time visitor today as a model of energy, cohesion, and unity in a divided continent and a fragmented world. Most of the infrastructure is impressive, the roads are superb, the telephones work, the cities are whistle-clean, and there is an infectious enthusiasm for life among ordinary people that seems uniquely Zimbabwean. Zimbabwean music throbs with a powerful soul. The prolific and gifted Zimbabwean sculptors working in stone reveal a deep seam of creative energy reaching far back into an ancient culture — a culture that is embodied most dramatically in the amazing ruins of Great Zimbabwe, a city created by the Shona people between the thirteenth and fifteenth centuries, whose beautifully engineered dry-stone walls are one of the wonders of Africa.

Standing in a street in present-day Harare, with its broad, tree-lined avenues, splashing fountains, well-kept parks and public gardens, smart buildings, and people in neat office clothes, it is hard to reconcile this image of Africa with the all-too familiar television images of famine, war, and destitution.

But whether one speaks of a land of contrasts or a land divided, the tourist brochures and the Oxfam publication are right: one should not be deceived by the appearance of central Harare into thinking that this is a country now enjoying a problem-free independence. The country has been forged out of one of the most bitter struggles in the post-colonial era. After independence in April 1980, the first decade of Zimbabwe's existence as a free country was marred by a civil war of extreme ferocity that left many thousands of people dead; it was provoked and fuelled in large measure by the destabilisation policy of the South African government at that time. In 1992 famine stalked large sections of the country as rains failed for the fifth successive year.

The Rhodesian colonial system was geared primarily for the benefit of a white minority for whom 'the whole economic system, on the farms as well as in the mines, rested on a cheap and plentiful supply of native labour'.[2] Both the educational system and the health service in Rhodesia were designed for this minority: ten times more money was spent on education for whites than for blacks. In Bulawayo in 1976 there were three general hospitals serving a population of 70,000 whites, while 400,000 blacks had access to one hospital; this was despite the fact that the health profile of blacks was substantially poorer.[3] Missions provided much of the preventive and primary care in rural areas, but more than half of them were closed during the struggle for independence and its ferocious bush war. In disability there was very little provision, and almost none provided by the government for black people.

So with independence there was an explosion of effort in

education and health. The government allocated 22 per cent of its budget to education, which it declared to be the birthright of every Zimbabwean. (This compares with an education budget of around 2 per cent in Britain in the same period.) Within ten years the total school population had jumped from 900,000 in 1979 to three million in 1989. The phenomenal expansion was achieved with the help of an enormous amount of community action, centred on building schools and running informal educational activities such as literacy and night classes for adults. There was a huge desire to get the country going under its new management, and to demonstrate the power of ordinary people to build it.

But the downside of educating so many people so suddenly is that there are very few jobs: to get the humblest position in Harare these days requires five 'O' levels. On the streets of Harare itself among the smartly-dressed and quick-stepping office workers are the unemployed and the beggars, many of them women with babies, and many of them disabled. The quiet and spacious suburbs with their swimming pools and magnificent flame trees, once home to white Rhodesians, are now the dwellings of a Zimbabwean upper-middle class who have made it. These are 'north of the railway line'. 'South of the railway line' lie the slums like Mbare and townships like Glenview, and the shanty towns made of packing crates and plastic sheeting that got bulldozed when the Commonwealth heads of state came to town in 1991. Every morning and evening there are long lines of patient people at each bus stop as the city workers wait for two, three, and sometimes more hours for the hopelessly inadequate buses to take them to and from their townships. 'No foreign exchange, no buses' is the excuse.

So there are huge problems. The bright promise at Independence of a free, equal, and just society has not been altogether fulfilled. But there can be little doubt that the long and bitter struggle leading up to Zimbabwe's independence has had a very significant impact on the general tone of the country, the aspirations of its people, the energetic communal action, and strong sense of civic consciousness. Against this background, developments in disability work have taken place which reinforce Zimbabwe's reputation as a country of unusual zest and imagination. Such developments owe much to the sense of struggle that accompanied the emergence from colonial rule, and are deeply affected today by the continuing struggle to build a nation in exceptionally difficult times.

Disability in Zimbabwe

There are three strong threads in the story of disability in Zimbabwe. First, from the 1950s onwards one name stands out as the pioneer and father of work in disability in the country: Jairos Jiri, who, starting from extremely humble origins, during his lifetime set up institutions for disabled people all over the country. Second, Zimbabwe has seen the birth and growth of one of the most vigorous disability movements in Africa, set up largely by people who came through the Jairos Jiri institutions and rebelled against them. Third, soon after Independence the government committed itself to a countrywide CBR policy which has brought rehabilitation to rural areas for the first time. The government is also committed to passing pro-disability legislation.

The Zimbabwe National Disability Survey of 1981, one year after Independence, found a total of 276,300 people with moderate to severe disabilities, out of a population at that time of some eight million — that is, 3.45 per cent were disabled. The survey estimated that one quarter of these, about 60,000, needed rehabilitation intervention.[4] This included people who had been disabled in the

David Zulu, accountant with the National Council of Disabled Persons of Zimbabwe.

violence before Independence, both civilians and ex-combatants. Existing facilities at that time catered for about 9 per cent of the 60,000. However, this survey was based on some rather questionable assumptions, relying not on house-to-house calls, but on disabled people identifying themselves by turning up at reporting centres; this presupposed that they knew about the survey, could physically reach the centres, and had the full co-operation of their families. (It also implied self-definition of disability, which is probably the most accurate way to measure such statistics.) However, despite such failings it was an expression of the new government's determination to tackle issues long left untouched and a measure of the energy with which it went about its business. Whatever the actual figure, what was clear from the survey was that existing services were seriously inadequate, especially in the rural areas.

The government's actions, especially its CBR programme, are clearly and interestingly documented in a recent book by Helen House, Mary McAlister and Cathy Naidoo: *Zimbabwe — Steps Ahead*,[5] to which the reader is warmly referred. This chapter will focus on the formation of the disability movement and its record. For the purposes of our enquiry into social action by disabled people we will briefly consider Jairos Jiri and his work, which set the scene for the emergence of the disability movement, before considering the movement itself.

The story of Jairos Jiri [6]

Jairos never went to school. As a teenager from a farm in the Bikita Reserve near Masvingo, he arrived in Bulawayo in the early 1940s looking for work; he had previously tended his family's goats and worked as a gardener. In Bulawayo he was stunned by the numbers of disabled beggars on the streets: begging horrified and humiliated him. His attitude to disabled people was the same as anyone else's in the rural areas of the country at that time: disablement came from the displeasure of ancestral spirits, or witchcraft, or, if congenital, was proof of a mother's infidelity. Disabled people in villages were certainly an embarrassment to their families for these reasons, but in rural areas begging was unknown. Jairos realised that the anonymity of the city and the breakdown of family structures within it made begging not only possible but, in the absence of any services, the only option for most urban disabled people.

He found a job in a bottle store in Bulawayo, but was gripped by the necessity of doing something about the disabled beggars. So he began. His job at the bottle store involved delivering orders on a bicycle; when disabled beggars came to the shop, he used the bicycle with its large carrier to take them to hospital for corrective surgery. The first person he picked up, a boy crawling along the pavement in rags, was eventually able to walk unaided after extensive treatment. Those whom the hospital could not treat, particularly blind people, he took home to his two-room house in a township. He had no finances other than his wages, but built a shack behind his house, where he got a friend to teach blind people to make baskets. He earned extra income for these activities by selling sweets on street corners, and opened a vegetable stall by his house. He then persuaded a shoe-maker to give instruction in shoe repairs to the growing crowd of disabled people who came daily to the packing-case workshop behind his little house.

People thought he was mad. The Municipal Authorities demanded that if he was going to do charity work, he should register as a proper organisation. When he tried to do just that, the Native Commissioner told him the idea was utter nonsense and he was not prepared to consider it; Jairos should not waste his time. It was not until a different Native Commissioner was appointed with more liberal ideas that Jairos finally managed to register the 'Bulawayo and Bikita Physically Defective Society' in 1950.

That was the start: one should not underestimate the measure of his commitment in what now seem like the dark ages. By the time he died in 1982, Jairos Jiri had spent 35 years, the whole of his working life, setting up centres for disabled people all over the country under the name of the Jairos Jiri Association. He had established seven children's centres, three training centres, three farms, six sheltered employment workshops, and one old people's home, plus commercial funding for craft shops. It was an extraordinary achievement by any standards, in a country where disability was almost totally neglected before he came along. It was the more remarkable given his background, complete lack of education, and the attitudes of the day. The work he set up continues.

Lessons from the Jairos Jiri experience
As a case study, the work of Jairos Jiri sheds light on the historical process behind work in disability that is common in many parts of the world: the transition from no services at all, to charitable institutions, to a growing political consciousness among disabled people (as we will see below) and the formation of a movement. It

also reveals the powerful tensions that exist between the 'charity industry', with its focus on individual need, and the movement of disabled people campaigning for universal rights.

With the awareness that we have now, focused on empowerment and equality, it is easy to be dismissive of past efforts that seem to stem from outdated notions of charity and paternalism. But we need to keep the historical perspective in mind. In Britain, Victorian philanthropy, with its gloomy, monolithic institutions and armies of determined do-gooders ladling out soup to the poor, laid the basis for present-day voluntary action, not to mention the establishment of the Welfare State. To criticise the Victorians now with our present attitudes is like saying that the USA should have put men on the moon in the 1920s: the time was not right.[7]

Similarly Jairos Jiri, with all his paternalism, played a vital role in preparing the ground for the response to disability that has developed in Zimbabwe over the last 15 years. To dismiss him as a misguided paternalist is to be unaware of the historical moment.

Forming a disability movement

The disability movement in Zimbabwe grew out of the institutions that Jairos Jiri created; the leaders of the movement themselves are nearly all graduates of them. Without Jairos Jiri it is very difficult to see how the movement could have started and developed as it did: he provided not only an education and training for hundreds of disabled people who would not otherwise have had one, but also the greenhouse in which the movement could take root and begin to grow, before transplanting itself into the world outside. Criticism of the institutions may well be fair, with the knowledge and awareness that now exists, but they were the test bed and the launch pad for what came next.

Alex Phiri, already quoted in Chapter 3, was abandoned by his parents when he lost both legs in a road accident at the age of eight. He was one of a group of people who became disillusioned with life in a Jairos Jiri institution in the early 1970s. He showed outstanding talent as a painter and was seen as a valuable asset by the institution where he lived: his paintings were prominently displayed, and added considerably to the impression made on visitors. They were also sold in the craft shops and brought in income for the Jairos Jiri Association. The Association therefore wished him to work for them permanently as an artist, but Alex had other ideas: he wanted to continue his studies, as far as university if possible. The institution refused his request to go to a school where he could work for his 'A' levels, so he went by stealth and by force of personality: he hid in the back of a truck that was going to the school, and demanded to be accepted.

During his time at a Jairos Jiri institution, Alex and others formed what they called the Kubatsirana Club (from a Shona word meaning 'to help each other'). This club organised excursions into the surrounding countryside for picnics, an activity supported and encouraged by the institution, which provided transport. But Alex and his friends used the outings as opportunities to discuss their problems as disabled people living in an institution. They then formed what they called the 'Inmates' Representative Council', an indication of how they perceived themselves at that time. Alex picks up the story:

> We decided to transform our club into a registered organisation, 'The Council for the Welfare of the Disabled'. The name confused Jairos Jiri because it sounded like a service organisation, but what we had in mind had nothing to do with service; it was an advocacy or pressure group. When Mr Jiri realised we were advocating power for disabled people, he suddenly felt threatened. 1974 was marked by a battle to get the organisation registered. We eventually got it registered in 1975.[8]

The response from Jairos Jiri was, perhaps, understandable but disappointing. His commitment to what he was doing was never in question. What had been achieved since the first rag-clad beggar had been scooped off the pavement into his bicycle carrier was indeed amazing, but his vision of the capabilities of disabled people was, for the new generation, much too limited. **Joshua Malinga**, now Secretary General of SAFOD (Southern Africa Federation of the Disabled), was another of the early members of 'The Council for the Welfare of the Disabled'. He himself had indeed been rescued from oblivion by Jairos Jiri as a non-walking village child with polio, but he describes with some despair how he was told by Jairos to learn shoe-repairing as his trade. Like Alex he wanted a proper education, and after a great deal of pushing he finally persuaded the institution to hire a teacher who would teach them 'with books'.

Joshua, Alex, and their friends felt that times had changed greatly since Jairos first started his work, but the Jairos Jiri Association had not changed with them. The struggle for national independence in which the whole country was engaged had its effect on their consciousness as disabled people, but the Association was not committed to and did not understand integration; rather its institutions tended to be terminal abodes for those who entered them, and they were touching only a minute proportion of the disabled people in the country: they held altogether about 1,000 people at any one time. Joshua and the others saw that such institutions would never be able to integrate those they did help, or reach the majority beyond the institutions, who were still untouched.

So they set off with their own organisation, without knowing where they were going, but with the conviction that certain principles were inviolable. The most important of these were that disabled people should be intimately involved in the planning of the services that affected them and that they had the same rights as any other citizen. Alex again:

We didn't have a clear plan of action. We operated on the enthusiasm of success rather than real structure. The constitution itself was very simple. It emphasised self-help for disabled people, but gave no guidelines as to how this should take place. Basically the organisation provided a monthly forum for disabled people in Bulawayo to protest against the shortcomings of the institutions and to share their personal problems.[9]

The National Council of Disabled People of Zimbabwe (NCDPZ)

By the end of the 1970s, with Independence in the offing, Jairos Jiri had become a highly revered figure; his name was a household word equated with work in disability. But Joshua Malinga and his friends were deeply concerned that this institutional approach, which depended on private charity, which was not committed to integration, which had a limited idea of what disabled people were capable of, which felt threatened by the idea of disabled people having a voice, and above all which made no demands on the government, would be adopted by the new government for lack of any better vision. Such an approach conveniently let the government off the hook altogether.

It was this fear in particular that spurred them to press on with forming their own organisation which would demonstrate an alternative: in September 1979, six months before Independence, they produced a paper outlining a policy on rehabilitation, containing 25 detailed points. The paper proposed the formation of a National Council for Welfare and Rehabilitation composed of government departments, voluntary agencies, organisations of disabled people, trade unions, and rehabilitation specialists. The council would take charge of all matters relating to disability in the country. In particular the paper strongly recommended pro-disability legislation, and community-based rather than institution-based rehabilitation. Such a council was never formed, but the proposals had an impact on government thinking and certainly contributed to creating the positive approach to disability that was demonstrated by the National Survey and the adoption of a country-wide CBR policy.

The next landmark in the development of the movement was when Joshua Malinga attended the Rehabilitation International Congress in Winnipeg in 1981, the watershed in the history of disability where Disabled People's International was born (already referred to elsewhere in this book). Before going, he had no idea what awaited him, but, like Mike du Toit from South Africa, he was fired in Winnipeg by the power of disabled people speaking out for their own rights against the weight of the medical rehabilitation model espoused by the professionals. Alex continues:

> *Before Joshua's trip to Canada we were simply a support group for one another; we had no political analysis. It was only after his discussions with the equally frustrated disabled people from around the world that we began linking our problems in Zimbabwe to social, economic, and political issues.*

The first thing they did was change their language. They dropped the word 'welfare' and called their organisation the 'National Council of Disabled People of Zimbabwe' (NCDPZ). From the start they saw its purpose to be primarily a pressure group to create new thinking about disability in the government, among professionals, in institutions, in the general population, and among disabled people themselves. The new thinking meant that disabled people should be able to contribute and be fully integrated into all aspects of life, share in the planning of rehabilitation services, and, crucially, have their rights recognised by pro-disability legislation on the statute book.

In order to function effectively as a pressure group, it needed to be a movement, which meant building a membership. Building a membership meant more than just talk: it meant practical projects. They began a small knitting and dress-making workshop, Afro-Knit, employing six disabled women in Bulawayo. But urban disabled people were better served by existing services than those in rural areas, for whom there was virtually nothing. Over 70 per cent of the country's population lives in the rural areas and, if NCDPZ were to make any impression there, they needed an office, full-time staff, and a vehicle. In 1982 NCDPZ started an outreach programme, the Rural Membership Development Programme, with support from Horticultural Therapy and funding from Oxfam (UK and Ireland).

The aim of this programme was to identify disabled people and their needs in the rural areas, conscientise them, help them to acquire medical and rehabilitation services, and enhance the general educational levels of disabled people through help with school expenses. They aimed to set up practical projects which would make disabled people more self-reliant, and also encourage integration through working jointly with able-bodied people. Such projects would give disabled people self-confidence and a moral boost. At the same time they would reveal to able-bodied people the potential rather than the limitations of disabled people.[10]

The Rural Membership Development Programme (RMDP) was started with a network of contact people in rural areas whose function was, and is, to assist in the implementation of the programme. They include disabled people, church workers, district councillors, chiefs, headmen, school teachers, hospital staff, and members of the Organisation of Rural Associations for Progress (ORAP). ORAP has been an important influence on the thinking behind the programme. After Independence many foreign development agencies established themselves in Zimbabwe, and funds flowed in, all aimed at 'projects'. ORAP is critical of this approach: it feels that a purely project-focused development strategy is artificial and neither recognises nor encourages the natural processes that are part of people's lives. ORAP does not see development in terms of buildings rising from the bush, or the number of wells dug, but in the gradual change in people's consciousness and ability to manage themselves and their environment successfully. 'Projects' should simply be a means to this end, not an end in themselves. This matched exactly the approach of NCDPZ when the rural membership programme started, which was to get away from concrete institutions and expensive infrastructures, and use existing structures to work with people in their own contexts.

Once disabled people in a particular area have been identified by the contact people, they form themselves into a branch of NCDPZ, supported by a development officer from the office in Bulawayo. Each local branch is responsible for identifying other disabled people, encouraging solidarity between them, facilitating their educational and rehabilitation needs, and setting up practical projects. A branch consists of an elected executive committee of disabled people which may co-opt others, including able-bodied people, as necessary. They may use a school, church building, council offices, local clinic, or the open air for their functions.

Ephraim Mafura is the chairperson of the Chirumanzu branch of NCDPZ. Chirumanzu lies about 250 miles south of Harare, and a little to the north of Masvingo and the impressive ruins of Great Zimbabwe. The area is scrub and bush, punctuated by widely scattered villages up to ten miles apart. In the centre of it there is a mission which runs a small hospital. Like many other parts of Zimbabwe it has been affected by drought, and at the time of my visit there to gather material for this book, the government was distributing food. Significantly, the disabled people I interviewed had not received anything.

Ephraim walks with a crutch as the result of polio, and spent his childhood in a Jairos Jiri institution.

I left the institution eventually and was employed by my brother, who had a grinding mill at home. I worked for almost ten years for my brother operating the grinding mill. But after ten years there were some problems between me and my brother: he was not paying me a proper wage. He said, 'I cannot pay you a proper wage, because I am looking after you.' But I said, 'How can you say you are looking after me when I am doing the work of any normal person?' You see, the attitude towards disabled people is like that.

So Ephraim left his brother's grinding mill and decided to start, with others, a branch of NCDPZ. It now has more than 100 members, scattered over an area about 50 square miles. With such a widely scattered population, the logistical problems of facilitating a group of disabled people are staggering. How do people move around, especially if they have mobility impairments? Ephraim explains:

We have a big problem getting people together. If you want to catch a bus, you have to walk at least ten or fifteen kilometres. If you can't walk, well, there are very few private vehicles, so it is extremely difficult to get lifts. It's a huge problem. We meet at the mission. They give us accommodation for the night. We pass word through schools and the Post Office agent. This works; we are able to meet, if people have enough warning.

What are the issues that face people in an area like Chirumanzu? In a rural area where people are not even able to grow enough food because of drought, the options seem limited: survival is what is at stake. **Simon Tevera** is 50, lost an arm in the war, and is a member of the Chirumanzu branch:

I have two cattle left now. I had eight before the drought. If these die, I don't know what I shall do. There is a government hand-out of maize every six months, but it is given to those who have participated in a food-for-work project, which usually means road building and maintenance. Disabled people cannot normally join in such schemes, so they get missed out at the food distribution.

So what is the meaning of 'disability politics' for Simon? What does being a member of NCDPZ mean? Simon is very forthright.

We do not speak about politics; we speak about survival.

But Ephraim explains that there is something that can be done 'politically' for people like Simon. He is pressing the NCDPZ office in

Simon Tavera, Chirumanzu District, disabled in the war before Independence:

Bulawayo to take up the case of food distribution at government level, and to ensure that disabled people are not missed out. He believes that this is exactly the kind of action the office should be taking.

There were some surprises in these interviews in Chirumanzu. Many of those interviewed were aged over 50 and had grown-up children. But none of them said that their children were helping them in their old age. **Michael Mhene**, for example, was forthright about large families:

> Let me tell you: it does not work, this idea of children looking after their parents. I have five sons and they do not even visit me, let alone look after me. I hope they do not make the mistake of having many children. Many children increase poverty.

Life in the rural areas of Zimbabwe is very grim indeed, especially when it does not rain for five years, especially when you get old, and especially when your children do not look after you.

The mechanics of social action for social change

An organisation like NCDPZ has an extremely difficult role. It was evident in these interviews that in such desperate circumstances the rural members of NCDPZ were looking to it for their survival. But the leadership of NCDPZ sees the organisation primarily as a pressure group, not as a service provider. This has led to much misunderstanding and not a little hostility on the part of disabled people, who say: 'We can't eat politics'. 'Politics' tends to be equated in rural areas with tribal rivalries and corrupt officials; the idea of a pressure group is not easy to understand for people who are not exposed in their normal lives to the mechanisms of power or the process of raising issues as matters of principle. They see NCDPZ receiving foreign funds, and wonder why these are not translated into practical help in the form of services.

What can NCDPZ offer to people like Simon Tevera by being a membership organisation? There is an obvious danger that the well-educated leaders of the organisation in Bulawayo develop a very different agenda from the rural members whom they claim to represent. But is that really the problem? An evaluation of the RMDP in 1988 pointed out that many rural members had, unsurprisingly, absolutely no experience of decision-making of any kind, and turned up at branch meetings in the hope that NCDPZ would be able to solve their problems. In other words, they did not have an agenda of their own, and were expecting the head office to provide one.[11]

So we are into the classic vicious circle of development: 'The active nature of under-development and poverty determines people's understanding of development, which in turn affects the kind of development work that can be done.'[12] In other words, to begin to break out of poverty and under-development requires awareness and understanding among those who are poor and under-developed, but it is precisely their poverty which prevents them from gaining awareness and understanding.

NCDPZ is faced with two very important issues here: the first is whether it can become engaged in real development work that will benefit people like Simon Tevera and Michael Mhene. The second is how to bridge the gap in awareness and understanding between the urban leadership and the rural membership. Jabulani Ncube was the director of NCDPZ for several years during the 1980s. He now works as a consultant for ADD (Action on Disability and Development). On the question of leadership he says:

> *There cannot be an NCDPZ without the existence of a coherent membership. If we are going to be talking about movements of disabled people, then we ought to define very clearly in our minds what it constitutes. A movement is not simply a few individuals at the top of an organisation conveniently calling themselves the leadership of a movement. I am not saying that that is precisely the situation, but this is a challenge for a number of organisations of disabled people that I know, not only in Southern Africa, but also in other countries where the creation of a true movement is threatened by such a situation.*

So the creation of a viable movement means a great deal of work with people in both the rural and urban membership programmes. It is not enough to tell people about their rights and expect them to be capable of securing them at once. If people are to become more independent and capable of fighting their own battles, time must be invested in training, orienting, and conscientising them about the issues and how to deal with them.[13] This requires considerable skill, patience, and tact in the development officers, who may often be tempted to deal with particular cases and individual matters themselves, rather than get the individual or local group to act. But every time the development worker does that, the person who should be learning is deprived of an opportunity to do so.

Then there is the question of 'projects'. It is significant that after eight years of experience in the RMDP with small-scale gardening, poultry, bakery, and sewing projects, disillusionment has set in. The number of people engaged in such projects has been small. Some of the projects have been over-ambitious, relying on outside inputs and advice. At the same time there is a clear recognition by the leaders of NCDPZ that without some material benefits, there will be no rural membership: indeed, people cannot eat politics. Sometimes the projects have failed because people do not have the mobility appliances to be able to function in them; the supply of essential appliances is a vital service at the base of any disability programme.

In urban areas the problems are different and on the whole have easier solutions. On the negative side it costs money to live in a town — to eat, to rent a house, and to move around. On the positive side the opportunities for income-generating activities are much greater. In 1991 NCDPZ opened a supermarket in Bulawayo which employs a dozen disabled people, and has a turnover of several thousand Zimbabwean dollars a month. It is a bold and ambitious project that has paid off and is a positive step towards making NCDPZ less dependent on foreign funding.

And what about relations with other players on the disability scene, like Jairos Jiri and the government rehabilitation programme? The abrasive militancy of the founders of NCDPZ, which certainly

The Freedom supermarket in Emakhandeni Township, the first big income-generating project to be set up and run by disabled people in Bulawayo.

did not win friends among many professionals, for example, has been replaced by a more constructive approach which sees the importance of close co-operation in order to build a unified service system in which disabled people have an important voice. For example, NCDPZ workers are involved in the training of government rehabilitation assistants (the equivalent of rural health workers). NCDPZ works closely with the government rehabilitation service for referrals and supply of appliances. With Jairos Jiri there is some co-operation: that Association has changed too, and is now more aware of the need to prepare people for life, rather than give them a permanent home; it has put itself on the line on several occasions to make this point, which has created painful confrontations with 'inmates'.

The problems faced by NCDPZ in the rural areas, the difficulties of building a cohesive movement, and the stresses and strains of trying to build an organisation not dependent on foreign funding are common to most (if not all) grassroots development groups struggling for social change in developing countries. These difficulties do not in any way obscure the successes of NCDPZ, which are considerable. At a general level it has succeeded in creating a new consciousness of disability issues in Zimbabwe. Access to buildings is far better now than ten years ago. Public transport makes some provision for disabled people. Integration in schools is a reality for many children. Pro-disability legislation is about to be passed. These are no mean achievements.

Let the last word here go to Jabulani Ncube:

The entire system of the world today needs to be questioned continuously, and possibilities for alternative strategies must be constantly explored. There are no easy answers; development has no recipe. What we require is commitment to action by people in the different nations and societies to develop themselves.[14]

CHAPTER 10

India: social action in a highly complex society

'One who always sees all living entities as spiritual sparks becomes a true knower of things.' (Sri Isopanisad)

Fact file

Population: About 850 million in 1991, increasing by 17 million (the number of people who live in Uganda) every year. The biggest state, Uttar Pradesh, has the same population as Egypt, Sudan, Ethiopia, and Somalia combined (134 million).

Languages: 15 official languages and more than a thousand other languages. The census of 1971 listed 1,652 languages spoken as mother tongues.

Religions: Hindu (82.64%), Muslim (11.35%), Christian (2.43%), Sikh (1.96%), Buddhist (0.71%), Jain (0.48%), others (0.42%)

Infant mortality rate: 97 per 1,000 live births (1988)

Life expectancy at birth: 58 years

Literacy: Men 64%, women 39% (1991)

Government: India is the largest democracy in the world, with a multi-party system and both federal and state legislative assemblies.

Background

Anyone approaching India from, say, Africa or the Middle East is in for a shock. Nothing compares with India, and nothing can prepare you for it: it is a universe of its own, with staggering numbers, distances, and diversity. The newspapers are littered daily with horrors never reported in the West. Even to attempt to write about India with any degree of clarity and cogency seems a hopeless task, especially for an outsider.

The difficulty in a book like this, which is trying to chart constructive pathways through the maze of social attitudes about disability, lies in identifying the agents of change in a highly charged, rigidly stratified, and extremely complex culture with many fault lines and zones of confrontation. India presents an immensely difficult problem in any discussion about development because, in approaching the subject of changing attitudes, it is impossible to disentangle culture from religion and politics. What constitutes 'local culture', and what is its part in creating change? To what extent is culture sacrosanct, especially when it is enshrined in religious dogma, and especially when that dogma seems to be the product of power games and domination by one section of society going back thousands of years? Aid agencies and development workers are often criticised for ignoring or undermining local culture in their desire to effect change; since these workers tend to be educated on Western models and their funders are usually from the West, this leads to the charge of cultural imperialism.[1] We have to confront the question of whether social action, including working for change in attitudes to disability, is just another form of cultural imperialism.

Gods, Gandhis, and film stars: the pantheon of modern India.

Culture, however defined, is not a static state, but the dynamic interaction of many forces, including interaction with other cultures. Western culture itself is undergoing constant change, in which the influence of Eastern philosophies cannot be ignored; it seems somewhat patronising to suggest that other cultures are immutable and should be preserved in some kind of time capsule. But in any case it is not as though social action is foreign to India: it was India that, under such moral giants as Gandhi, pioneered it as a strategy for change on a national level. India has set an example for social action on the grand scale which has remained an inspiration to millions throughout the world.

Not only is modern India the largest democracy in the world in terms of an elected government. Throughout the country there is also a vigorous culture of social action over a range of issues, from deforestation to bonded labour to atrocities by landlords. 'Social action centres round mobilisation of oppressed people through a sense of moral outrage against injustice and inequality, for survival and identity.'[2]

One of the main arguments of this book is that a change in attitudes to disability is not just for the benefit of disabled people themselves, but is an important indicator of a wider, deeper growth in consciousness among human beings which is part of valuing the planet and those who live on it. Injustice is not confined to any one culture, and nor is the moral outrage that tries to counter it: both occur everywhere. Although social action on disability is comparatively new in India, it follows logically in the pattern for action already established in other areas of the struggle for social justice in the country.

Despite the bewildering complexities of India and the huge risks inherent in any simplified analysis, some attempt must be made to set the context for the very important experiments in social action on disability that are taking place in the country.

Rich and poor

After Independence in 1947 the Indian government embarked on a series of five-year plans which were aimed primarily at tackling poverty. The country has made rapid strides in industrialisation: there is hardly a car on the roads which has not been assembled within the country. India has its own nuclear and space programmes. The Indian film industry is the largest in the world, in which moguls amass colossal fortunes, while rags to riches for stars and starlets is a proven possibility. In agriculture the green revolution of the 1960s and 1970s has made India more than self-sufficient in food: overall surpluses are available not only for its own regional shortages, but also for occasional relief to other countries. These successes have not, however, made a significant impact on the problem of poverty: out of the total population, half (that is at least 400 million, which is about a twelfth of the world's population) are living below the poverty line. Eighty per cent of the population lives in villages, where the poverty is most apparent. The technological successes in agriculture have simply widened the gap between rural rich and poor, since improved agricultural techniques frequently mean more mechanisation and less human labour. Those who have fertile or irrigated land have done well; the landless and those on marginal or dry land have been left behind. It is the yawning divide between rich and poor in the rural areas, or rather those who have land and power and those who do not, that has created the need and the context for social action in much of India.

Caste

Caste is essentially a Hindu characteristic; the whole Hindu world-view is based on circumstances of birth, not on belief as understood in the West. Hinduism is inseparable from community and family. There is no one set of scriptures revealed at a particular moment in history, but a whole shared experience going back thousands of years which is still evolving; it is a shared culture rather than a religion, with the family and social relationships at its heart.[3]

For traditional Hindus, caste is an integral part of their entire world view: status is acquired by birth, not achieved by effort, and cannot be changed, not even through education and taking on sophisticated jobs. The only real option to escape from this structure is to renounce Hinduism in favour of another belief system, as was done by a famous *harijan* ('untouchable') leader, Dr Ambdekar, who became a Buddhist in the 1920s, taking about three million other *harijans* with him. But even among non-Hindus in India the influence of caste can still be felt.

There are four main caste groups and many sub-groups. These derive originally from the broad separation of the populace, dating back four thousand years, into occupational roles: priests (*Brahmins*), warriors (*Shatrias*), merchants (*Vysias*), and servants (*Sudras*). Others, notably the tribals and people referred to historically as 'untouchables', are considered outside and beneath the caste system.

Gandhi insisted that the 'untouchables' should be referred to as *harijans*, or 'children of God', and the term 'untouchable' is no longer used. The term *harijan* itself has now been officially discarded in favour of 'Scheduled Castes'. This term derives from a government policy of positive discrimination in favour of these people in the job market, where they are allocated (or 'scheduled') a certain percentage of jobs in the government sector. (Confusingly the term 'Backward Classes' is the official designation of the lower castes, the *Sudras*.) But such positive discrimination has, many Indians would contend, served only to perpetuate and indeed solidify the caste system, because it means that people get jobs on the basis of caste rather than merit.[4] It is seen as a sop to keep the masses from grumbling too much.

The term *dalit* is used to include all oppressed people: the scheduled castes, landless labourers, bonded labourers, and tribals. It is not therefore congruent with *harijan*, although *harijans* are *dalits*. Since most *dalits* live in villages, it is a term most often heard in reference to issues in rural areas. But we are not speaking of a minority: over 50 per cent of the population of India is composed of *dalits* — *harijans* and tribals, people who are technically 'beneath' all the other castes. There are thus more people outside the caste system than within it.

Whereas cities provide some general anonymity and therefore a potential weakening of the caste system, village life is still dominated by it. 'Scheduled castes' live in clearly defined areas of the village, and most land is in the hands of higher-caste people. In extreme forms of the system, a high-caste Brahmin will not only avoid associating with the scheduled castes, but will regard everything they touch as unclean. Violence between castes in rural areas is commonplace, mainly atrocities by landowners against *dalits*.[5]

Caste encapsulates politics, religion, and culture in one overarching structure that poses a formidable obstacle to constructive change. As a *harijan* leader in Tamil Nadu put it, 'All men are born unequal, and women hardly count.' The greatest difficulty of all is that caste is more or less universally ingrained in the entire social and cultural fabric, including that of its victims. This has a devastating effect on the self-image of those at the bottom of the ladder. The perception of themselves as inferior beings is very common among *dalits*:

Ironically the victims have internalised the values about their status as born unequal. They have legitimised the mythical destiny imposed by their *karma* to live out the punishment for the guilt accumulated in their past lives. The resulting damage is so deadly to the whole of their personality that a profoundly wounded psyche is the prime characteristic of the *dalits*, whether they are highly educated or totally illiterate.[6]

A profoundly wounded psyche is not a characteristic only of *dalits*. A social and religious belief system which ranks human beings from 'pure' to 'impure' would appear to carry a built-in prejudice against disabled people, who are not perceived as 'whole'. In traditional Hindu belief, disability is a punishment for misdeeds in a former life. If a change in attitude and consciousness on disability has to start with self-esteem and a positive self-image on the part of the disabled person, the belief in *karma*, or destiny, that inflicts disability as an inevitable and deserved punishment for failures in past lives, is not a very encouraging starting point.

The wounded psyche is the result of centuries-old traditions, beliefs, sanctions and customs. The disabled person herself has to change; she has to claim within her family and environment the space for this change. These processes involve a Herculean task. True integration requires much energy and time.[7]

Father Cutinha, Director of the Divine Light Trust for the Blind at Whitefield, Bangalore, describes the situation of caste as it relates to disabled people in this way:

Disabled people form a sort of fifth caste, below the other four. But among disabled people themselves, disability does to some extent cut across caste boundaries, so that high-caste and low-caste disabled people may be happy to be in the same group. But where the economic cake is small, there it acts. For example in the rural areas it operates. And among higher castes, although they do not say this, their behaviour indicates that it does operate over marriage. A disabled woman, for example, stands very little chance of getting married in the higher castes. I have spoken to Brahmins, blind, who have been through this school, and I have said to them, 'I have a feeling that your parents did not accept you.' And they have broken down and said, 'Yes, that is so.' I am inclined to think caste does operate strongly with disability, especially among the higher castes.

Women

The position of women in India places them among the most oppressed in the world. This oppression begins with the Hindu texts, which contain numerous categorical statements emphasising women's inferior status. Thus Manu, a famous law-giver of c. 200 BC: 'In childhood a woman must be subject to her father, in youth to her husband, and, when her lord is dead, to her sons. A woman must never be independent.'[8]

Most women in India, especially in the rural areas, lead an existence of extreme subservience, with very little control over their own lives. The few (mainly urban) women who have succeeded and risen to prominence in a completely male-dominated society do not indicate a general improvement, at least not in the rural areas.[9]

A disabled woman therefore suffers a multiple handicap. Her chances of marriage are very slight, and she is most likely to be condemned to a twilight existence as a non-productive adjunct to the household of her birth. At best she may be the object of misplaced sympathy which regards her as helpless and unable to do anything for herself or for the family; or she may well be kept hidden in order not to damage the marriage prospects of siblings; alternatively she may be turned out to beg. It is small wonder that many disabled female babies do not survive.

The Association of the Physically Handicapped in Bangalore runs a training programme in its main centre for both disabled men and women. The problem of what happens to young disabled women when they leave is acute; usually they return to what amounts to the prison of their own families, with no prospect of marriage. That is why Hema, a founding member of the Association, has recently started encouraging women leavers to form their own separate independent living groups away from their families.

Parvathi, Vasanthi, and Hamsaveni are one such group, who live together in a house on the outskirts of Bangalore, earning their living through tailoring. **Hamsaveni**, aged 20, explains her motivation for taking this option:

If I was at home, my parents would be very protective and not give me any freedom. Being at home is a trap. In this group I can come and go as I like. We feel free in this group and we also feel secure. We earn our living by making school uniforms and making clothes to order. We have good relations with our neighbours; we do all our own shopping. We feel good about ourselves and our neighbours respect us.

Women waiting for the start of a disability sangham meeting, near Bathallapalli, Andhra Pradesh.

This is a triumphant story. Centres for Independent Living (CILs), which have become an important feature of the disability movement in the West, starting in California in the 1960s, are certainly an option for disabled people all over the world, especially in urban settings, and especially for women with little chance of marriage.

Women also act as carers for disabled children. As we will see in the case study of Jordan and the Occupied Territories, neglect of disabled children by their mothers is not usually a deliberate choice, but one forced on them by lack of services; as soon as services are available, they are seized upon. In India such services as exist are generally available only in the towns. Most women in rural areas have no access to services for their children; in the last part of this chapter we will see examples of where social action groups are trying to address this problem.

Social action on disability: the background

On the basis that 3 per cent of any population is disabled to a degree which needs specialised services, there are, at the very least, well over 25 million disabled people in India. It would be quite impossible here to survey the whole scene, and in any case comprehensive statistics do not exist: even the number of institutions is not known accurately.

The Indian government divides disabled people into four categories: blind, deaf, orthopaedically disabled, and mentally retarded. Both government and private institutions for all these categories exist in cities, but cater for a tiny fraction of the number who need services. The rural areas have very little provision for disabled people.

There is no single cross-disability movement in India which unites all disabled people. Blind people, deaf people, and those with orthopaedic impairments have their own single-disability national federations, but there is very little linkage between them. The logistical problems of organising a single cross-disability movement, with so many languages, such vast numbers, and distances so great, are formidable. With over 14,000 indigenous rural development NGOs working in India, the task of coordination and information-sharing about any aspect of development becomes daunting.

As it has done for the Scheduled Castes, the government has allocated a percentage of jobs within the government sector to disabled people: blind people, deaf people, and those with mobility impairments get one per cent each. But apart from the fact that these percentages are not properly applied or monitored, the same problem occurs as with the other job allocations: these measures are regarded as a sop by the higher castes to stop the moaning lower down the ladder; rather than abolish the hierarchy, such measures reinforce it. Father Cutinha again:

> Take job reservations for disabled people. The higher castes say, 'Yes, give them these things, no problem, but so far and no further', just as they do with the reservations for the lower castes. So there is a lack of seriousness in understanding the problems of disabled people, just as there is a lack of seriousness in understanding the problems of the dalits. It's the same thing.

These allocations are not enshrined in law, but have the status of general agreement. They do not constitute an inalienable right.

However, weighed against all the negative factors of caste, violence, and the oppression of women are the counterbalancing factors of a society which has a culture of democracy that would be the envy of most other developing countries. Government structures reach into the remotest villages, and many of the thousands of indigenous voluntary agencies working in rural development receive government funding. In the state of Tamil Nadu alone, there are over 1,500! There is an enormous interest in and prodigious work on social change in rural areas, based on a wide range of philosophies. We will see three contrasting examples in detail below.

Breaking the mould of charity

Although there is a vigorous and impressive debate and committed action on development issues in general in India, disability is still dominated by the charitable approach based on large, often privately funded, institutions for a limited number of people. The task of breaking this mould and treating disability as a social and political issue seems formidable. Father Cutinha has been Director of the Divine Light Trust for the Blind in Whitefield, Bangalore for over forty years. Able-bodied himself, with a keen perception of the structural causes of disability, he charts with great clarity how his own consciousness has evolved over the years from charity to the social model:

> At the beginning my only motivation was to help out. We opened as a school. I taught different things. I had no concept of development at that stage. The social-work concept at that time, which I was schooled in, was to play a key role in helping others, but the potential of these others was not fully recognised. Helping a person was the philosophy: taking them off the streets, providing food and clothing, giving them education, that kind of thing. I do not now deny that the help is required, but it is not the engine of development itself. This attitude did not begin to change until the early 1970s. So when I started, I was part of that social-work culture. But later on the socio-political analysis came through to me, not in relation to disability per se, but in relation to poverty generally.

The 1960s and 1970s saw the development of a strong Marxist trend among some development workers in the analysis of poverty in India. Father Cutinha was influenced by it, but had reservations:

> Although I agreed to a large extent with the kind of Marxist analysis of poverty, there was one major thing missing from it, and that was the cultural context. It is not just a question of rich or poor here: there are cultural and religious determinants such as caste. And apart from caste there are cultural patterns like early marriage, which causes disability because women are often not mature enough physically to give birth safely, a situation worsened of course by the absence of ante-natal and post-natal care.

But another problem of the Marxist analysis was that it simply
stopped at 'the deprived'. It did not consider the particular situation of
disabled people, who actually form a kind of fifth caste. So I said to the
Marxists, 'You are ignoring a tenth of India's population.' They
replied that they are simply part of 'the deprived'. But I said, 'No, they
have special needs, they are in a group by themselves. They are
marginalised among the marginalised.'

So the thought was: why not build up a movement who would claim
their rights as disabled people? We thought:' Nobody's going to help,
so we should stand up and fight ourselves.'

In the decision to work for the establishment of a disability
movement, Father Cutinha and his group were heavily influenced
by one major factor: the question of grant in aid for institutions. By
the end of the 1970s a number of institutions and schools for
disabled children had been founded. They decided to request the
same facilities and funding as those working with normal children.
It meant adding just one sentence to the legislation. But despite
intensive lobbying with legislators, they met with indifference:

We went to every leader of every party and explained to them the
position. We said, 'This is a common factor; disability has no party.'
We worked for six months like this. We must have approached nearly
200 politicians of different parties. It was just a matter of adding one
sentence to the code. We waited with great apprehension for the
crowning of our work. But when it came to the crucial moment, not a
single person in the legislative assembly raised the matter. It just was
not mentioned. No one, just no one mentioned it.

I had a good friend among the Communist Party members, a very
progressive man. He called me and asked, 'You are disappointed?' I
said, 'Of course, bitterly disappointed.' He said, 'Tell me: how many
votes can you give me?' I replied, 'Well, four or five perhaps.' He said,
'You must learn this lesson: unless disability becomes a movement on
its own, it will not survive as an issue. It must become part of the civil
rights movement.'

This was a turning point in Father Cutinha's own understanding of
political processes. In his opinion it is impossible even today to talk
in terms of political action by disabled people in the way that this
Communist friend meant it. There are a few exceptions, like the
National Federation of the Blind in Delhi, which takes political

action at the national level on behalf of blind people; but nobody else, says Father Cutinha, among Indian disabled people is prepared for political action. There are, according to him, two reasons: first, disabled people themselves are not yet ready for it. Second, institutions are still the dominant gathering point for disabled people, but those in these institutions, lulled by inertia, do not even question the assumptions of their own boards. The boards consist mainly of people, both able-bodied and disabled, who have made an emotional and charitable response to disability. A familiar response from the boards of institutions is: 'We are doing something. Need we do more? We don't want to rock the boat'. Father Cutinha comments:

By and large the boards that manage the services are no different from what they have always been. Nothing will change until aware disabled persons themselves come up and run their programmes. But this will take a long time, because when disabled people try to take over the services, the boards react by saying they are ungrateful. Even when disabled people get on to one of these boards, they tend to be those who are not yet sensitised or aware politically.

When I approached one of our board members here to take direct political action, he demurred. He said he didn't want to upset government officials, and said he would approach 'his contact' in the relevant department. It is always like that. You work with 'your contact in the department'. So we don't think in terms of demanding it as our right, but in terms of getting it because 'our boy' is in the department. And if you don't have a boy in the department, you don't get it. Generally this is how things work, and most boards function on that basis. They don't see the need for more principled work. A serious intellectual commitment is not there, either among disabled people or among able-bodied people.

From institution to response centre

Father Cutinha then quotes the first draft of the national policy on education published by Rajiv Gandhi in 1985, in which there was no mention of disability at all. But to his amazement, people working in disability were not only not aware of this, but they did not even know that a new national education policy had been published. They were not alert to the strategic importance of keeping an eye on such things. So he and his group sent telegrams asking why it had been left out; the result was that in the final draft in 1986 there was a mention of 'the handicapped'. Unless there is an awareness of the mainstream political issues as they affect disabled people, no meaningful change is likely.

There was a moment of truth for Father Cutinha himself when it dawned on him, 35 years after starting his school for blind children, that only about 5 per cent of blind children were recognised as having special needs through government provision in India:

I just could not believe it. After 40 years of independence all the efforts of the government and the NGOs were not able to reach more than 5 per cent. At this school we could take only about 8-10 new pupils each year. We were not even beginning to touch the problem.

This realisation was the final milestone on the road from charitable concern to strategic action, based on an awareness of the actual size of the problem and its structural causes: he turned the school into a resource centre for training teachers from ordinary schools in how to integrate blind pupils into their classes.

There could not be a more telling testimony to the importance of developing a strategic political consciousness: the result of the change from school to resource centre is that now, with the same budget and the same staff, they reach out to almost the whole of India.

We motivate ordinary teachers to start services, and they come here for training. So we have made our point and proved ourselves by de-institutionalising. We are infinitely more productive now.

Political consciousness is not an optional extra 'for those who feel that way': if the aim is integration and better services, then there must be a proper understanding of how existing structures marginalise disability and how inadequate the charitable, institution-based approach is. Unless these structural causes are understood, says Father Cutinha, 'We are still at the level of charity, but simply more sophisticated than before.'

So, in his view, the situation is that the field of disability in India is dominated by both able-bodied and disabled people motivated mainly by charity, and in their own understanding they are doing a reasonable job within that framework. Most disabled people and those who work with them have not reached the stage of consciousness where they really understand the political process. The question therefore is: how can disabled people and those who work with them become politically aware? Father Cutinha says:

It will happen. We have to build up a consciousness in a small group capable of interacting with a bigger group. They have to discover their own strength and potential before they can interact with the larger issues and a wider group.

As we saw in Chapter 3, the change in consciousness and approach has to begin with disabled people themselves. It is the building of self-awareness and political consciousness in small groups of disabled people in rural areas that forms the substance of the rest of this chapter.

Social action on disability in rural India

On the face of it, the task of trying to deliver services to disabled people in rural India is so daunting that it has not generally been attempted: it is hard enough, it is argued, to deliver services to non-disabled people, so disabled people are off the end of the scale. But the breakthrough comes when it is realised that the medical and institutional model of service provision itself is inappropriate. A model of self-help in which disabled people take responsibility for their own development is required. Furthermore it is not a question of creating extra projects or building new organisations to deal with disability: existing rural development organisations can include disability in their current programmes, especially if those programmes are based on the principle of animation for social action.

It is Action on Disability and Development (India), under the direction of B. Venkatesh (interviewed in Chapter 2), which has been pioneering the concept of integrating social action on disability into existing programmes. In 1988 ADD India persuaded three well-established rural development organisations of very different character, working in Andhra Pradesh and Tamil Nadu, to take on disability in their current programmes. The principle for each was the same: stimulate the formation of disability *sanghams* (associations) in each village which would assume responsibility for the needs of disabled people in that village. The members of these *sanghams* would be disabled people themselves.

The three organisations are: the **Young India Project** (YIP), the **Rural Development Trust** (RDT), both in Andhra Pradesh, and **PREPARE**, working in villages around Madras in Tamil Nadu. These three organisations provide contrasting styles and ideologies of rural development work. It is enough to summarise their approach without offering judgements on their particular philosophies. The important point is that, despite being so different, they all incorporate social action on disability into their existing programmes.

The Young India Project

The Young India Project is an amalgamation of 25 activist groups working in Andhra Pradesh, Karnataka, Tamil Nadu, and Orissa. With an ideology which is mainly Marxist but which also owes a good deal to Gandhi for inspiration on non-violence, it works with the rural poor, especially *dalits*, to form unions and to press for the implementation of government pro-poor policies through direct action and non-violent mass struggle. It is working to establish 'liberated zones' which are free of atrocities, free of land seizures, and free of police collusion with exploitative practices. It does not believe in and does not run 'development projects' in the way that RDT and PREPARE do: it is an example of a radical social-action organisation committed to struggling for the rights of oppressed people through unionisation and mass action. YIP started working with ADD (India) in 1988 and has now fostered the formation of 44 village disability groups (*sanghams*) with a total membership of about 1,421 in August 1991.[10]

The Rural Development Trust

The Rural Development Trust was set up in 1969 and is now an enormous organisation employing over 700 people. It began as a classic project-focused organisation, digging wells and providing help to very poor people, but has now evolved into both service provision and social action. It works in 300 villages in the area around Anantapur with an average population of 2,000 per village; it runs clinics, supplementary schools, and three hospitals. Its cadres of development workers are busy working on literacy, vocational training, community health, and ecological issues such as tree-planting and soil conservation; they also work to establish and animate social action groups of women and landless labourers. RDT's approach to development can perhaps be described as social mobilisation and compassion, in which the provision of services and social action are given equal importance in the total package of integrated rural development. It began social mobilisation of disabled people in 1989, and by the end of 1991 had fostered the establishment of disability groups in 44 villages.

PREPARE

PREPARE was set up in 1983 in response to annual cyclone disasters on the Tamil Nadu coast near Madras. From initially training people to survive, it then began working with tribal people in the area, and later started training villagers in community health. Within the community health programme, immunisation against polio and referral for cataract patients were important features which led to reflection on disability as an issue. The director, Dr Daisy Dhamaraj, says that at the beginning they regarded disability as an individual medical and welfare problem, where immunisation and referral for surgery was the limit of what they saw as necessary. But as their regular development work progressed, they had already begun social mobilisation around women's issues and the situation of tribal people and fishing communities. They were aware that work with disabled people could not remain at the individual welfare level, but were uncertain how to move matters forward. They looked in vain for models of community-based schemes in self-reliant strategies for disabled people. Then they discovered ADD India in 1988, and PREPARE embarked on the process of social action described below.

In each case the agreement between ADD India and the rural development organisations is that ADD India provides disability training to the organisations' cadres, carried out in the field and at appropriate institutions such as the Divine Light Trust for the Blind and the Association for the Physically Handicapped, Bangalore. ADD India staff also make regular field visits to give training in social analysis, communication skills, leadership skills, *sangham* management and administration, and help with planning and evaluation. ADD India has a staff of two field workers, besides Venkatesh, who undertake these tasks. One of them, Saraswadhi, works only with disabled women, in clear recognition that, within disability *sanghams*, domination by men is a problem.

'The sangham gives me energy and strength'

The rural development organisations provide cadres specifically designated to work on disability, funds raised from their own sources to cover the work, training in animation techniques, and background assistance to disabled people to obtain benefits from the government. The most important part of their work is to encourage the formation of village disability *sanghams*. In the case of YIP, these *sanghams* can then become part of regional unions. YIP also provides training for the disabled members of the agricultural labourers' union.

The aims of this approach are very clear: to mobilise disabled people to take action on their own behalf, and to use existing structures to secure services and benefits. It was a completely new approach to the disabled people involved; at the beginning they tended to misunderstand what was intended. The charity model prevailed in all minds. When Venkatesh first appeared in a village and gathered the disabled people together, their first reaction was typically, 'What are you offering? What can you give us?' His answer was: 'I am offering nothing. I as a blind person have worked on myself, have found my place in society and can make a contribution. You can too.' Venkatesh also insisted from the beginning that none of the three umbrella organisations should contribute financially to these *sanghams*: the *sanghams* should raise their own money for any expenses, such as bus fares, from their own resources. This was essential to break the expectation of reliance on external agencies.

The idea that disabled people should take charge of their own lives, including their own rehabilitation needs, was completely revolutionary — not only to the disabled people, but also the cadres assigned to work on disability. It takes a long time to train people who are already committed to and skilled in one model of direct intervention to stand back and simply act as a resource and facilitator. In the Young India Project, for example, the person assigned to disability in one area had previous experience as a social worker in another organisation, and saw his new role with disability *sanghams* as similar: he thought he was required to work on individual cases to ensure that they got the government benefits and services they needed. So he would accompany individual members of the *sangham* to hospital for operations or to local government offices for loan applications. For him it was stimulating and rewarding to work like this: he could see instant results, the disabled person in each case was very grateful, and he enjoyed a general acclaim in the community as an efficient, persevering, and caring worker. He had spent three years of his life as a wandering ascetic before becoming a social worker, and now felt he was building up spiritual credit for such 'good work' with disabled people. But the disabled people themselves were not gaining much in enhanced self-perception or psychological strength through that approach: it was simply delivery of services and a perpetuation of the individual charity model.

The field research for this book included many days sitting in villages in Andhra Pradesh and Tamil Nadu talking to disability *sanghams*. They ranged in size from half a dozen to 20 members; they included women, children, men, and parents, coping with a wide variety of disabilities. The pattern of replies to questions revealed a substantial change in self-perception and self-confidence. The wounded psyche of disabled people in India can be repaired.

In the village of Dampetla near Penukonda in Andhra Pradesh, the disability *sangham* has nine members with different impairments: blindness, polio, leprosy, hemiplegia, deafness. **Ramu** is a 35 year-old woman who contracted leprosy ten years ago; but the disease has stopped progressing as a result of treatment. She is the leader of the *sangham* and lives on her own with her daughter, aged 8; her husband has left her. She has no land and her 'house' is a palm-leaf hut, probably the poorest dwelling in the village. And yet she has a radiant smile, a strong sense of humour, and a spotless sari. A year ago she applied to the government for a loan to buy a pair of goats. Initially it was refused, but with pressure from the *sangham* and YIP it was eventually granted. Ramu explains:

By myself I did not have power to persuade the bank to give me a loan for the goats, but when the sangham came in behind me, they eventually agreed. The sangham gives me energy and strength. But it is not only because we can get loans through it: we are more confident in ourselves now. And because we are in a group, the other people in the village respect us more now. Before, we were just forgotten individuals. Now we are people who can do something.

This kind of testimony was repeated in almost every disability group discussion. The tradition of forming *sanghams* based on other issues is well established: there have been women's *sanghams*, *sanghams* of landless labourers, and others for many years, all founded for the same purpose: group solidarity and pressure for social justice in jobs, loans, and land allocation. The fact that disabled people have now formed their own *sanghams* places them on a similar footing to these others, and attitudes towards them are changing accordingly: they too are seen to be striving for social justice, like everyone else.

Being in such a group also enables disabled individuals to be heard, perhaps for the first time in their lives. Ramu had gained enough confidence through being in the *sangham* to express herself forcefully in an open meeting on the caste system: 'I am opposed to it and think it should be abolished. I would like to see an India without a caste system.'

As with other *sanghams*, it is the lower-caste disabled people who tend to join, because they obviously have reason to. In Dampetla the group reported that there was a blind Brahmin girl in the village, but her father didn't want her to join. They were sad about this and felt that, given a free choice, she would have joined.

The three young women in Bangalore quoted earlier formed their own independent living centre in order to escape the trap of their over-protective families. Over-protection is possibly the most disabling cultural behaviour pattern in these villages: cases of neglect are rare (although there is no way of assessing the number of disabled infants who are killed or allowed to die). For example, in the village of Mannur near Madras one interviewee was an 18 year-old girl with one arm, whose mother refused to let her do anything in the house, even though she was clearly capable; she had been pulled out of school early and was quietly vegetating at home — a sad waste of human potential. The explanation her mother gave was that she was afraid of what the neighbours would say if she were put to work: she feared they would accuse her of mistreating her daughter. This indeed was the usual explanation for over-protection. But the presence of a disability *sangham* in the village means that this kind of attitude and practice in families can be challenged.

The most common benefits applied for through the *sanghams* are loans, reduced-cost bus passes, pensions, and scholarships for school children. The availability of these benefits again places India in a rather different position from most poor countries in the South: it is remarkable that, in a nation of 850 million people, one disabled person in one village can apply for and get a loan from the government to buy a goat. But these benefits tend to be applied selectively, or to applicants who can 'pay'. Loans tend to be refused on the grounds that a disabled person is 'not a good risk'; the *sangham* can play a part there in showing that if the disabled person has sufficient support, he or she is just as good a risk as anybody else. And if a local official is seen to be guilty of corruption, the embarrassment of having a posse of disabled people camped on his doorstep is considerable, and likely to be an effective prod to a decent response. In Dampetla one member of the group is deaf and speaks in sign language, but he has made it his speciality to accompany other members on their forays into officialdom and see that the officials deliver. If they do not, the matter is discussed with the *sangham* and action taken.

A barber's shop in a village near Anantapur, set up with a loan obtained through the disability sangham.

These experiences of forming a group, lobbying officials, and taking action over their own affairs are themselves greatly empowering for disabled people in Indian villages. They report a new-found confidence in themselves and a new respect from their community. They vividly illustrate the philosophy espoused by Venkatesh and many others, which was discussed in Chapter 3: that a change in attitudes to disability must begin with disabled people breaking out of low self-esteem and forming positive self-images. The vicious circle can be broken, even where the weight of cultural behaviour and attitudes seems at the start to be insuperable.

ADD India has made a significant start on a revolutionary way of working with disabled people in rural India. The costs are extremely low: for ADD India itself, they amount to the salaries and travel expenses of the three field staff; for the rural development organisations the cost is almost negligible, since they use existing staff as animators of the disability groups. That such effective work can be done so cheaply has come as a startling revelation to, for example, the Rural Development Trust: **Anne Ferrer**, wife of the founder, says:

Social action is so cheap! For the price of one salary we have seen the formation of groups in 44 villages. Hundreds of disabled people are finding a new purpose in life, and community attitudes are changing.

Jordan and the Occupied Territories: community action with disabled children in refugee camps

'Equality is not created by hand-outs.'
(Yusuf Hiliqawi)

Fact file on the Occupied Territories

Population: 1.8 million
Religions: Muslim 90%, Christian 10%
Population growth rate: 3.5% per annum
Refugee population: West Bank 15%; Gaza 60%
Adult literacy: 87% for men, 62% for women
Life expectancy: 60 for men, 64 for women
Infant mortality: 45 deaths per 1,000 live births
Annual gross domestic product: West Bank £686 million; Gaza £243 million

Background

Disabled children, especially those with mental disabilities, form a special category in community and social action on disability. In the nature of things it must be their parents and other members of the community who take action on their behalf. This chapter examines the particular issues affecting children with disabilities, and the attempts by their families and the community at large to respond to them within a particular social and political context: that of Palestinian refugees in long-term camps.

In many ways the Palestinian refugee camp context is unique: the problem which gave rise to it certainly has few rivals for intractability. But it obviously has parallels with other refugee situations where people are living in temporary, high-density camps or ghetto-slums without being fully integrated into the host country. Refugee situations give rise to particular problems of development, in particular the problem of how far people can go in taking charge of their own development within a closely circumscribed political context. The reason for considering it in this book is to examine how, even in such very unpromising circumstances, there is the possibility of genuine community action on social issues, and in particular on behalf of disabled children. The implications of this kind of action are far-reaching, having an impact not just on attitudes to disabled people but on the whole psychology of oppression for those involved.

There are some 2.1 million Palestinian refugees living in Lebanon, Syria, Jordan, the West Bank, and the Gaza Strip; nearly 800,000 of them live in camps. Some of them, or their parents, became refugees in the first Arab-Israeli war of 1948; others arrived as refugees as a result of the war of 1967. The 'camps' are actually rural or urban slums consisting of densely-packed cement-block dwellings with corrugated tin or asbestos roofs. They have electricity, but sewage disposal is usually via open drains down the middle of the street. Most streets are not paved. There are 61 camps in the five 'fields',

Palestinian refugee camps have been in existence for more than 40 years. This girl belongs to the third generation born in a camp in Jordan.

with populations that range in size from a few thousand in the small camps to over 100,000 in the largest.

Two years after the Palestinian refugee crisis arose as a result of the 1948 war, a special United Nations agency was created to take care of them: the United Nations Relief and Works Agency for Palestinian Refugees (UNRWA) is mandated every year by the United Nations to provide for the health, education, and welfare needs of these refugees. Unlike any other UN agency, UNRWA has a fully operational role: it runs schools, clinics, hospitals, and other services, and is the largest employer in the Middle East, having a total staff of about 30,000 people and an annual budget of some US$250 million.

The attitude of each host country to these camps is that they are temporary, pending a 'solution' to the problem of Israel and Palestine. The camps have always been perceived by the host governments in each country as centres of actual or potential unrest as the refugees find themselves discriminated against in jobs, status, nationality, and opportunity. In consequence the camps are generally heavily controlled, either by the State security apparatus in Jordan and Syria, or by the Israeli military in the West Bank and Gaza Strip. Lebanon is a different case: the camps are on the whole under the control of Palestinians themselves, now watched over by Syria and a reborn Lebanese government, but Palestinians in Lebanon suffer worse discrimination than anywhere else in the region.

There are striking parallels between the overall Palestinian refugee context and the situation of disabled people all over the world. Development (in the sense used in this book) is the process by which people become empowered to take decisions and make choices which affect their lives. Throughout the book we have been examining how that process applies to disabled people, and have stressed that the process of empowerment must begin with a strong sense of positive identity and self-esteem in those who are oppressed. So the development process becomes a quest for how to break out of the vicious circle of oppression resulting in low self-esteem, resulting in victimisation, resulting in further weakness and further oppression. The starting point for change, as we have seen, is self-esteem in the person oppressed. This applies to Palestinian refugees just as much as it does to any other oppressed group, including disabled people.

The Palestinian refugee context also illustrates the problem of what roles should be played by the community on one hand and the State on the other. In this case, the State role is taken by UNRWA, which provides most of the services that one would normally expect from a government. UNRWA was set up primarily as a relief organisation and a provider of basic services. Some people who work in it see its role as limited to that function, but an increasing number point out that its title contains the word 'Works' as well as 'Relief', and that its mandate does imply a developmental role. This argument is conducted with particular intensity over disability and what role the agency should play in providing services for disabled people.

The issue of 'community' in the Palestinian camp situation also brings into sharp focus the question of who controls the development process in a highly charged political environment. Over the years three layers of service provision and development activity have emerged in these camps: first, there is UNRWA, which provides the basic neutral infrastructure for people to live, get educated, and stay reasonably healthy; second, the provision of services is a key part of the struggle for the hearts and minds of camp dwellers, and thus 'development' becomes a tool in the hands of Palestinian political factions vying for influence, territory, and credibility; third, there are efforts outside either of these first two to set up development activities by foreign NGOs and non-aligned local groups and individuals.

In the minds of most camp Palestinians there is a high degree of ambivalence about the role of UNRWA. On the one hand, the agency stands as a symbol of their refugee status, and they regard the services it provides as a minimal right in the face of the injustice of being made refugees in the first place. On the other hand, they readily agree that UNRWA, by concentrating on relief and not development, has, over the forty years of its existence, created a 'hand-out' mentality that has undermined the spirit of initiative and self-development, and done considerable damage to the collective self-esteem of the refugees. UNRWA itself, recognising this dilemma, has made efforts over the past ten years to play a more developmental role by encouraging income-generating projects aimed at individual self-sufficiency. Its approach to disability has also been conducted in the spirit of development rather than relief, as we will see below.

This scenario applies to each of the five fields in which UNRWA operates: Lebanon, Syria, Jordan, the West Bank, and the Gaza Strip. This chapter focuses only on Jordan, the West Bank, and Gaza, which have certain specific conditions of their own. In Jordan the camps are kept under very tight surveillance by the State security apparatus, and any community activity is closely watched. The formation of a local committee requires a list of names to be submitted to the Jordanian security department, which routinely rejects those it does not approve of. But there is a 'Catch 22' here: without a properly registered charitable society with its own officially approved board, it is illegal to raise or receive donations from any quarter, either local or foreign. This clearly acts as a severe restraint on properly organised community action.

In the West Bank and Gaza Strip a similar situation prevails, but the surveillance is of a different kind, because there is a clear dividing line between Palestinians and the Israeli military; in other words, Palestinians fall clearly on one side of a political divide, whereas in Jordan the line is not so clear: in Jordan Palestinians are part of the government as well as the governed, and so the form of control is more subtle than it is across the river.

The contrast in control systems was dramatically illustrated for me recently on visits to camps on both sides of the river: while visiting a community disability centre in Jabaliya Camp in the Gaza Strip, I witnessed a classic battle between Israeli soldiers with rifles and children with stones just outside the centre itself. An Israeli soldier was hit in the face by a stone, and a boy from the camp was hit in the head by a bullet; he later died. In Jordan a few days later on a visit to a similar centre, I was shadowed by a State security agent who I thought at first was a parent, and who insisted on sitting in on a local committee meeting.

Such control mechanisms, whether by brute military force or subtle infiltration, make these camps far from ideal places in which to embark on the process of community development, but there are strong counterbalancing factors. In particular there is a heightened sense of communal and national consciousness, and thus an enhanced willingness to work for the common good. The history of development in the West Bank and Gaza Strip reveals, since 1967, a process in which people, both in camps and in the community at large, have increasingly managed to shed the role of passive recipients of aid and take charge of their own activities. There has been a growing realisation that nothing can be gained by waiting for peace to arrive before beginning development, and that the peace process is more likely to succeed if there is some equality between the parties; but equality is not created by hand-outs. Consequently there was a phenomenal growth of home-grown development efforts during the 1980s, to promote such activities as pre-school education, agriculture, health care, and women's groups. The Intifada (Uprising) that erupted in late 1987 was a result of this new assertiveness and self-confidence, and also served to develop it. The parallels with the situation of disabled people everywhere are only too clear: breaking the vicious circle of oppression entails refusing to play the role of victim.

Disability in the West Bank and Gaza Strip

The situation for disabled people in the West Bank and Gaza Strip is an illustration of outdated concepts dominated by professionals and those involved in a major rehabilitation industry. There has for a long time been institutional care available for some (but by no means all) disabled people, however, these institutions have been strongly characterised by the 'charity' model, and the removal of disabled people from their own environments. Some of these institutions have tended to operate behind closed doors, with a reluctance by their staff even to co-operate with surveys or to allow access by researchers to their disabled 'inmates'.[1]

Although there have been a few attempts to introduce CBR (Community-Based Rehabilitation) in some form in some areas, the general attitude towards disability among people and groups working in development up to the mid-1980s was that it was not a priority, and that it was part of welfare rather than development. Developmental priorities were concerned with the establishment of basic services in primary health care, agricultural extension, women's activities, and early childhood education. Disabled people were generally either ignored or confined out of sight in institutions.

But with the advent of the Intifada in December 1987, there was a sudden explosion of interest in disability: it became politically important.[2] Confrontations between young people with stones and soldiers with rifles produced a dramatic increase in permanent impairments such as spinal-cord injuries, loss of eyes, and amputations. The injured were regarded as heroes and the whole 'industry' of rehabilitation received a dramatic boost. Millions of foreign dollars were poured into creating large and extremely well-equipped rehabilitation centres, but without thinking of needs beyond the medical, and without being able to construct an interconnected referral system of which these centres were a part. In addition the needs of other disabled people, not the 'Intifada-injured', who formed by far the largest proportion, were eclipsed.

This failure was caused partly by the fact that there is no

Palestinian government and therefore no central planning authority, and partly by a concept of rehabilitation and an approach to disability which is almost entirely medical. The political dimension, in so far as the 'Intifada-injured' were disabled in a political struggle, did nothing to alter this perception; in fact it enhanced it. The failure was as much the fault of foreign funders as anybody else's. The Swedish government, for example, provided millions of dollars for an extremely well-equipped rehabilitation centre in Ramallah, which at the time of writing has only ten beds filled. The same sum would have been enough to fund dozens of neighbourhood rehabilitation centres for years.

The testimony of many of those injured is that medical rehabilitation, despite its undoubted quality, has not addressed their real needs. The sense of heroism soon wears off after the initial visits by well-wishers to the hospital and after the injured person arrives home to find that he or she is an economic burden on an already hard-pressed household and, furthermore, is doomed to spend the rest of his or her life doing absolutely nothing.

For example, **Nihad Mansour**, who lives in Jabaliya refugee camp in the Gaza Strip, is now paralysed from the waist down after being shot in the back by an army patrol:

> I had treatment and rehabilitation in various places. I spent a while in the Abu Raya institution in Ramallah, which was nice and very well equipped, but when they had finished with me, they just sent me home. There was no attempt to provide me with training or to plan for my life as a paraplegic, or even to counsel me on what would be involved. Their approach was purely medical. What's the use of that? I knew people in the Abu Raya centre who made sure that their bedsores did not heal so that they would not be sent home.

The real needs of a paraplegic like Nihad begin when he gets home, not when he is receiving treatment.

The interest in disability created by the Intifada was not, after all, a change in attitude, but simply a perpetuation of the old attitudes, with more attention and more money. As we have already seen in Chapter 3, it is of no service to disabled people to regard them as heroes; they need to be treated like anybody else, rather than placed on a meaningless pedestal. At no point have disabled people themselves in the West Bank and Gaza Strip played a role in the process of designing services or planning strategies; the national committee on disability, formed in 1990, contains not a single disabled member, and none of the main institutions has any disabled members on its board.

The control over policy and resources for disability in the West Bank and Gaza Strip is firmly in the hands of professionals and those with a stake in the rehabilitation industry. There is an urgent need for disabled people to be included in the planning process, precisely to deal with the kinds of problems faced by Nihad and many others. At present there is an unseemly willingness to make political and financial capital out of the Intifada-injured without understanding or catering for their real needs, or involving them in planning as people with needs beyond the medical, and with experience that could be tapped.

Why has there been no mobilisation of disabled people in the West Bank and Gaza Strip? In a society where political consciousness is so highly developed, this lack is (on the face of it) surprising: it is particularly surprising because people injured in the Intifada, regarded as heroes, generally escape the stigma that usually attaches to disablement. There seem to be a number of reasons for this failure to mobilise.

First, most grassroots activity tends to be undertaken in the name of one Palestinian political faction or another, and it is not at all easy for spontaneous activity to avoid being patronised in this way. There *is* a genuine 'popular movement' but it is fragmented between at least five factions, four political and one religious.

Second, moving around in these territories is extremely difficult, even for non-disabled people: there are continual curfews and road blocks; going to Jerusalem, a central point, requires special permission, and being allowed to leave the Gaza Strip for anything other than casual labour inside Israel is rare. Hence building an organisation of any kind has very practical, logistical obstacles.

Third, because it is hard for people to travel, links with and knowledge of other models are slight. Hence thinking on disability in the West Bank and Gaza Strip, among both disabled people themselves and those relating to the issue, remains at present stuck in the format that relies on professional rehabilitation and charitable institutions.

Fourth, the formation of groups run by disabled people implies, in the minds of many disabled people, that there is a State authority from which such a group can make demands. Where that does not exist, there is much less incentive to form such groups. **Ibrahim Tilbani**, now in his forties, lives in Jabaliya camp in Gaza and was blinded as a child; he is the head of the local disability committee and has given thought to the question of forming a blind union; but, as he observes:

It comes down to the question of a government, or the absence of a government. If you have one, it can create laws and regulate society. In the absence of a law, nothing can happen. In Gaza there are workshops and things like that which employ blind people, and I could set up a union of blind people tomorrow, but my question is, 'What would it offer me?'

Another disability committee member, **Yusuf Hiliqawi**, agrees:

Consider: who shall we demand our rights from? What body will give disabled people their rights? There is no body here to award rights under the law.

However, as we will see in the case of Lebanon, the absence of a law-giving authority does not mean that disabled people cannot or should not mobilise; indeed rather the contrary, since disabled people can add a very important dimension to the whole discourse about civil and human rights. In Lebanon, despite the virtual absence of a government for fifteen years, disabled people have mobilised to considerable effect, especially against the war and the absence of rights for disabled people — which includes the absence of a government to give those rights. A peace march by disabled people in Jerusalem would be a very powerful expression of a desire for and commitment to peace and social justice.

In Jordan the overall situation in disability is similar, with a fairly high-tech rehabilitation industry attracting large funds, especially from wealthy individuals, and a focus on institutional care, especially for children. But there are important differences from conditions prevailing in the West Bank and Gaza Strip. In the first place there is a government which has made a commitment, through legislation, to creating opportunities for disabled people. Secondly, groups of disabled people have started to form in Jordan. However, we are concerned here not with Jordan as a whole, but with the refugee camps which form a separate community under different constraints; these constraints ironically make effective local mobilisation even more difficult than it is in the West Bank and Gaza Strip. Confrontations with the Israeli army in camp communities west of the river have a strong unifying effect and provide a powerful incentive to undertake community action in the teeth of such difficulties. But where the control is more subtle, there is less incentive.

However, it was in the Jordanian camps in the early 1980s that the seeds of a new approach to disability were sown which are now bearing fruit in Jordan, the West Bank, and Gaza Strip: the mobilisation of whole camp communities to deal with the issue of disabled children.

Community mobilisation and disabled children

In 1981 UNRWA decided, in the light of the International Year of Disabled Persons, to 'do something for disabled refugees'. It proposed the setting up of a low-cost community centre for disabled children in one smallish rural camp in Jordan, Suf, with a population at that time of 11,000. A house-to-house survey was conducted which revealed a population of about 150 disabled people in the camp, of all ages and disabilities. Of these, 40 children with mental disabilities were seen as needing specialised services. An old tin building was renovated by the local youth club, two women from the camp were given basic 'training' for a month at an institution in Amman, and the first Community Rehabilitation Centre (CRC) in these camps was born.

The central objective was to provide a basic service and to change attitudes to disabled people within the community. The concept was to keep costs low, to involve the community through a local committee and the use of volunteers, and to provide a non-professional day service for those who could benefit from it. As far as the usual rules of community development went, it broke the most basic: the initiative came from the outside (indeed very early meetings with camp elders produced the response, 'We don't have a problem with disability here'), and UNRWA provided the administrative support. Running costs came from a European funding agency (Oxfam/UK and Ireland). Understanding about disability issues was minimal at the beginning in all three parties: UNRWA, the European funder, and the local community. But despite these apparent drawbacks and the undeniably amateurish way in which the whole thing was approached at the beginning, it was the start of a learning process between these three parties which, ten years later, had prepared the ground to shape a policy on disability for the refugee population for which UNRWA is responsible.

The story that has unfolded since 1981 illustrates many valuable lessons in the development process, especially as it relates to disability. Because of its hidden nature and the stigma that it carries, disability has not been an issue around which these refugee communities (or any other communities for that matter) have naturally mobilised. The response of the elders in Suf, denying that disability was even a problem, is not unusual. So an outside initiative was justified: there needs to be a trigger for community mobilisation, and in this case it was provided by UNRWA.

Once the centre in Suf had been opened, attitudes did indeed change dramatically: the pessimists had said before its opening that people would not be prepared to bring their children to the centre, because they would not want it generally known that they had a disabled child, especially if the disability was mental. They told stories of mentally disabled children being kept chained to a bed in a dark room. But it turned out that such stories, if true, were not at all typical, and that parents for the most part were desperate for some help with their children — help which the centre was now able to provide. They flocked to the centre. Children appeared who had not been detected in the initial survey, testifying perhaps to the 'dark room syndrome' but also to the desire of their parents to remedy the situation.

Other camps took note. The foundation of the Suf centre sparked within a few years the establishment of four other centres in camps in Jordan, supported by different foreign NGOs and administered by UNRWA. Attitudes in UNRWA changed too. In 1989 UNRWA decided to establish the posts of Disability Programme Officers in all five fields; these DPOs would be responsible for instigating community action on disability in the refugee populations of their respective fields. This was a major shift in UNRWA: it was a clear indication that the agency was now taking disability seriously.

But there were important points of principle which had not been sorted out. The most crucial were:

- Who owns these centres: UNRWA or the community?
- What role could local committees play in running the centres?
- Should the centres rely entirely on volunteers? Should the volunteers be paid anything — and, if so, how much?
- How 'professional' should the services be? To what level should the volunteers be trained?
- What about provision for disabled people who did not attend the centres?
- What would happen to children once they had left the centres?

In Jordan there were real difficulties in forming local committees, for the reasons stated earlier: all names had to be approved by the security authorities, which cut out more or less everyone except the most conservative and ineffective. Early committees were soon disbanded. So the centres in Jordan have remained in a kind of limbo, with no real control by the community at all, under the UNRWA flag but not recognised as part of UNRWA's essential services.

Top-down control or bottom-up development?

Across the river in the West Bank and Gaza, however, there was the opportunity to approach the task differently, and also to break with the usual heavy emphasis on institutional care dominated by disability industry magnates. **Abdul Qadir Awad**, the DPO for the West Bank, perceived from the beginning that the key to constructive community action on disability lay in the formation of an effective local committee, and that his role was the establishment and support of these committees. He describes how he set about the task of forming local disability committees:

From the outside it is important to identify those who have some influence in the community. Then you have to look at what already exists in the camp or community in the way of associations and bodies which are doing things. It is important to assess how effective they are. Once you have assessed who the effective people are, you can enter the community through them. Through them I can get to know others. The most important thing is to choose people who have a good reputation in the community and who are effective.

What is his own role once the committee has been formed?

I don't want to put all the responsibility on the local committee, nor do I want to put it on myself. It must be shared and balanced. The local committee needs to be the main entr)e to the disabled people in that community for any organisation that wants to deal with them. They have to have the power to make decisions. That is very important. Most programmes in the Occupied Territories are run from the top down. We want this to be bottom up.

Secondly, they must have the freedom to shape the programme as they see fit. They know the needs of the community much better than I do. My role is advisory on the professional level. I can advise on technicalities. I can also help them with funding; that's very important. I am a facilitator in the programme, not an implementer.

My third very important role is to open them to other experiences, both in the Occupied Territories and beyond. This society is very closed. People do not know about what is going on elsewhere; they need to be told and shown.

By late 1992 there were eleven committees in West Bank camps and four in Gaza. **Ahmad Amaasi**, a member of the Fawwar camp disability committee, describes how they got started:

We formed a local committee and started to work on the issue of disability. The first thing we did was undertake a survey. The total number of people in the camp is about 4,000. We used volunteers from the camp to do the survey. We divided them and the camp up into groups. We went house to house, every house. We found 366 cases of different disabilities of all ages. Our definition was as wide as possible: we included, for example, asthma cases.

We arranged for those with mobility problems to see specialists in hospitals and get aids and appliances and physiotherapy. We tried to arrange for hearing aids for deaf children, but they are very expensive. We realised that there was a small number of children, about 15, who would benefit from the opening of a centre. These were mainly children with cerebral palsy, and mental disabilities.

We first thought of building or renovating a building, but could not get any funding for it, so that idea had to be cancelled. But the youth centre was not being used, so we decided to use that, at least temporarily. There was no glass in the windows, the place was a mess, so there was a lot of work to be done.

Well, we started by collecting money from people locally, from the zakat [religious tithing system], for example; we bought some furniture and some toys. We opened the centre at the beginning of this academic year, in September. It is equipped with basic furniture and also a small kitchen where we can make sandwiches for the children.

All this has been done in Fawwar without any external funding. In Jabaliya camp in Gaza there was a similar process. A committee was formed, and UNRWA made available an old, derelict building once used as a supplementary feeding centre. The committee began to collect individual donations from the camp community: a receipt book recording local donations revealed a remarkable story of interest and enthusiasm: 'Hassan Shqeir — one bag of cement; Ibrahim Bseiso — ten shekels;[3] Fatima Murad — fifteen shekels;

A volunteer from Jabalia refugee camp in the Gaza Strip prepares a door for the community disability centre.

Muhammed Musa — 20 cement blocks; Ahmad Nasrallah — five sheets of corrugated iron' ... and so on.

Within a few months of the committee's formation, the derelict building had been transformed into a smart centre with three classrooms, freshly plastered and painted. As in Fawwar, the committee had already done a survey of Jabaliya, a very much larger camp containing about 60,000 people. **Tammam Ashqar** is the only woman member of the Jabaliya disability committee:

> *The survey came up with 1,800 people with disabilities in the camp out of a population of 60,000. Of these, 70 were deaf children. Then we thought, which group of disabled children is not served in the Strip at all? We realised it was the deaf: there is no institution for the deaf in Gaza. This is the most difficult group to deal with here, because there is nobody with experience in teaching them. But so far we have made good progress, and many of the children have started to acquire some speech. We are pleased with what we have done.*

> *To start with, we accepted 24 in two classes, and we are now planning to open a third class with a further 12. Eventually we hope to absorb all the deaf in the camp.*

Voluntarism versus professionalism

So far, so good. But the question of expertise immediately comes to the fore. All these centres have started with volunteers who have had minimal training, or none at all, in any form of special education. Such an 'amateur' approach has received fierce criticism from people running 'professional' institutions, who argue that if teaching non-disabled children requires trained teachers, how much more important is it to have well-trained specialists working with disabled children? Can untrained volunteers do any more than just keep the children occupied? If boredom sets in because the teachers do not know what to do, the whole concept of a rehabilitation centre is undermined.

This is an extremely important question which has enormous implications for any community action on disability. Working with mentally disabled children in particular requires higher than average levels of creativity, imagination, and understanding of child development. The experience of the centres so far, since the one in Suf first opened in 1983, has been that raw volunteers from the camp, with no previous experience or training, can reach more than satisfactory levels of expertise through their own experience, reinforced by regular training inputs by specialists. In the Jordan programme several in-service training experiences have been arranged over the years which have, to varying degrees, transformed perceptions and expertise.

In the early days of the Suf centre, mentally disabled children were sat in rows in desks in front of a blackboard, while the teacher struggled to work through a curriculum that was taken straight from a primary school: that was the only kind of 'teaching' which the volunteers themselves had ever experienced. But gradually, with input from specialists and especially those who opened windows on to discovery learning and tapping inner sources of creativity, the volunteers have acquired skills which make many of them now the equal of (or superior to) trained teachers in better-equipped and better-funded private institutions.

But this increasing expertise in the volunteers has raised another fundamental issue. Many of them can now legitimately claim to have impressive skills, and they feel that they should be duly rewarded. Are the centres not exploiting them by using them as volunteers for either no pay or very low honoraria? Is this not another case where disability and indeed women — since nearly all the staff are women — are being given a raw deal yet again.

This matter has a bearing not only on the quality of work being done in the centres, but also on their sustainability: it is one thing to collect donations from a refugee community, where unemployment usually runs as high as 40 per cent, for bags of cement and roofing materials and small cash contributions to renovate an old building. It is quite another to expect the same community to support a system where the staff are being paid proper salaries. Should foreign agencies pick up the tab, or, in the case of these centres, UNRWA itself? It brings us back to the role of the State versus the role of the community, the role of the State in this case being taken by UNRWA. Somehow a balance has to be struck between service provision by UNRWA which does not involve the community and which therefore perpetuates the 'hand-out' mentality, and a truly vigorous local initiative whose survival is precarious.

There is also the question of where disability fits into the planning and thinking of governments or government surrogates like UNRWA. It may be legitimate to ask why disability should be relegated to low-key, unofficial community initiatives relying on low-paid volunteers when the regular school system, for example, is properly funded with paid and trained teachers.

On the other hand, there has been a marked change in consciousness within UNRWA, generated by the establishment of these centres among other factors, which was noted by many of those interviewed, for example **As'ad Daud**, a blind person from Ain el Hilweh camp in Lebanon:

It's extraordinary what has happened inside UNRWA over the past few years in terms of disability. Now you can sit with UNRWA people and talk about it, and they understand. Five years ago they would not even have been prepared to listen to you. There is a new climate; people are interested and knowledgeable.

This new awareness has created a willingness among the educationists, for example, to discuss integration, a willingness that was not present ten years ago. Integration into normal schools for those who can be integrated is now an increasing reality for numbers of disabled children in these camps.

But it is not a question of whether UNRWA should take sole responsibility for these centres; it is not *either* UNRWA *or* the community: there can be real partnership between the two. It is possible, certainly in the situation we are dealing with here, to have vigorous local initiative with long-term sustainability and high standards. Clearly community participation and 'ownership' of such services is an immensely valuable prize, not just because there is a greater sense of empowerment for the people concerned, but also because the service is more likely to be effective, human, and appropriate. It would be an entirely retrograde step to operate these centres on the same basis as the schools, in which there is no community participation and little attempt to cater for the needs of the individual child. But at the same time, UNRWA has an outright obligation to see that disabled children have the same chances as any others, and it can fulfil this responsibility by ensuring the financial sustainability of local initiatives, just as governments do in other countries, including Lebanon. A government subsidy does not mean government control.

Beyond the centres

There remains the challenge of those who do not attend the centres, and the question of what happens to the children when they leave the centres. There are also other fundamental problems, in particular the lack of both women and disabled people on the local committees in numbers that could be considered significant.

The danger of opening a centre is that the efforts of the local committee become focused on it to the exclusion of other responsibilities. We have seen that in Jabaliya camp, for example, the centre is at present dealing with only 24 children out of a total population of 1,800 disabled people. There are many other things to be done: home visits, provision of appliances, modifying houses to make them accessible, raising awareness, improving health and transport services, integration into mainstream education. The committee is responsible for these and anything else relating to disabled people and their needs. The establishment of a centre was not the first thing which the committee in Fawwar thought of or undertook. Ahmad Amaasi explains:

Besides the centre we also have a programme for helping slow learners in normal school. Forty students in the regular school are being given supplementary lessons, a very important activity. This programme runs after school. We focus mainly on Arabic and arithmetic. But the teachers doing this have received no payment either.

In activities outside the centre we have installed toilets in the regular school which can be used by people in wheelchairs. We are also working with families who do not send their children to the centre. We arrange transport for disabled people who need to go to hospital, for x-rays, for example. So there are three programmes at present: in homes, at the school, and in the centre.

These activities too have been supported by contributions from the camp population. **Abdul Qadir**, Disability Programme Officer in the West Bank, illustrates:

The Fawwar committee sent me a note saying how much the community had contributed: 500 shekels as a contribution towards running the centre, 500 for food, 850 shekels for furnishing the centre, 700 shekels for training and for transporting the trainees. That all adds up to 3,400 shekels [£618] from the local community.

Jenin the same: they rented a place for 700 dinars [£700] a year; 17 dinars for transporting a disabled person from his home to the institution for computer studies where he is studying; 80 dinars for x-rays; cassettes for 20 dinars; 23 dinars for stationery.

These little things all add up to an effective approach which builds trust among people in the community. The local committee opens doors into the rest of the community. For example, in Jenin there is a merchant who donates 50 dinars every month to the committee.

Another gives 70 dinars per month towards aids and equipment. People realise that the local committee is much more in touch with the needs of disabled people than anybody in Jerusalem, and they can see to them properly.

The aim of the committee is to reach the biggest number of disabled people possible. They do that partly through the centre, but also through other activities.

The issue of what happens to children after they have left the centres remains the single biggest unsolved question. There is an absolute need for vocational training and possibly for sheltered workshops for those who cannot live independently. But no real steps have been taken in this direction, perhaps because the whole enterprise seems too big for the rather low-key and low-cost approach that has been the main characteristic so far, and also because there is a very high unemployment rate anyway. But it cannot be left unaddressed.

Lessons from the Palestinian experience

Some development workers consider that community mobilisation and participation 'is only possible when the community has reached a certain threshold in economic, social and educational awareness'.[4] This seems a very curious approach to community development and, if accepted, it presumably rules out a large number of communities in developing countries from even starting on their own development, because it assumes that some have passed the threshold and some have not; and in any case, who is to decide when a community has reached that threshold?

The story of community action for and with disabled children in the Palestinian context gives the lie to such an idea. The local initiatives in disability described in this chapter are a clear demonstration that, even in the most difficult economic and political circumstances, community mobilisation and full participation are possible. Indeed, the story of these efforts illustrates that the process of acquiring social awareness occurs when people themselves take positive action for change *despite* all the obstacles, without waiting for the economic or political situation to improve. It is yet another example of change having to start with the oppressed.

CHAPTER 12

Lebanon: rebuilding civic consciousness

*'Is this all? Just rehabilitation exercises, and eating and sleep?
Isn't there anything else?'*

(Hassan Bsat)

Fact file

(Note: these figures are even more approximate than most statistics: there has been no national census in Lebanon since 1947.)

Population: 3.3 million
Religions: Christian and Muslim in approximately equal proportions. The exact balance is subject to debate. There are also sects within the major religions (for example, Sunni, Shi'ite, and Druze Muslims) which are an important aspect of the confessional mosaic of Lebanon.
Languages: Arabic; English and French are also widely spoken, and Armenian among the Armenian population (5% of the whole).
Population growth rate: 1.1% per annum
Refugee population: 300,000 Palestinian refugees. There were probably at least one million internally displaced people at the height of the war.
Urban population: 80%
Life expectancy: 65 for men, 70 for women
Infant mortality: 50 deaths per 1,000 live births
Annual gross national product: £1,273 million
Annual GNP per capita: £378.00

Sister Sonia is a nun who has worked all her life with mentally impaired children. Until February 1991 her life was the special school which she ran in the mountains above Beirut in an old monastery on the edge of the village of Qal'a. It overlooks a deep, wooded valley reaching down to the Mediterranean 3,000 feet below, a magical — and strategic — spot.

Then the shells came, from three directions, for 48 hours without stopping, without giving the children a chance to get out. Every room was destroyed. Gaping holes were smashed in the cut stone walls; the roof fell in; the beautiful building with its arches and vaulting which had watched over the valley for more than three hundred years was reduced to a ruin. Miraculously no one was killed. By an extraordinary piece of luck, Sister Sonia found a secret passageway under the kitchen floor, an opening to a flight of steps which had been tiled over and hidden by a chest; the steps led down into a small chamber below ground level, where everybody in the building, staff and children, huddled as the explosions thudded and roared above them and the foundations shook.

On a recent visit Sister Sonia showed me the secret passageway, and upstairs the shattered rooms where the children had slept, now deep in debris from collapsed walls and roof; the occasional sodden blanket and decapitated dolly peeped from under the rubble, the only signs that this had once been a place alive with children's laughter.

Within two months of being bombed out of this magnificent building, Sister Sonia had set up the school in another building in a nearby village.

Background

Lebanon has paid the price for being, once, the freest state in the Middle East. Here was the heart of intellectual liberalism in the Arab world, where the press was free, books were published without censorship, and the universities produced creative and seminal thinkers. But it was — and is — also the cockpit where the different ideologies and power interests of the Middle East and the world at large clash. Add to this gross inequalities in the social, economic, and political life of the country, and the scene was set, in the early 1970s, for the wrecking of what was once a unique and beautiful country, often then referred to as the 'Switzerland of the Middle East'.

Outsiders now perceive Lebanon as a place of unrestrained and incomprehensible violence, of war which has long since lost sight of its original aims and which defies analysis. But that sensationalised and over-simplified image is far from being the whole story. There is also a story of individual and collective courage that struggles against the chaos to create and maintain an alternative based on co-operation and civic consciousness.

In the mid-1970s Lebanon had a population of about three million. Since the beginning of the war in 1975, 144,240 people have been killed, 197,506 injured, and 17,415 listed as missing, presumed dead.[1] Hundreds of thousands have been displaced. The number of people disabled by the war has never been counted. The Lebanese pound exchanged at four to the US dollar at the start of the war in 1975. The exchange rate in September 1992 was about 2,000 to the dollar.

The war is officially over, the militias mostly disarmed. The Taif Agreement of 1991 which ended it gives Muslims one more seat in a cabinet balanced precariously across the sects. The 'global' war, representing the clash of Middle Eastern and world power interests fought out by proxy in Lebanon, is perhaps over for the time being, with the end of the Cold War, the neutralising of Iraq, and the re-drawing of the political map of the Middle East. But in south Lebanon the Arab-Israeli war rumbles on, as intractable as ever.

Sister Sonia in the ruins of her centre for disabled children. Fifteen years of civil war have come to an end. Now the task of building the peace is immense.

Fifteen years of civil war have left scars which will take decades to heal. A whole generation of children has grown up knowing nothing but war, with their education severely disrupted or largely absent. The fracture lines in Lebanese society remain, and it will take a long time before trust and confidence across these lines are regenerated. For fifteen years there was virtually no central government authority, and scant respect for the rule of law. The political process has been largely discredited. The task of building a democratic, civil society from this base seems, to say the least, daunting.

Disabled people have already started, however, to make a significant contribution towards rebuilding civic consciousness. The disability movement in Lebanon, the most vigorous in the Middle East, makes its claim to be part of a constructive and positive culture, creating a consciousness that is against violence, against the sectarian divide, and for the development of human potential.

Disability in Lebanon

In war situations in particular, disability is perceived as a medical problem. Funding for medical rehabilitation, which does not address the long-term or social needs of disabled people, is the easiest to obtain. The war disabled thousands of people in Lebanon and also created the general sense that 'we must do something about disability'. But this sense, instead of leading to a cool appraisal and an accurate assessment of the overall picture based on a real understanding of the needs of disabled people, resulted in the funding of expensive medical rehabilitation centres within the sectarian framework. **Nawaf Kabbara**, paralysed in a car accident in 1980 and now president of the Friends of the Handicapped in Tripoli, observes:

> *This emphasis only on medical rehabilitation is exactly the opposite of what is needed. That's why this sense of 'We must do something for disability' is very dangerous. Instead of using what could actually be positive in terms of reaction and good will, it is turning out to be our prison. 'Rehabilitation' has become an industry based on the medical model which has not addressed the real situation of disabled people at all in terms of their rights and long-term needs. It has only served to reinforce the trap that we are in.*

There is also the question of how disabled people are perceived in Lebanese society as a result of the war: has the increase in the number of disabled people created a new awareness and better understanding? **Muhammed Halabi**, a member of the Lebanese Sitting

Handicapped Association in Sidon, sums up attitudes as follows:

There are three ways in which people relate to disability and disabled people: some people are aware, but very few of them; these are usually people who have some personal experience, but not all those who have personal experience are aware. There are other people who regard you with pity, who say, 'God cure you' when they see you; these people do not allow you to contribute or to give of yourself. There is a third sort who simply ignore you; they just do not take any interest in you at all, they are embarrassed, they treat you as though you are not even part of society. These are the majority.

Personally I have the following experience. Education? I got educated. Employment? I got employed. With a great deal of effort a disabled person can achieve these things. There is just one thing that I have not been able to do, and that is to get married. This is the clearest indication that disability is not acceptable in this society. People accept you as a teacher or a pupil, or as an employee; but, as a brother-in-law or a sister-in-law, that's something else. That's where I am. It's a very important point.

Muhammed Halabi, a teacher of computing. 'People accept you as a teacher or a pupil, but not as a brother–in–law.'

Attitudes to disabled people, in other words, are pretty much the same now as they were before the war. As should by now be abundantly clear, just providing medical rehabilitation services does not amount to a positive attitude towards disabled people. One of the central themes of this book is that disabled people have to take the initiative in changing attitudes, starting with themselves, because if they don't do it, no one else will. In Lebanon this task has taken on a particular dimension because of the war and the circumstances that created it, and the stupendous task of trying to build a society that will not easily revert to the grinding attrition of the last fifteen years. This requires, in a word, the building of a civil society, which means a society which functions by the rule of law, by principle rather than private interest, by a civic consciousness which has a vision of the common good, and by tolerance of ideological and religious differences.

What has this got to do with disability? Simply this, that the disability movement in Lebanon is committed to addressing these problems both within itself and within the country as a whole. These are problems that affect everyone, not just disabled people. But a solution will not be found until the problems have been defined and a commitment made to building a culture that opposes their causes. The situation of disabled people and the disability movement provides a visible and tangible model that can illuminate the problems and act as a laboratory for doing things differently.

For example, many people working now for these aims in Lebanon, especially in the disability movement, point to the problem of individualism as one of the main obstacles to the creation of a civil society: things get done and jobs secured through personal contacts and favours, rather than through a system based on rights or objective principles. This feature, known as *wasta* in the Middle East, is present in all societies to some degree; but, where it is the norm rather than the exception, it makes the raising of serious issues and matters of principle highly problematic or downright impossible.

Nada Azzaz, a blind person living independently on her own on a tenth-floor flat in Tripoli and an active member of Friends of the Handicapped, explains the problem like this:

> *The State is absent in Lebanon. Everything the State should do is done by individual initiative. A few disabled people have got jobs with the government, but they have got them as favours because of personal*

contacts, *and they are not necessarily secure in these jobs; they have them on sufferance, as it were.*

The problem is exacerbated, as far as jobs are concerned, by Lebanese law, which, as Nada points out:

... explicitly discriminates against disabled people: the law states that no one can be employed by the government who is not physically fit and 'free from deformities and defects'.

Despite this law, it has been a tradition for some time in Lebanon that blind people can work as telephone operators in banks and government departments. But, as **Mu'nis Abdel Wahhab**, another blind person from Tripoli, points out:

This is done on the basis of pity, not rights. These people have no job security, they are not properly integrated into the employment system; they can be dismissed at any time and have no pension rights, for example.

For **As'ad Daud**, also blind, from the Ain el Hilweh Palestinian refugee camp near Sidon, jobs by right are the key to a change in consciousness throughout the whole of society:

I was just crossing the road now on the way to this interview and a girl tried to give me money instead of helping me to cross the road. She thought I was a beggar. How should I react to that? Lecturing this girl is not going to make any difference. What will make a difference is when blind people can have jobs like everyone else. Even if I lectured this girl for three hours and then she goes out and sees a disabled person begging in the street, what is the point of the lecture? But if she saw me working, she would understand.

You cannot give disabled people their rights by giving them money. Money does not give anybody their rights. I cannot solve the problems of a disabled person by giving him 3 million dollars. That amount of money does not defend him. What defends him is his job, his work. If he has a job, he is living proof that he is a human being like everyone else.

But we disabled people have to change, in the sense that in whatever field — shaving, crossing the road, going from place to place — one has to depend on oneself to the greatest extent possible. This society has to respond to the new century and show that it can treat disabled people as full human beings, and disabled people also have to respond to the changes and work hard to get jobs.

So building the peace means building a civil society where issues are placed above personal interests. But unless there is a commitment by the government to giving legal rights to disabled people, there is little hope of creating major changes in perceptions and attitudes throughout society. At present discrimination is enshrined in the law, with apparently no accessible mechanism for correcting it: the politicians have other priorities, and disability does not swing votes. What to do?

Across the world the movement towards civil and social rights has to focus on specifics if it is to be heard. It is no use declaiming slogans and banging on a drum. Action for change on social and civil issues needs to be both strategic and tactical, with the insight to spot the points on which to stage a confrontation, and also a flair for creating events that grip the public imagination. Unless the public imagination is gripped, nothing will happen. It can be exciting stuff. The disability movement in Lebanon is not short of examples.

The disability movement

Throughout the war there has always been a commitment to holding on to essential human values, a kind of dogged rearguard action by those who have refused to bow to the madness of the political gangsters and the militias. This has been particularly true among disabled people, many of them victims of the violence. The overall aims of the disability movement in Lebanon have been focused on two levels: at the level of disability itself there is the problem of *ad hoc* and inappropriate rehabilitation services — as just one example of a very poor understanding of disability issues in the population generally; at the level of Lebanon there is the problem of how to create a climate where a civic maturity can develop. The two are closely linked. If disabled people had rights under the law, this would indicate both a better general understanding of disability as an issue, and would also imply a civic consciousness on which sound policy could be built.

The history of the movement starts from 1981. **Hassan Bsat** from Sidon became paralysed in 1979 not as a result of the war, but through a diving accident. His experience of rehabilitation was like so many others: it stopped at the medical response, and after that there was nothing. He stayed in the rehabilitation centre for three years of treatment and rehabilitation:

> *It was also a time of coming to terms with my disability — a very difficult period, I cannot say it was not. Every day I lived in the hope*

that tomorrow I would walk. There was some progress in my ability to cope during that time. I learned how to get undressed, wash, go to the bathroom, and so on all on my own. But that is as far as it went. After that, the way seemed to be blocked. I asked myself, is this all? Just rehabilitation exercises, and eating and sleep? Isn't there anything else? I decided I had to get a job.

He managed to get himself trained as an architectural draughtsman, but had great difficulty finding a job afterwards. In 1981, the International Year of Disabled Persons, he joined with others to start various activities with and for disabled people.

We eventually set up the Lebanese Sitting Handicapped Association at the end of 1981. I was a member of the founding committee. There were six people at the start on this committee, plus sixteen people in Sidon who were members.

Then came the Israeli invasion of Lebanon in the summer of 1982. Two months before, he had finally found work in an architect's office in Beirut, but the invasion put an end to that: it was impossible to reach Beirut from Sidon. So he set up his own home-based business with a machine making plastic signs for hospitals, offices, and other business premises. He began to earn a living from this, and also to work on the activities of the Association.

The Lebanese Sitting Handicapped Association

So was born the first organisation run by disabled people in Lebanon. The Lebanese Sitting Handicapped Association (LSHA) now has about 300 members in Beirut, the Beqa'a Valley, and the south. The main trigger for its formation was the enormous increase in the number of disabled people as a result of the war, and the absence of any rehabilitation services which went beyond the medical. Hassan again:

At that time in 1981 there was no one to speak in the name of disabled people. There was no one who could give advice about integration and the mechanics of it. No one came round the hospitals to give advice to people newly disabled. If there was any attempt at that, it was very individual and random. We saw the need to do something on a general and organised level which would have official recognition.

LSHA started as a response to the needs of people who suddenly found themselves disabled. It also attracted people who had been disabled since childhood and who had become interested in the issue of rights. They perceived that work with individual disabled people was never going to address the heart of the problem if fundamental rights remained out of sight and ignored. But they also realised that the chances of securing fundamental rights in Lebanon with a civil war going on and the country divided up among militia fiefdoms was very remote. **Sylvana Laqis**, disabled by polio as a child, is deputy director of LSHA:

The main reason for our existence today is to lobby. But the war has meant that this part of the programme has been asleep, because the government has not been there to ask our rights from. We have asked many things from the State, in particular to establish a special department in the government for disabled people. On this point we worked with other disabled associations, for example Friends of the Handicapped. But the situation was not ready for that. We are hoping to start now that the war is over.

So lobbying is our main aim. But we have found that if we want to strengthen the view of disabled people towards themselves, we have to have some services. We must be realistic. Not everyone who is disabled understands the need for lobbying.

So they have branches in different parts of Lebanon: the south, the Beqa'a, and Beirut. They visit disabled people at home with a team including a physiotherapist. Those who were injured in the war have a particularly hard time adapting to their new situation.

Sometimes we try to contact them as soon as they have been injured before they have left the hospital, and sometimes they refuse to see us then, because they do not want to believe that they are going to be like us. Most people take at least a year to come to terms with, for example, paralysis.

The families of those disabled are profoundly affected too, and Sylvana says that their work is probably more with the families than with the injured people themselves. The families have widely differing attitudes towards the disabled person in their midst:

There was one family whose son, aged 12, was disabled by a shell blast, and his parents put him in a dark room where visitors could not come. They did everything according to their own understanding. We worked with that family for two years before they were convinced of the need to let him go to a special school. On the other hand there are families who take very good care, and who go to great lengths to get their children to a special school, even though it may be a long way away.

Another example was a young man who had been paralysed and who had been in bed for 15 years at the time we visited him. Fifteen years! Can you imagine? After a year we managed to get him out to a summer camp, and sometimes we take him on home visits to see other disabled people. Now he is much better. He is beginning to study electronics.

All the members of the Lebanese Sitting Handicapped Association are disabled; it has no paid staff and operates entirely with volunteers. This is both a strength and a weakness: it means that everyone is on an equal basis and there is a strong spirit of co-operation and communal endeavour. It also keeps costs low. But against these huge advantages must be set the inevitable inefficiency of an entirely volunteer system, where no one is under the obligations of a contract. **Muhammed Halabi**, a member of LSHA quoted above, has a degree in computer studies and runs a computing course for disabled people. In his view:

The wheelchair workshop run by the Lebanese Sitting Handicapped Association.

Among the volunteers there is a problem of understanding between
those of different educational backgrounds; it is hard to reach a
consensus, and you cannot give orders. Working with volunteers is
difficult; it is not as efficient as working with paid people whom you
can depend on. But paying people would be an enormous problem.

Following the initial impetus of LSHA there are now four
organisations working on the social and political aspects of
disability in Lebanon: LSHA, the Youth Association of the Blind, the
Friends of the Handicapped and the National Association for the
Rights of Disabled Persons (NARD).

The Youth Association for the Blind

One of the leading lights behind the formation of the Youth
Association for the Blind was **Amer Mukaram**, already quoted in
Chapter 6. His life experience illuminates many of the issues
discussed in the first half of this book: the effects of being brought
up in an institution; the problems faced by a blind person trying to
succeed in a sighted learning environment (the American University
of Beirut — AUB); the question of integration versus separation for
disabled people; and the need to lobby the government to legislate
for fundamental rights.

Amer spent his childhood at a school for blind children with only
rare visits home, and was kept almost completely cut off from any
meaningful contact with the world beyond the confines of this
institution until he went to university. At university he wanted to
study Maths, but found that it was almost impossible to record the
material at that level either in Braille or on tape, and the lecturers
made no concessions for him. He had to abandon Maths and change
to Arabic literature and philosophy.

To begin with, other students were not very helpful, and the first
person to show him round the campus was another blind student.
He found this very disappointing, feeling that if blind people
formed themselves into a clique within the student body, they
would be even more cut off from the sighted world, as they had
been at his school. He was convinced from the start that integration
would not be achieved by forming a separate movement of people
like himself, and so for the whole of his time at AUB he avoided
associating with other disabled people. His thought constantly was
how to reach out from the isolated 'world of the blind', as he had
experienced it through his childhood, to the real world beyond, with

its newspapers, books, cinemas, debates, politics, and relationships:

People say that there is a world of the blind, as though we inhabit a separate world from 'normal' people. But we must dispel this idea. We must have access to the same culture, magazines, etc. There must be a way of doing this.

In 1987, at the end of his student years, he heard about a camp for disabled people and decided to see what went on. He was appalled that all disabilities were lumped together 'in the name of integration'.

The people who ran this camp talked about integration, meaning integration of all disabled people with each other. But where on earth did they get this idea from? Who says that there should be a separate world called 'the world of the disabled'? We are supposed to integrate with society, not with other disabled people only.

After the experience of this camp, he and another blind person decided to run a summer camp for blind and sighted people together. It was at this camp that the idea of the Youth Association of the Blind took root, in 1988. Amer continues:

Let's look at the history of disability politics in Lebanon. Up till 1988 there were welfare associations for the blind which ran blind schools. But there was nobody saying that blind people should be integrated into society. A blind person spends all his or her formative years in one of these schools and then must leave; but they are totally unprepared to go out into society. There is no association which concerns itself with what happens to a blind person after they have left the school. And nor is society prepared to receive them. Society has not been involved in the blind person's development up to that point, and does not see it as its duty to do anything.

That kind of institution creates enormous problems. A specialist blind school is the root cause of the problems. Blind pupils should go to ordinary schools.

It was the need to introduce blind and sighted people to each other which was and remains the main impetus behind the Youth Association of the Blind.

We reject the idea of forming an organisation only for blind people. We must enlist sighted volunteers in our organisation and develop friendships between blind and sighted people so that they understand each other.

YAB is also now working to lobby the government to legislate for integration of blind people in mainstream education: 'The State has the responsibility to create the circumstances through which that can happen.'

Amer is adamant that a separate organisation of blind people is not the way forward if integration is to be achieved:

> You hear much these days about the need for disabled people to form
> their own organisations to demand their rights. We reject this idea.
> That simply reinforces the idea that there is a dividing line between the
> two worlds of able-bodied and disabled people. But if we form
> associations which are mixed between able-bodied and disabled people,
> this is giving a clear signal that we need to work together on this.

YAB works through such activities as summer camps, a talking magazine, and the involvement of sighted volunteers to widen its circle of contacts and reach more blind people in Lebanon. It also recognises that transport is a huge problem for blind people and it wants to start a project to do something about it. Amer concludes:

> There is no State in the world that has the right to say to a person,
> 'You have no right to enter that building to get educated.' So why
> should the State say that to disabled people? The law must make it
> possible for disabled people to enjoy all the rights that other people
> have. It is society that should insist on this: the government works
> with their money: they should insist on spending it on these rights.
> Only the means are different for disabled people.

The Friends of the Handicapped

This perspective, and also the concept of disabled people and able-bodied people working together, are shared by the Friends of the Handicapped, an organisation which was founded in Beirut in 1978, originally concerned with the issue of mentally disabled children. One of the founders was Dr Musa Sharafeddin, who has two children with multiple disabilities, physical and mental. But it has now evolved into an organisation working for the rights of all disabled people. It owes much of its inspiration since the mid-1980s to **Nawaf Kabbara**.

Nawaf, quoted in Chapter 3, was paralysed in a car accident in 1980 in his early twenties. Already active in student politics before his accident, he went to England to complete his post-graduate studies in 1981, and during the four years that he was there was exposed to ideas on disability as a social and political issue. In 1984 he returned to Lebanon and started to work with the Lebanese Sitting Handicapped Association. He was then invited to join up with the Friends of the Handicapped to form a branch in the north of the country, working on disability generally. This marked the beginning of a remarkable series of initiatives and projects by Friends of the Handicapped, working with LSHA and other organisations: in 1985 there was the first demonstration by disabled people against the war in Beirut; in October 1987 the Peace March from Tripoli to Tyre, described very briefly in the opening chapter of this book, which attracted international attention; in 1988 the formation of the National Association for the Rights of Disabled People and, with that organisation, the launch of its Arabic magazine *Asda' al Mu'awwaqeen* (*Echoes of Disabled People*); in 1988 too a major week-long festival in Tripoli run by Friends of the Handicapped.

Friends of the Handicapped (FoH) is an organisation of both able-bodied and disabled people which works on several fronts. Its main aim is to create the climate for integration through lobbying, social action, and raising awareness both locally and nationally. Like LSHA and YAB, it sees the importance of providing services to disabled people, both for their own sake and in order to create awareness among disabled people. It too relies heavily on volunteers, mainly young people, both disabled and non disabled, who can drive cars, transport disabled children to school and adults to places of work, read to blind people, help children with their lessons, see to the supply and repair of aids and appliances, do home visits, and run group activities. FoH has a core of paid staff, most of whom are disabled.

Seventy per cent of the organisation's funds come from a variety of foreign donor organisations, the rest from local and government contributions. This funding has enabled them to run an efficient service-delivery system, but the fact that such a large proportion comes from foreign donors creates anxiety about sustainability: they are fully aware of the precarious nature of foreign funding relationships, and are now laying the basis for self-sufficiency through a number of income-generating projects. The most visible is a town taxi operation, The White Taxis, which when started in 1990 was the only telephone-request taxi fleet in Tripoli. (It has since attracted competition from the normal commercial sector.) They have also started a machine-knitting project employing nine disabled people making jumpers. Their most ambitious project is a proposed shopping complex on land donated by the municipality, the shops to be run by disabled and non-disabled people. It is planned to include a library, a citizens' advice bureau, a hostel for independent living, and sports facilities.

The story of FoH so far has been one of growing confidence and discovery about the reality of social and practical action. They have gained experience about what works and what does not through trying bold and imaginative ideas, some of which have been successful and some not. Among the successes it is worth looking in detail at one particular example of direct social action, less eye-catching than the Peace March, but perhaps just as significant in its way. It involved intensive social action over a sustained period to bring reform to the only institution dealing with disabled people in Tripoli, the Abu Samra Centre.

This place was a kind of total institution where old people, people with both mental and physical disabilities, and those whom their families would no longer look after were incarcerated. Conditions were by all accounts horrendous: there was no heating, no hot water, very little privacy, most of the 'inmates' slept in a vast dormitory, and there was no respect from the staff. When the war broke out in 1975 and international money became available for 'rehabilitation', the management set up a physiotherapy unit. But, according to one former 'inmate', **Nasir Halabi**,

> ... *they didn't change their attitudes. They kept all the physiotherapy equipment in a cupboard, locked away. The director said to someone who asked why: 'We don't have anyone here who is worth using it on.'*

> *Look, I am a person. I exist. I have my rights. I have as much right to the institution's resources as anyone else. In that place you only got treated if you had some kind of influence with the director.*

From 1975 to 1986 Abu Samra was the only rehabilitation institution in north Lebanon. Then in 1986 Friends of the Handicapped arrived on the scene. They thought at first that they could make use of Abu Samra and refer some of their people there for physiotherapy. This led them to understand the conditions in the centre and they tried to create improvements through pressure on the board, but to no avail. After the Peace March in 1987 and the Tripoli Festival in 1988 (both run by disabled people), FoH in Tripoli felt more confident and more determined to do something about the conditions in Abu

Nasir Halabi, former 'inmate' of the Abu Samra Institution, at home with his daughter. 'Look, I am a person. I exist. I have my rights.'

Samra. Some of its 'inmates' joined FoH and worked for them 'on the inside'. Nasir Halabi was one of them:

> *The director didn't like this and tried to get rid of what he called the trouble-makers. He started by cutting off the water and then said we had to be in bed by 7 pm. It was very insulting to treat us like that.*

This crisis provoked a confrontation with FoH. They gave the director an ultimatum:

> *Either we sort this out through negotiation or through direct confrontation. If it comes to confrontation, society will be your judge.*

Negotiation did not work; the director did not listen. He threw the 'trouble-makers' like Nasir out of the institution. FoH immediately contacted other groups in the town, women's groups, youth groups, and people in key positions, and told them what had happened. Nawaf Kabbara takes up the story:

> *We used a number of tactics. One was to get a friend who was a journalist to go in with a video camera, not for real, but just to scarethe director and show that this was a serious business. The same with another journalist who did an interview with him. All this was to put pressure on him. He got more and more anxious.*

At the end of the fasting month of Ramadhan there is a special festival where traditionally people give presents. FoH picked this day as an appropriate moment for their next move. Members of FoH turned up at six in the morning to take people from the institution to the mosque for prayer, but were denied entry by the director. They again alerted groups and individuals in the town to what had happened, then they announced their intention of visiting Abu Samra in the afternoon to spend a few hours with the 'inmates'. The director panicked and asked the Syrian forces to intervene. But the president of the board got wind of what was happening, and, to avoid embarrassment, sent someone to open the door and let them in for the afternoon visit. Nawaf remembers:

> *But the whole thing created a huge furore in the city and raised a campaign against the director. This created a lot of pressure on him, and he eventually resigned.*

> *These were the tactics we used. The important thing was that it showed that people in the city, and in particular the disabled people, were not prepared to tolerate that kind of institution any more. That's why it was a turning point as far as disability was concerned.*

Nawaf Kabbara in his office at Friends of the Handicapped.

What happened in Abu Samra? First they changed the director and the president of the board. Then they partitioned the large dormitories, removed all the petty regulations, and improved the food. Next they recruited professional social workers to work with them. Today Abu Samra is still an institution, but it is no longer inhuman. This story shows some impressive skills in social action. There are two key points: first, FoH had a sense of timing, of how to provoke a confrontation and of when to go for the show-down. Second, strong alliances with other groups and key individuals in the community provided the crucial pressure to force the director out; having able-bodied members and volunteers undoubtedly made these alliances easier, since FoH were not perceived as an exclusive group consisting only of disabled people, but as an open organisation of people with a commitment to bringing about change.

This example created a positive reform in one institution and also demonstrated that disabled people and their friends could change things if they went about it in the right way. Other examples of social action initiated by FoH have shown a similar sense of visible theatre and timing, and of picking the ground that people beyond the disability movement can relate and respond to. The Peace March in 1987 was the most notable.

The Peace March had three aims: first, to show an overwhelming will for peace and unity; second, to create a network of civilians all over the country that could organise and lead further civil protest activities; third, to end the marginalisation of the disabled community and ensure its place in the new civil Lebanon.

The march took months to prepare, and had to overcome a great deal of scepticism in Lebanon itself. The critics accused the organisers of, among other things, 'using disability for political purposes', as though disabled people are somehow outside and immune from the political process. Contacts were developed with organisations outside Lebanon, and arrangements made to film the whole thing. It was routed to pass through the main crossing points between the fracture zones on Lebanon's mosaic map. Fifty-six people in wheelchairs started from Tripoli in the north, joined by more than a hundred walking disabled and able-bodied people who acted as pushers and co-marchers. Those who took part were from all confessions in Lebanon. At each militia checkpoint there was a point of tension as hardened militiamen wondered how to react. In the major towns, rallies with music and dancing were held. By the time they reached Tyre in the south, the publicity they got en route, both nationally and internationally, ensured a huge crowd and an impressive welcome from the local dignitaries and politicians.

The march was a leap of courage, faith, and imagination at a very dark moment; there were not many signs of hope at that time in Lebanon. It did not stop the war, which went on for another three years, nor did it spark a groundswell of civil protest as intended. But it restored faith both inside and outside the country that people were prepared to put themselves on the line for deep and basic principles, in a country were many had lost hope of sanity ever returning. And, perhaps almost by the way, it put disability as an issue firmly on the map in Lebanon.

It was important to keep the momentum going. In 1988 FoH drew up a list of principles, in addition to the original aims of the march, which it felt the march had demonstrated and which needed to be kept in view with further planned events:

- to reactivate civil defiance to the state of violence and military control over the country;
- to encourage young people in particular to express their concerns through non-violent civil action as a platform for new ideas, commitment, and potential;
- to encourage different interest groups to work together for the common interest of peace and a civil society;
- to show that disabled people could play a significant role in creating the will and climate for a non-violent civil society.

With these goals in mind, almost a year later in August 1988 FoH launched a Festival of Peace in Tripoli. The somewhat unlikely venue of a disused railway station set in a large open space, long since taken over by nature, was turned, for a week, into a sort of medieval market *fest* where stalls were set up by glass blowers, potters, sweetmeat makers, and traders in various other handicrafts. The emphasis was on Lebanese culture and the need to treasure it when everything seemed to be falling apart. A cafe was set up with water pipes and traditional coffee-making. Story telling is an old tradition in Lebanon; a story teller (*hakawati*) was on hand to recount the exploits of heroic figures like Antar, Leila, and Abu Zeid al-Hilali. Plays and music were performed, and in one corner was an ancient *sandouq al ferjeh*, the Middle Eastern equivalent of a kind of magic lantern, where a story is told by a story teller who rolls illustrations across a drum set on a special stand.

More than 6,000 people attended the Festival of Peace. For the first time in Tripoli in five years there was something which drew people out of their homes after dark; in the transformed environment of an old railway station, a sense of life and of the heritage of this ancient land had returned. Not an insignificant contribution to the rebuilding of a civil society.

The National Association for the Rights of Disabled People
The fourth organisation of disabled people in Lebanon is NARD, the National Association for the Rights of Disabled People. This was founded in 1988 by four people active in FoH and LHSA, to coordinate and focus efforts on lobbying and advocacy among the other organisations. It also intended originally to establish a research centre on disability in Lebanon and the Arab world generally. Its main achievement to date has been the production of a high-quality quarterlymagazine, *Asda' al Mu'awwaqeen* (*Echoes of Disabled People*), which is distributed throughout the Middle East.

In the light of the arguments in Chapter 6 over the role of the State and the role of private voluntary action, Lebanon represents a society where the collapse of the State has indeed been replaced by private initiative, but the balance has swung too far in that direction. Without a legal framework and recognition of rights which provide a baseline for mutual understanding and discussion, it is not possible to raise issues as matters of principle. The creation of a civil society can only succeed if the general intent towards the common good is enshrined in a civil code; it cannot be left entirely to individual good will and initiative.

The disability movement in Lebanon provides a microcosm of this perhaps obvious fact. The main thrust of the movement now is to get disability legislation on to the statute books. But now that the war is over, disability ranks low in the priorities of politicians. The only way the movement is going to succeed is to continue to raise awareness among the general public by imaginative and creative events like those described, coupled with systematic and dogged efforts in approaches to politicians.

The way of social action in Lebanon is already impressive: it has not ghettoised disability, but has enabled disabled and able-bodied people to work together on a common project, the most important project of all, which is the re-establishment of mutual trust and cohesion after seventeen years of war.

PART FOUR

Conclusions

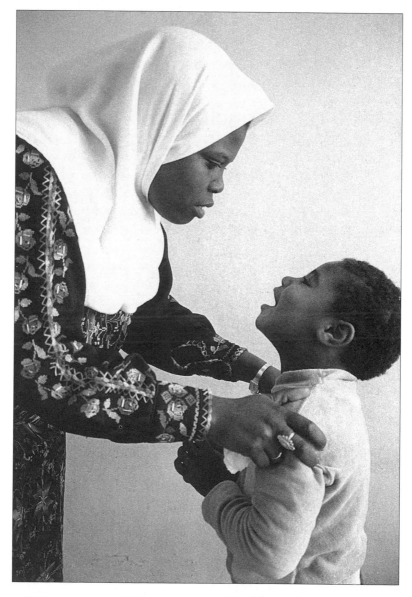

In'am, coordinator of the Jarash community disability centre, Jordan, works with Murad, an autistic child.

CHAPTER 13

Disability and liberation

'The problem is not how to wipe out all differences,
but how to unite with all differences intact.'
(Rabindranath Tagore)

For me the process of researching and writing this book has been one of the most significant experiences of my life. I feel I have travelled a long way into the realms of human development and have emerged with a whole new awareness of the resources of the human spirit. I have tried to be an objective, committed witness, intensely interested in the outcome but with no pre-conceptions, no axe to grind. As the Tao Te Ching says, 'The truth waits for eyes unclouded by longing'.

Whether I have succeeded is another matter. Did I really start with no pre-conceptions, no axe to grind? The most illuminating part of the process has been the discovery of my own prejudices. Even someone starting out with full sympathy and the intent to champion the cause of disability finds himself falling into the very traps that create the problem in the first place.

Levels of awareness

My own awareness has moved through three phases, three concentric circles of understanding.[1] The first and outer circle is the understanding that the 'problem' of disability is created by an able-bodied and disabling world that refuses to accept disabled people on their own terms. Prejudice and discrimination are the result.

The next circle is the understanding that change has to start with disabled people. That was the main message transmitted by nearly all the disabled people interviewed and is the central message of this book, suggested in the first half and illustrated by the case studies in the second. It neither negates nor eclipses the first circle of understanding, but rests on it.

The third circle has to do with the question of integration versus segregation, and the dynamics within the disability movement. This is the most difficult area in which to reach an understanding, because it touches very specifically on the question of power and control. Who controls? What is the relationship between the disability movement and the rest of the world? Cannot prejudice operate in both directions? The question of how power is handled once it is acquired is as important for the disability movement as for any other liberation movement.

There are other issues which, if you have stayed with the arguments and examples so far, you will be aware are not fully resolved. Is the social model of disability really sufficient to deal with the whole thing? Is it realistic, for example, to imagine the day when the birth of a disabled child will be greeted with the same joy as that of a non-disabled child? If you were told tomorrow that you had multiple sclerosis, what would your reaction be? It is prejudice that disables, but if prejudice is at base driven by fear, how do you get rid of fear, the fear of what might happen to you? Is this not a very individual matter, this fear? Is it not, when it comes to the crunch, a matter between you and your soul, and not between you and society? Pain and impairment exist, and that is not the fault of society but the condition of a particular body. It has to do with 'the unbearable heaviness of being', to adapt Milan Kundera's phrase. This perhaps is the fourth circle of awareness and understanding, not fully accessible to someone who is not disabled; each disabled individual will make his or her own response at this level, and it is here that individual personality plays the largest part.

There are parallels with other liberation movements, especially the women's movement, but disability is undoubtedly different in some respects. In the final analysis, what is the relationship between disability, liberation, and development?

Then there is the question of 'specialness'. I have said that disabled people do not want to be regarded as special, and yet at various points in the book I am saying they have something special to offer, something which non-disabled people do not have. I have said they are not heroes or heroines — but clearly some of those quoted are exceptional people.

We have to hold all these things in tension. There is no neat resolution. In this final chapter I do not want to attempt a resolution, so much as draw things together into the different circles of understanding.

Basic needs and the quest for meaning

In the opening chapter I said that disability provides a way in to a deeper set of values. We need to return to that idea. Consider the matter of basic needs. Basic needs are lacks which need to be supplied, like food, shelter, and health. But there is a fundamental problem in seeing 'development' primarily as a process of meeting needs in this way. The problem lies in the fact that such needs are passive: if these needs are met, so this approach asserts, then 'development' has happened.[2]

But there are other needs which are just as basic: the need to be creative, to make choices, to exercise judgement, to love others, to have friendships, to contribute something of oneself to the world, to have social function and purpose. These are active needs; if they are not met, the result is the impoverishment of the human spirit, because without them life itself has no meaning. The most basic need of all is the need for meaning.

It is true that none of these active needs can be met unless life itself is not at risk of being extinguished by starvation; the quest for meaning requires, at minimum, knowing that there is a tomorrow. But to focus only on the bare maintenance of life as the object of development is to miss out completely on most of what human endeavour aspires to.

The quest for meaning is both a deeply spiritual and a profoundly political matter. The active needs listed above go unmet, are not even on the horizon, when people are no longer in control of their own lives in any meaningful sense, when the political, social, and economic forces that affect them are out of their reach and toss them about like chaff in the wind. The unequal distribution of resources, the growing gap between haves and have-nots, the insecurity of employment at many levels, corruption and incompetence in high places, major political decisions made only on economic grounds and out of narrow self-interest — these injustices wipe out the sense of meaning in poor people's lives and reduce life to a bare and grinding business of grim survival.

Our fulfilment as individuals is largely dependent on our relationships with those around us. Lola, a sighted friend, reads to Yahya, a blind student, in Tripoli, Lebanon.

It comes down ultimately to a question of rights and justice, but also of relationships. In theory rights and justice are reflected in laws; but the most enlightened laws are worthless unless in practice they are reflected in the way we relate to each other. Human life finds its meaning in relating. Our fulfilment as individuals is largely dependent on our relationships with those around us, set within an overall context which officially acknowledges our rights.

All this goes without saying. But it applies to everybody. We cannot use such arguments for some and not for others. We cannot say that such arguments do not apply to a portion of the population that is categorised as disabled. The liberation of disabled people is ultimately a question of justice and rights enshrined in law, made real by the empowering relationships that come from a genuine understanding by the rest of us.

An enquiry into disability and the social and political forces surrounding it brings us face to face with the purpose of survival, the way justice does or does not happen, and the central question of human relationships. The areas of life marked 'spiritual', 'developmental', and 'political' are concepts that amount, ultim-ately, to different facets of the same thing, which is the quest for meaning.

Identity, suffering, and 'privacy'

I think much of the apparent confusion and contradictions about disability issues can be resolved through the realisation that disability provides, for the disabled person, a certain experience or set of experiences that are not shared by other people. These experiences do set disabled people apart, but they also bind them, as it were, closer to life itself and its purpose. This needs some explanation.

Suffering brings insights. In my own life, a week spent in captivity in Lebanon is not something I would wish on anybody else, but I do not in any way regret the experience: it was of course brief in comparison with the experiences of other hostages, but it gave me insights into myself and the human condition which I could not possibly have gained in any other way. In that sense it was a 'given' experience, an experience which has formed part of the fabric of me as a person, an intensely personal experience. Most people can point to incidents of major trauma which are theirs alone. Everybody is shaped by the experiences that occur through their lives, and the apparently negative experiences often turn out to be the most formative. The same point has been made by a number of disabled people quoted in this book: they would not wish their disability on anyone else, they agree that it would be better for a child not to be born disabled, but their own disability is an essential part of their experience and their identity.

And yet saying that 'suffering brings insights' is problematic, because it reinforces the linkage between disability and illness. The only 'suffering', in the view of some, is knowing that people relate to you differently when you are disabled. In other words, if negative attitudes did not exist and if no barriers were placed in the way, permanent impairment would not be a problem. It is fear of the attitudes and the barriers that is the real fear, not fear of the impairment itself, which creates such negative feelings in the not-yet-disabled about becoming disabled. It is not so much fear of being unable to do things, but more of being rejected, unable to form normal relationships, left on the sidelines, being dependent on other people who do not understand your needs, losing control of basic choices in day-to-day living. That is what disability seems to amount to and that is why it is feared. And so this fear is expressed in prejudice, awkwardness, cold-shouldering, pretending the problem does not exist, which all serve to perpetuate the cycle. The crucial task is to break the cycle.

We can start by accepting that disability exists. It is part of human life, part of the way things are. Let us engage with it, enquire into it, make friends with it. Disabled people do this from the inside, people who are not yet disabled need to do it from the outside. One way or another we cannot ignore it; if we ignore it, we place ourselves outside the human condition in some kind of unreal, aseptic world that cuts us off from our very humanity.

> Privacy exacts its costs. How quickly it turns to loneliness and alienation. Our defense against one kind of suffering, ironically, turns out to have invited in another. We somehow feel safe from the troubles of the world, but we also begin to feel dry, empty and alone in our isolated havens. Gone is the mutuality and spontaneous support that arise naturally when lives are led in common. With doors closed to the pain of others, we banish that which would release our compassion and engagement with life. We need heart-to-heart resuscitation.[3]

Integration means recognising differences

Impairment does entail a loss. But let us not be misled: it is mainly a loss when measured against the standards of an able-bodied world. That is the point. We have a notion that disabled people are more dependent than non-disabled people. We think that a wheelchair, for example, underlines this dependency. But for most people in the able-bodied world material success is measured by the number of gadgets on display in a person's house. A TV must come with a remote control so that you don't even have to move from your chair to change the channel — a feature of modern life (at any rate in the West) that is now accepted as standard. A high salary is used to buy a state-of-the-art motor-car with electric windows, temperature control at the touch of a button, and ergonomically designed seats to avoid back-ache in the exhausting business of sitting down. Such a car is admired, while a wheelchair — by comparison an extremely utilitarian mobility device — is derided as a symbol of dependency. But who, we should ask ourselves, is dependent?

The world we inhabit has been designed by able-bodied people, and it is they who have in large measure invented the 'problem' of disability. In truth, dependency and inter-dependency are part of the substance of all our lives to a high degree, and yet disability is seen as bringing extra dependency. The only thing that makes disabled people more 'dependent' is that they have fewer choices.

But saying that confronts us with another paradox: the difficult question of integration and separateness. If the 'problem' of disability is an artificial social construct and would be instantly solved if the able-bodied could only get rid of their tunnel vision, then what is all this about a separate disability movement, and even a separate disability culture?

'The problem,' wrote the Bengali poet Rabindranath Tagore, 'is not how to wipe out all differences, but how to unite with all differences intact.' Why should everybody be the same? Real integration of disabled people can be achieved only on the basis of a full recognition of their differences. This in turn depends on their being able to make a free choice to identify themselves as a distinct social group. How can disabled people express and celebrate their different-ness? By coming together in groups, by forming a movement, by developing their own culture, which then becomes part of a multi-cultural society.

In an early chapter of this book we considered the two extremes of a fascist society in which uniformity and conformity are prized and difference is damned, and (in contrast) an open society in which the whole spectrum of human life and experience is celebrated. A carnival in which everyone wears the same costume would be no fun at all; it would be a contradiction in terms: a carnival is made a celebration precisely by the diversity of the costumes. To prepare their costume and then come forth to join in the general celebration, people need to be able to 'retire back into their chambers' (as Jabulani Ncube of Zimbabwe put it in Chapter 6). Retiring into the chamber and coming forth are both necessary parts of this process: there is nothing to come forth with if the costume has not been prepared in the chamber first.

Disabled people need to be able to 'retire into their chambers', that is, meet among themselves as a distinct group, in order to develop their own culture as a contribution to the sum of human experience and expression. It is in such a distinct group that change can begin, where disabled people can feel the strength of being with others faced with the same difficulties, where an actual experience of empowerment can happen through a shared understanding. Change does have to start with disabled people themselves in this way: the case studies in this book illustrate that point above all others. With this new strength they are then better equipped to come forth and make their contribution to the totality of human experience. 'The celebration of difference, we will then discover, is the celebration of humanity, of being members of the human family.'[4] The same is true for any group of oppressed people.

Links with other liberation movements

It is important to see the connections between disability issues and other struggles for social justice, for example the women's movement. The double disadvantage which disabled women experience has been touched upon in various places in the book, but not given anything like the treatment it deserves. It is a failing. I myself was not sensitive enough to the way that gender-imposed inequalities operate among disabled people, and I did not insist sufficiently on finding disabled women to interview.

The reason why the women's movement has not previously dealt with the issue of disabled women is, according to one writer, because 'they reinforce traditional stereotypes of women being passive and needy',[5] the very stereotypes from which feminists are trying to escape. That is also a reason, I suspect, why other groups struggling for their own liberation have not generally linked up with the cause of disability in any significant way. But that too is part of the ignorance and prejudice that pervades the whole of the able-bodied world about disability.

Other parts of the women's movement have recognised the obvious links, not only with disability, but also with all other struggles for social justice by oppressed people. A letter to the magazine *Spare Rib* of September 1992 puts it succinctly:

> ... if you really are involved in the cause of ... feminism, whether you like it or not you are also involved in the ANC, Intifada, gay liberation, disabled people's rights and similar 'causes'. Whoever the oppressed and the oppressor are, there is only one freedom.

It is clear that disability does lie in close parallel with other liberation struggles, and other such struggles have something to learn from the disability movement. The women's movement (as I understand it) is not trying to make women more like men. It is, on the one hand, trying to define, express, and celebrate 'womanliness' as an essential and integral part of the human experience, and on the other hand to show that a sense of a common humanity must regard the person inside the body as of far greater importance than the body itself. So with disability.

Able-bodied women can learn from the disabled, who have had to learn this before they can truly cope, that the physical body is not as important as the person that lives inside; ... that every woman who is honestly involved in her own personal growth is making a contribution to the women's movement whether she is aware of it or not.'[6]

The role of able-bodied people

So what about me as a non-disabled, 'temporarily able-bodied' person? What is my role? One of the ways in which segregation has been most blatant is in assigning 'specialists' to 'look after' disabled people, as though non-specialists are incapable of doing so. This is all part of the baggage of the medical model, where control over health is kept in the hands of trained professionals. Besides disempowering disabled people, it disempowers able-bodied people, who feel that they 'don't know enough' to 'deal with disability'. This is nonsense. Micheline Mason writes:

> The truth is we do need you, not to be the 'experts' or managers of our lives, but to be friends, enablers and receivers of our 'gifts' to you. We need you to admit cheerfully what you don't know, without shame; to ask us what we need before providing it, to lend us your physical strength when appropriate, to allow us to teach you necessary skills; to champion our rights, to remove barriers previously set in place, to return to us any power you may have had over our lives. We may also need you to remind us of our importance in the world, and to each other, at times of tiredness and discouragement. We can live without patronage, pity and sentimentality, but we cannot live without closeness, respect and cooperation from other people.[7]

The truth is, as well, that able-bodied people need disabled people in order to re-engage with the totality of human experience. Unless we can relate constructively to disabled people, we ourselves are impoverished. It is a question of partnership.

Ruth and Stephen

Towards the end of my research for this book I found a remarkable example of such partnership.[8] Ruth Sienkiewicz-Mercer has severe cerebral palsy, hardly any movement in her limbs, and no speech. For thirteen years, from the age of six to nineteen, she lay in a State institution in Baltimore in the USA, treated like an object with no mind, no thoughts, no feelings, no opinions, no wishes, no dreams. The only attention she received in all that time was to be fed and toileted. Through all these years inside this immobile and silent body her lively mind kept track of time, people, events, characters, her own emotions and development — without being able to communicate any of this; her 'carers' had not the faintest inkling that anything was actually going on inside her head. She was classified as an 'idiot'.

It was not until a volunteer, Stephen Kaplan, interested in the problems of the speech-impaired, realised that she was bursting to say something that Ruth was 'discovered' as a person. By using word boards held up in front of her and asking her to say 'yes' by raising her eyebrows or 'no' by pursing her lips, he drew from her her story, word by word and line by line, and set it down. The whole writing took years to complete, covering perhaps a few paragraphs in each session. The book they wrote together is rich in texture and full of penetrating insights from a person who did all her learning and growing in almost complete isolation. Without Stephen, Ruth would never have emerged, doomed for life to be a silent, imprisoned witness of a world that refused to acknowledge that she even had something to say.

Ruth's contribution to the sum of human experience is profound. If anyone still has lingering doubts about the value of an individual severely impaired life, I suggest that this book will put those doubts to rest for ever. That is the good news. The bad news is the shock of realising that Ruth is one of the lucky ones: how many other Ruths are there who have never been 'discovered', who are living their lives trapped inside a body with no way of relating to people on the other side of it, and assumed to have nothing to say?

Ruth's story illustrates all the major issues raised by disability. It is about the ignorance, prejudice, and fear that create the climate of hostility experienced by disabled people; it illustrates dramatically the dismal paucity of the medical model and the institutional approach; it reveals the profound insights that come as a result of suffering; it reveals Ruth as indeed someone extremely special — but not as someone claiming to be a heroine. But above all, it is about an empowering and liberating relationship, a relationship free of all prejudice and fear, and full of understanding which set her free; it also brings us back to the struggles by other oppressed groups for recognition, dignity, and liberation, particularly the women's movement.

The examples of social action recorded in this book, like the pressure for change on the Abu Samra institute in Tripoli or the formation of disability *sanghams* in India, illustrate what is possible when disabled people and able-bodied people work together with respect and understanding. Disabled people are engaged in a liberation struggle, but a liberation struggle that does not presuppose a zero-sum game — *if you win, I lose*. It is *if you win, I win*. The liberation of someone like Ruth, or the sense of their own worth newly discovered by disabled people in an Indian village, is a liberation which enriches us all. Such liberation is possible once disabled and able-bodied people understand that how we relate to each other is the key. We all, both able-bodied and disabled people, need to be liberated from our fears and prejudices, our misunderstandings and tunnel vision, and our ability to oppress each other. It is a process of liberation that continues for the whole of our lives.

> *The earth does not argue,*
> *Is not pathetic, has no arrangements,*
> *Does not scream, haste, persuade,*
> *threaten, promise,*
> *Makes no discriminations, has no*
> *conceivable failures,*
> *Closes nothing, refuses nothing,*
> *shuts none out.*[9]

Notes

Chapter 1

1 *Webster's Collegiate Dictionary*, fifth edition, London: Bell, 1947.
2 See the suggestions for further reading at the end of this book.
3 Lucy Elman: 'Barely human', *Guardian*, 15 August 1992.
4 It has become fashionable in some circles in the USA to refer to non-disabled people as 'temporarily able-bodied'.

Chapter 2

1 A paise is one-hundredth of a rupee; 45 rupees were worth £1.00 at 1992 values.

Chapter 3

1 The words 'disability', 'impairment', and 'handicap' are discussed in Chapter 7.
2 Rachel Hurst of DPI expresses this view particularly strongly.
3 M. Fine and A. Asch: 'Disabled women: sexism without the pedestal' in M. Deegan and M. Brooks (eds.): *Women and Disability: The Double Handicap*, New Brunswick, NJ: Transaction Books, 1985.
4 ibid.

Chapter 4

1 cf. the comment made by the UK Social Security Minister, Nicholas Scott, during a debate in the House of Commons on the Civil Rights (Disabled Persons) Bill on 31 January 1992. This Bill would have outlawed discrimination against disabled people, but was effectively killed by the Minister's attitude, which he stated as 'benevolently neutral'.

2 Colin Barnes: *Disabled People in Britain and Discrimination*, London: Hurst and Co., 1991.

3 Paulo Freire: *Pedagogy of the Oppressed*, London: Penguin, 1984.

4 David Robinson: 'Self-help groups', *British Journal of Hospital Medicine*, August 1985.

5 Vic Finkelstein: 'A tale of two cities', *Therapy Weekly*, 22 March 1990.

Chapter 5

1 Diane Auret: *A Decade of Development: Zimbabwe 1980-1990*, Harare: Mambo Press, 1990.

2 See, for example, *Disability Statistics Compendium*, New York: United Nations, 1990.

3 Colin Barnes: *Disabled People in Britain and Discrimination*, London: Hurst and Co., 1991.

4 Rachel Hurst: 'Self-help for disabled people', in *Yearbook of Cooperative Enterprise* 1992, Oxford: Plunkett Foundation.

5 I am aware that this view is contentious, and that there is substantial evidence to the contrary. I can only report what my interviewees told me!

6 Esther Boylan (ed.): *Women and Disability*, London: Zed Books, 1991.

7 J. Baker: 'The Ethics of Disability Prevention: A Parent's Point of View', paper read at the 16th Congress of Rehabilitation International, Tokyo, 1988.

8 David Werner: 'Arguments for Including Disabled People in Primary Health Care', unpublished paper.

9 See Colin Barnes, op. cit., for a very comprehensive discussion of this point.

10 Vic Finkelstein: 'Disability and the helper/helped relationship. An historical overview' in Brechin et al.: *Handicap in a Social World*, London/Milton Keynes: Hodder and Stoughton/The Open University, 1981.

11 Anne Borsay: 'Personal trouble or public issue? Towards a model of policy for people with physical and mental disabilities', *Disability, Handicap, and Society*, Vol. 1, No. 2, 1986.

12 Particularly recommended is *How Can I Help?*, by Ram Dass and Paul Gorman (London: Rider, 1985).

13 ibid., quoted with permission.

14 Vic Finkelstein, op. cit.

15 ibid.

16 ibid.

17 Ram Dass and Paul Gorman, op. cit.

18 Erika Schuchardt: 'The crisis as an opportunity to learn', quoted in Boylan, op. cit.

19 Pam Zinkin, personal communication, October 1991.

20 Veronica Brand: 'Socio-economic factors affecting the rehabilitation of paraplegics in Zimbabwe', *The African Rehabilitation Journal*, Vol. 1, No. 4, 1984.

21 Address by Marilyn Baikie to the Disabled People's International 8th Asia-Pacific Leadership Training Seminar, Suva, Fiji, 25 June 1990.

Chapter 6

1 Technically the word 'rehabilitation' implies restoration to a previous level. In the case of children disabled from birth, it would be more accurate to speak of 'habilitation'. However, for the sake of simplicity I have used 'rehabilitation' throughout this text.

2 Unpublished report by ADD.

3 See the Suggestions for Further Reading at the end of this book.

4 See especially Mike Miles: 'Why Asia rejects Western disability advice', in Diane Dredger (ed.): *Disabled People in International Development*, Winnipeg: Coalition of Provincial Organisations of the Handicapped, 1991.

5 The prime text which defined it was Helander, Mendis and Nelson: *Training Disabled People in the Community*, Geneva: WHO, 1979.

6 Brian O'Toole: 'Community-Based Rehabilitation: Problems and Possibilities', paper written at the University of Guyana, undated.

7 Helander, Mendis, and Nelson, op. cit.

8 This is a common practice in some Western countries such as Britain.

9 David Werner: 'Project Projimo: a programme for and by disabled people', in Dredger (ed.) op. cit.

10 Especially the writings of Mike Miles, e.g. 'Where There Is No Rehab Plan', Peshawar: Mental Health Centre, 1985.

11 Lena Saleh: 'Initiating Action. Proceedings of the 7th World Congress of ILSMH on Mental Handicap', Vienna 1978.

12 Quoted in Frank Prochaska: *The Voluntary Impulse: Philanthropy in Modern Britain*, London: Faber, 1988.

13 ibid.

14 ibid.

15 Livion Nyathi: 'The disabled and social development in rural Zimbabwe', *The African Rehabilitation Journal*, Vol. 1, No. 4, 1984.

16 Justin Dart, Chairperson of the President's Committee on Employment of People with Disabilities in the United States, quoted in *Vox Nostra*, May 1992.

17 Ram Dass and Paul Gorman: *How Can I Help?*, London: Rider, 1985.

18 ibid.

19 Justin Dart, op. cit.

Chapter 7

1 Thomas Harris: *I'm OK, You're OK*, Avon Books, 1969.

2 *Disability Statistics Compendium*, New York: United Nations, 1990.

3 Dr Daisy Dhamaraj: 'PREPARE's Work with the Disabled', paper presented to a workshop on disability and development, October 1991, organised by ADD India.

4 Oxfam files.

5 Personal communication from Pam Zinkin, Institute of Child Health, London.

6 Examples can be found in Mike Miles: 'Where There Is No Rehab Plan', Peshawar: Mental Health Centre, 1985.

7 David Werner: 'Visit to Angola', *Vox Nostra* No. 1, 1990 (published by DPI).

8 Zimbabwe National Disability Survey, 1981.

Chapter 8

1 Robin Palmer and Isobel Birch: *Zimbabwe: A Land Divided*, Oxford: Oxfam, 1992.

2 A settler politician quoted in Palmer and Birch, op. cit.

3 ibid.

4 Helen House, Mary McAlister, and Cathy Naidoo: *Zimbabwe — Steps Ahead: Community Rehabilitation and People with Disabilities*, London: Catholic Institute for International Relations, 1990.

5 op. cit.

6 Information about the early life of Jairos Jiri is taken from *Jairos Jiri, the Man and his Work* by June Farquhar (Harare: Mambo Press, 1987).

7 Frank Prochaska: *The Voluntary Impulse: Philanthropy in Modern Britain*, London: Faber, 1988.

8 Extract from an interview with Alex Phiri by Yutta Fricke, published in *CBR News* No. 5, April 1990.

9 ibid.

10 Peter Nyathi: 'Evaluation of the Rural Membership Development Programme of NCDPZ, May-June 1985'.

11 Report of the participatory evaluation exercise of the NCDPZ rural membership development programme.

12 Jabulani Ncube: 'Evaluation Report on the Development Studies Course, Selly Oak, Birmingham, September-December 1987, and its Relevance to my Work with NCDPZ', Oxford: Oxfam files.

13 NCDPZ Evaluation Report, 1988.

14 Jabulani Ncube, op. cit., 1988.

Chapter 10

1 For example, Thierry Verhelst: *No Life Without Roots — Culture and Development*, London: Zed Books, 1990.

2 Pramod Unia: 'Social action strategies in the Indian Sub-Continent', *Development in Practice*, Vol. 1 No. 2, pp. 84-96, 1991. This is a useful critique of the approach and effectiveness of social action groups throughout the sub-continent.

3 Judith Brown: *Modern India: The Origins of an Asian Democracy*, Oxford: Oxford University Press, 1985.

4 Jacob Dhamaraj, personal communication.

5 Untitled paper by PREPARE, Sripermabudur, Tamil Nadu.

6 A *dalit* leader in Tamil Nadu, quoted by PREPARE, op. cit.

7 Dr Daisy Dhamaraj: 'PREPARE's Work with the Disabled'. Paper presented to workshop on disability and development organised by ADD India, October 1991.

8 Quoted in *Silver Shackles: Women and Development in India*, by Maitrayee Mukhopadhyay (Oxford: Oxfam, 1984).

9 ibid.

10 Paper presented by Narinder Bedi, YIP, at a workshop on disability and development, organised by ADD India, October 1991.

Chapter 11

1 Rita Giacaman *et al.*: 'Towards the Formulation of a Rehabilitation Policy: Disability in the West Bank', Birzeit University, October 1989.
2 ibid.
3 2.7 shekels = 1 US dollar.
4 Michael Miles: 'Where There Is No Rehab Plan', Peshawar, 1985, quoted by Rita Giacaman, op. cit.

Chapter 12

1 Figures released by the Beirut Police Department and reported in the *Guardian*, 11.3.92.

Chapter 13

1 I owe to Chris Underhill of ADD the insight which resulted in the picture of these concentric circles.
2 The paucity of the basic-needs approach is well described by Jeremy Seabrook in his article 'Development and human needs', published in the newsletter of the Gandhi Foundation, *The Gandhi Way*, No. 32, Summer 1992 (The Gandhi Foundation, Kingsley Hall, Powis Road, Bromley-by-Bow, London E3 3IIJ).
3 Ram Dass and Paul Gorman: *How Can I Help?*, London: Rider, 1985.
4 Vic Finkelstein: 'Disability and the helper/helped relationship: an historical overview', in Brechin et al.: *Handicap in a Social World*, London/Milton Keynes: Hodder and Stoughton/The Open University, 1981.
5 M. Fine and A. Asch: 'Disabled women: sexism without the pedestal' in M. Deegan and M. Brooks (eds.): *Women and Disability: The Double Handicap*, New Brunswick, NJ: Transaction Books, 1985.
6 Y. Duffy: *All Things are Possible*, Michigan: A.J. Garvin and Associates, 1981.
7 Micheline Mason: *Disability Equality in the Classroom: A Human Rights Issue*, London: Disability Equality in Education (78 Mildmay Grove, London N1 4PJ).
8 Ruth Sienkiewicz-Mercer and Stephen Kaplan: *I Raise My Eyes To Say Yes*, London: Grafton Books, 1990.
9 Walt Whitman: 'A song of the rolling earth', 1860.

Some organisations dealing with disability and development in developing countries

The organisations listed below are those with an international mandate. There are many hundreds of national and local organisations which are beyond the scope of this book. For additional addresses and descriptions of programmes, see *ICOD Compendium: Facts about the Members of the International Council on Disability and Related Agencies of the United Nations System*, published by Rehabilitation International (q.v.). A complete register is being compiled by The Hesperian Foundation (q.v.).

United Nations system

International Labour Organisation (ILO)

Willi Momm
Vocational Rehabilitation
Branch
4 Route des Morillons
CH-1211 Geneva
Switzerland

Supports projects and programmes dealing with economic aspects of work in disability. Its support is through training, consultancies, and funding.

UNESCO

Lena Saleh (Disability)
Special Programmes Section
7 Place de Fontenoy
75700 Paris
France

UNESCO's disability unit produces excellent booklets on a variety of topics related to disability in several languages.

**United Nations Centre for
Social Development and
Humanitarian Affairs**
Mamadou Barry
Disabled Persons Unit
Vienna International Centre
PO Box 500
A-1400 Vienna
Austria

**United Nations Relief and
Works Agency for
Palestinian Refugees
(UNRWA)**
Director, Relief and Social
Services
Vienna International Centre
PO Box 700
Vienna
Austria

*UNRWA, mandated to work with
Palestine refugees in the Middle East,
encourages the formation of local disability committees and community-
run disability centres in refugee
camps in Lebanon, Syria, Jordan, the
West Bank, and Gaza Strip.*

UNDP
Einer Helender
United Nations Development
Programme
1 UN Plaza
New York
NY 10017
USA

*Helender, the author of the World
Health Organisation's CBR
manual, coordinates the Inter-
Regional Programme for Disabled
People.*

**World Health
Organisation (WHO)**
Dr Pupulin
Rehabilitation Section
20 Avenue Appia
CH-1211 Geneva
Switzerland

*WHO provides advice and
financial support especially to CBR
programmes. It is the originator of
the term 'CBR', and the producer
of the principal CBR training
manual.*

Non-governmental organisations working on disability in developing countries

ActionAid
Hamlyn House
Archway
London N19 5PG
tel: 071 281 4101

*An aid and development agency
which supports disability projects
in developing countries.*

**Action on Disability and
Development (ADD)**
23 Lower Keyford
Frome
Somerset
BA11 4AP
UK
tel: 0373 473064   fax: 0373 452075

A development agency which gives

advice and financial support to groups and projects run by disabled people. Its work is focused on Africa, Central America, and Asia (through ADD India).

ADD India
PO Box 2598
Bangalore 560 025
India
tel: 91 812 217802
fax: 91 812 215508

ADD India is a separate sister organisation working in India, Nepal, and Bangladesh; it is beginning to develop a regional approach.

Appropriate Health Resources and Technology Action Group (AHRTAG)
1 London Bridge Street
London SE1 9SG
UK
tel: 071 378 1403

Has an excellent resource centre covering both health and disability. Produces CBR News (see Suggestions for Further Reading).

Caritas Internationalis
Piazza S. Calisto 16
00153 Rome
Italy

Funds and operates programmes and training in disability work.

Cerebral Palsy Overseas, CPO
Derek Lancaster Gay, Director
6 Dukes Mews
London W1
UK
tel: 071 486 6996

Advises on setting up projects, particularly related to cerebral palsy.

Handicap International
ERAC 14 Ave
Berthelot 69361
Lyon Cedex 07
France
tel: 78 69 79 79
fax: 78 69 79 94

Specialises in orthopaedic work, using expatriate volunteers. Many of its programmes are in war-affected areas.

Hesperian Foundation (David Werner)
PO Box 1692
Palo Alto
California 94302
USA

David Werner is the author of Disabled Village Children *and runs the Projimo Project, a CBR programme organised by disabled people. The Hesperian Foundation is also compiling a register of organisations relating to disability.*

IMPACT
c/o World Health Organisation
Room L 225
20 Avenue Appia
CH-1211 Geneva
Switzerland

An international initiative against avoidable impairment, working mainly in prevention.

l'Arche (Jean Vanier)
Trosly Breuille
603 350 Cuise La Motte
France

A world-wide organisation which provides an alternative to institutional care for people with mental impairments. Disabled people live in small family groups with non-disabled people.

Oxfam (UK and Ireland)
274 Banbury Road
Oxford OX2 7DZ
UK
tel: 0865 311311
fax: 0865 312600

An aid and development agency which includes support for disability in its work in Africa, the Middle East, and Asia. Decisions to support projects or programmes are made in field offices located in about 40 countries.

Radde Barnen
(Swedish Save the Children)
Tegeluddsvagen 31
Box 27320
S-102 54 Stockholm
Sweden
tel: 010 46 8 6650100

An aid and development agency

with a particular interest in disability projects.

Rehabilitation International
432 Park Avenue South
New York
NY 10016
USA

A co-ordinating body for people working in disability, mainly practitioners and professionals.

Royal Commonwealth Society for the Blind
Commonwealth House
Haywards Heath
West Sussex
RH16 3AZ
UK
tel: 0444 412424

Save the Children Fund (SCF)
17 Grove Lane
London SE5 8RD
UK
tel: 071 703 5400

Supports disability-related work in many different countries where it is represented. The focus is on CBR and integrating disability within its general programmes. Unlike most other development agencies, SCF has a Disability Adviser operating worldwide.

Organisations providing training courses on disability and development

Institute of Child Health
30 Guildford Street
London WC1
UK
tel: 071 242 9789

Runs, under the direction of Pam Zinkin, a one-year diploma course (to be changed to a Master's) in CBR.

Handicapped Education and Aid Research Unit (HEARU)
Ken Westmacott (Director)
Walburgh House
56 Bigland Street
London E1 2NG
UK

Organises overseas workshops on appropriate technological aids for disabled people.

The Open University
Milton Keynes
MK7 6AA
UK
tel: 0908 653414

Offers a distance-learning course on disability which raises in great detail the issues treated in this book, but in a British setting.

Organisations networking globally on disability

Disability Awareness in Action (DAA)
Rachel Hurst
11 Belgrave Road
London SW1
UK
tel: 071 834 0477
fax: 071 821 9539

An international public education organisation campaigning in support of the UN Programme of Action Concerning Disabled Persons.

Disabled People's International (DPI)
101-7 Evergreen Place
Winnipeg
Manitoba
Canada R3L 2T3
tel: 204 287 8010
fax: 204 287 8175

The world-wide co-ordinating body for cross-disability organisations, run by disabled people with the goal of achieving full and equal participation for disabled persons.

Initiatives for Deaf Education in the Third World
Doreen Woodford
9 Church Walk
Much Wenlock
Shropshire
TF13 6EN
UK

An important initiative, with partners all over the world. It also does training.

International Centre for the Advancement of CBR (ICACBR)
Queens University
Kingston
Ontario
Canada K7L 3NG

International League of Societies for Persons with Mental Handicap
Ave. Louise 248 bte 17
B - 1050 Brussels
Belgium

Suggestions for further reading

There are not many books which set out to deal with disability in developing countries in the way that this book does — which is why I wrote it! But the following is a list of publications which I have found particularly helpful in developing my arguments. They are not necessarily concerned with developing countries, nor even with disability as such.

Books

Colin Barnes: *Disabled People in Britain and Discrimination. A Case for Anti-Discrimination Legislation*, London: Hurst & Co., 1991.

A detailed and scholarly account which warns against complacency in a Northern country which still has no anti-discrimination legislation on disability.

Esther Boylan (ed.): *Women and Disability*, London: Zed Books, 1991.

A useful collection of articles covering both the developed and developing world.

Ram Dass and Paul Gorman: *How Can I Help?*, London, Sydney, Auckland, Johannesburg: Rider, 1985.

The best book I have come across for insights into the role of helper and helped. Essential reading for anyone who takes these roles seriously, whether professionally or privately.

Diane Dredger: *The Last Civil Rights Movement*, London: Hurst and Co., 1989.

Explores the origins and history of Disabled People's International.

Diane Dredger: *Role of Organisations of Disabled People*, Winnipeg: Disabled People's International.

Helen House *et al.: Zimbabwe Steps Ahead. Community Rehabilitation and People with Disabilities*, London: Catholic Institute for International Relations, 1990.

Referred to in Chapter 9 of this book.

Mike Miles: 'Where There Is No Rehab Plan', Peshawar: The Mental Health Centre, 1985.

A fierce attack on CBR and the claims made for it. Somewhat extreme, but it provokes thought.

Milton Keynes World Development Education Centre: *Challenging a Disabling World*, available from Milton Keynes World Development Education Centre, Stantonbury Campus, Milton Keynes MK14 6BN, UK.

A well-produced package designed to help groups to think about the social model of disability.

Jenny Morris: *Able Lives*, London: The Women's Press, 1989.

The testimonies of disabled women.

The Open University: Course materials on *The Handicapped Person in the Community*, published by the Open University, Milton Keynes, MK7 6AB, UK.

Very thorough treatment of the British context.

Frank Prochaska: *The Voluntary Impulse: Philanthropy in Modern Britain*, London: Faber, 1988.

A brief, helpful overview of the way in which private voluntary action and 'charity' have developed in Britain. It is interesting to compare trends in Britain with those in developing countries.

Ruth Sienkiewicz-Mercer and Stephen Kaplan: *I Raise My Eyes to Say Yes*, London: Grafton Books, 1990.

Described in Chapter 12 of this book. Written with extraordinary simplicity and power, it describes Ruth's experiences in a total institution, illuminating the obstacles to personal development faced by disabled people in a world of profound ignorance and entrenched prejudices.

Marigold Thorburn et al.: *Practical Approaches to Childhood Disability in Developing Countries: Insights from Experience and Research*,

obtainable from 3D Projects, 14 Monk Street, Spanish Town, Jamaica, West Indies; or Dr Kofi Marfo, College of Education, 405 White Hall, Kent State University, Kent, Ohio 44242, USA.
A valuable collection of articles on a range of topics, mainly on programme issues. Includes a powerful critique of CBR.

The United Nations Economic and Social Commission for Asia and the Pacific (ESCAP): *Self-help Organisations of Disabled Persons*, New York: United Nations, 1991.
A useful compendium (in large print) relating to the Asia and Pacific Region.

Ellen Wilkie: *A Pocketful of Dynamite*, London: Hodder and Stoughton, 1990.
A lively and poetic disabled person tells her own inspiring story.

Journals and newsletters

Listed here are the major periodicals produced for a global audience. In addition there are many regional and national newsletters.

CBR News: newsletter/journal published by AHRTAG (see Appendix for address).

Disability, Handicap and Society: an academic journal published three times a year. Subscriptions address: Carfax Publishing Company, PO Box 25, Abingdon, OX14 3UE, UK.

Disability Now: monthly newspaper published by the Spastics Society, 12 Park Crescent, London W1N 4EQ, UK.

Disability Rights Handbook: produced annually by Disability Alliance. Recognised as the most comprehensive guide to rights, benefits, and services for all disabled people and families.

New Internationalist Special issue on disability, No. 233, July 1992: a brief introduction and good summary of some of the issues. Available from New Internationalist, 55 Rectory Road, Oxford OX4 1BW, UK; fax 0865 793152.

Vox Nostra: newsletter/journal published quarterly by DPI (Disabled People's International). Available from DPI (see Appendix for address) in several languages, including Arabic.

Index